BANKING REGULATION IN TIMES OF CRISIS

European Studies in Law and Economics Series

1. *Group Litigation in European Competition Law. A Law and Economics Perspective,* Sonja E. Keske
2. *Behavioural Economics in Consumer Policy,* Hanneke Luth
3. *Ex-Post Liability Rules in Modern Patent Law,* Rosa Castro Bernieri
4. *Competition and Innovation in the EU Regulation of Pharmaceuticals: The Case of Parallel Trade,* Claudia Desogus
5. *The Law and Economics of Organ Procurement,* Fırat Bilgel
6. *Law and Economics in the RIA World. Improving the use of economic analysis in public policy and legislation,* Andrea Renda
7. *Regulatory Competition in European Corporate and Capital Market Law,* Lars Hornuf
8. *Economic Criteria for Criminalization: Optimizing Enforcement in Case of Environmental Violations,* Katarina Svatikova
9. *Definition of the Relevant Market. (Lack of) Harmony between Industrial Economics and Competition Law,* Hila Nevo
10. *Patents as Protection of Traditional Medical Knowledge? A Law and Economics Analysis,* Petra Ebermann
11. *Rethinking the New York Convention. A Law and Economics Approach,* Shen Wei
12. *Towards a Better Assessment of Pain and Suffering Damages for Personal Injuries,* Vaia Karapanou
13. *Comparative Analysis of Merger Control Policy. Lessons for China,* Jingyuan Ma
14. *Does Law Matter for Economic Growth? A Re-examination of the 'Legal Origin' Hypothesis,* Guangdong Xu
15. *Committed to Reform. Pragmatic Antitrust Enforcement in Electricity Markets,* Małgorzata Sadowska
16. *Civil Liability of Securities Underwriters. Enforcing the Gatekeeping Function,* Olia Skripova

BANKING REGULATION IN TIMES OF CRISIS

An Economic Analysis from Turkey and Russia

Deniz Akün Ergun

intersentia
Cambridge – Antwerp – Portland

Intersentia Ltd
Sheraton House | Castle Park
Cambridge | CB3 0AX | United Kingdom
Tel.: +44 1223 370 170 | Email: mail@intersentia.co.uk

Distribution for the UK:
NBN International
Airport Business Centre, 10 Thornbury Road
Plymouth, PL6 7 PP
United Kingdom
Tel.: +44 1752 202 301 | Fax: +44 1752 202 331
Email: orders@nbninternational.com

Distribution for the USA and Canada:
International Specialized Book Services
920 NE 58th Ave. Suite 300
Portland, OR 97213
USA
Tel.: +1 800 944 6190 (toll free)
Email: info@isbs.com

Distribution for Austria:
Neuer Wissenschaftlicher Verlag
Argentinierstraße 42/6
1040 Wien
Austria
Tel.: +43 1 535 61 03 24
Email: office@nwv.at

Distribution for other countries:
Intersentia Publishing nv
Groenstraat 31
2640 Mortsel
Belgium
Tel.: +32 3 680 15 50
Email: mail@intersentia.be

Banking Regulation in Times of Crisis. An Economic Analysis from Turkey and Russia
Deniz Akün Ergun

ISBN 978-1-78068-300-3
D/2015/7849/33
NUR 827

British Library Cataloguing in Publication Data. A catalogue record for this book is available from the British Library.

ACKNOWLEDGEMENTS

I would like to express my gratitude to several people who have contributed significantly to this book. First and foremost, I would like to thank Prof. Alessio Pacces and Dr Özlem Olgu without whom this research would not have been possible. I must acknowledge Prof. Alessio Pacces for his patient help, insightful advice, motivation and guidance. Prof. Pacces carefully and expertly honed my efforts in applying legal theory to a financial analysis. I am also wholeheartedly grateful to Dr Özlem Olgu, who helped shape the econometric analysis in this work and assisted in developing it by encouraging me to further immerse myself in in-depth analysis. Her never-ending support for my needs and ideas, her encouragement to believe in success, and her understanding of the hardships one can encounter helped me to keep going.

I am also indebted to Prof. Gabriela Chiesa for her comments on the earlier drafts of this book.

Special thanks must also go to Prof. Jonathan Klick and Prof. Thomas Crossley for their comments that greatly improved the quality of this work.

I would also like to take this opportunity to express my gratitude to Dr Murat Ucer for always supporting, encouraging and believing in me throughout my academic journey. I am especially grateful for his analytical suggestions and motivation.

Prof. Michael Faure, Prof. Luigi Franzoni, Dr Ann-Sophie Vandenberghe and Marianne Breijer are also deserving of recognition for their encouragement and especially as they were instrumental in the development of my research ideas.

Many thanks to my dearest friends Chris, Seray, Ahmet, Gözde, Can, Cicek and Oya for generously sharing the burden of this experience with me and for their constant moral support under all circumstances.

I would like to present my greatest appreciation and thanks to my sister Merve and to my lovely aunts Ela and Isil, and my uncles Kevin and Mehmet for always being there for me.

Furthermore, I would especially like to give my warmest thanks to my parents, Suheyla and Avraham Shamir and to my grandparents Dr Faruk and Sabiha Tezer, and great uncle Prof Ercan Tezer for their unconditional support and for believing in me from the beginning to the end. Their continuous encouragement gave me the strength to pursue my research.

My special thanks go to my mother to whom I owe all my accomplishments in life.

Most of all, I would like to thank my loving husband Devrim Ergun. Dear Devrim, your guidance throughout this journey was at all times invaluable, and your love, your friendship, your absolute patience and support, and above all, your belief in me, were instrumental in achieving completion of this work. I love you.

Istanbul, February 2015

CONTENTS

LIST OF ABBREVIATIONS

BAT	Banks Association of Turkey
BCBS	Basel Committee on Banking Supervision
BIS	Bank for International Settlements
BRSA	Banking Regulation and Supervision Agency
CAR	Capital Adequacy Requirement
CBR	Central Bank of Russia
CBRT	Central Bank of the Republic of Turkey
CDO	Collateralized Debt Obligation
CEE	Central and Eastern Europe
CRD	Capital Requirements Directive
DEA	Data Envelopment Analysis
DIA	Deposit Insurance Agency
EBRD	European Bank for Reconstruction and Development
ECB	European Central Bank
EU	European Union
FSAP	Financial Sector Assessment Program
GDP	Gross Domestic Product
GMID	Euromonitor International
G-20	The Group of Twenty
IAS	International Accounting Standards
IOSCO	International Organization of Securities Commissions
IMF	International Monetary Fund
LOL	Lender of Last Resort
NPL	Non–Performing Loans
OLS	Ordinary Least Squares
SDIF	Savings Deposits and Insurance Fund
US	United States
UK	United Kingdom
WB	World Bank

LIST OF TABLES AND FIGURES

TABLES

FIGURES

INTRODUCTION

1. THE NEED FOR REGULATION

The importance of banks and financial markets relies on the fact that they promote economic efficiency by allocating savings efficiently to profitable investment opportunities. Banks intermediate funds from people who do not have a productive use for them to those who can achieve a higher expected return, hence facilitating financial intermediation in an economy. A well-functioning financial system contributes to the economic growth of a country. More importantly and as this research emphasises, other than contributing to economic growth, an efficient banking system is a key determinant for the financial stability.

A stable banking system is capable of withstanding financial shocks and imbalances, thereby alleviating the disruptions in the financial intermediation process. The importance of financial stability became evident during the 2007–2009 global financial crisis. The financial crisis that started in the US subprime mortgage market in 2007 spread quickly to Europe and became a global crisis. It led to a global recession in the world economy with a higher detriment in some countries than others. Among the advanced economies, the GDP growth rate of the US economy was -2.8% in 2009 and -0.05 in 2010. In the EU this ratio was on average -4% in 2009 and -0.3% in 2010. Compared to advanced countries, emerging market economies displayed remarkable resilience and maintained robust rates of economic growth. The GDP growth rates in Emerging Market Economies[1] have remained positive in the same years; 0.01% in 2009 and 3.2% in 2010 (IMF, 2009). Given the lessons from the crises of the past 15 years, developing countries have adopted measures to become less vulnerable to external shocks that are likely to emerge from more developed countries.

The theory of market failure forms the basis for understanding financial regulation. Following the detrimental economic and financial consequences in the aftermath of the crisis, academics and policymakers started to focus their attention on the construction of an appropriate regulatory and supervisory framework of the banking sector. During the 2007–2009 global crisis, banks were engaging in excessive risk-taking. Prudential banking regulation and supervision

1 Emerging Market Economies are grouped as such: Emerging Asia, Emerging South Asia, Emerging Europe, Emerging Americas, Emerging Middle East, Emerging Africa, newly Industrialised Asia, Developing Asia, China and India. Among these groupings, Turkey and Russia belong to the "Emerging Europe" classification (IMF, 2009).

aim to curb excessive risk-taking of banks because engaging in excessively risky transactions is the ultimate source of instability. Hence, banking regulation is needed to deal with the failure of markets to police banks' risky behaviours.

2. RESEARCH QUESTION AND THE RELEVANCE OF THIS BOOK

This work aims to understand the impact of regulations and supervision on banks' performance focusing on two emerging market economies, Turkey and Russia. The goal is to examine the way in which regulations matter for financial stability and banking performance from a law and economics perspective. A review of the theory of banking regulation, particularly as applied to emerging economies, shows that the efficiency of certain solutions regarding banking regulation is open to debate. Therefore, in the context of emerging countries, whether a certain approach is efficient or not will be presented as an empirical question to which this research will try to find an answer.

The research question of this work is whether stricter banking regulation leads to better performance by banks. The relevancy of this question arises from the fact that banking regulation and supervision has been the subject of discussion due to the global financial crisis. Since the start of the global financial crisis, numerous papers and studies, as well as many academics, journalists and policymakers drew attention to the weaknesses in regulation and supervision, pointing to examples such as lax regulation, insufficient capital and poor supervision as factors that contributed to the crisis. More importantly, the global crisis urged regulators all around the world to consider changes in regulation and supervision (Čihák et al., 2012; Beltratti & Stulz, 2011).

In order to answer the research question, the book will first start with a theoretical discussion of banking regulation and discuss the efficiency of certain solutions in this context. This part will be followed by an empirical analysis where a comparison of the performance of Turkish and Russian banks will be made. I chose these emerging countries as they both experienced severe banking crises at the end of the 1990s, followed by major restructuring and regulatory reform in their respective banking sectors. However, Turkish banks have been resilient during the 2007–2009 global crisis, experiencing no bank failure whereas Russian banks were strongly influenced by the global financial crisis in terms of major bank failures.

After having derived the efficiency scores[2] of both countries' banks, a regression analysis will be carried out to investigate the regulatory determinants of these banks' performances. Lastly, the regulatory variables that make the

2 For the purpose of this research, technical efficiency measures the ability of a bank to perform financial intermediation.

difference in my empirical analysis will be explored across the two geographical dimensions of variability, namely Turkey and Russia between 1999 and 2010.

To my best knowledge, the literature on banks' efficiency analysis is in its infancy regarding the regulatory environment. Most of the studies (e.g. Pastor et al., 2007; Dietsch & Lozano-Vivas, 2000; Carvallo & Kasman, 2005) use economic environment variables, industry concentration levels, or simple banking profitability ratios. Besides, several studies that study the impact of regulations focus on individual countries rather than providing international evidence (e.g. Drake et al., 2006; Berger & Merster, 2003). In recent years, a smaller but growing number of studies (e.g. Pasiouras, 2008; Pasiouras et al., 2007, 2009, 2011; Beltratti & Stulz, 2011; Čihák et al., 2012) started to investigate different banking regulatory and supervisory regimes around the world using "The Bank Regulation and Supervision Survey" carried out by the World Bank (WB) in order to provide a more comprehensive analysis on the impact of regulations. This survey is a unique source of comparable world-wide data permitting international comparisons of a wide range of issues related to banking regulation and supervision. It was conducted by Barth, Caprio and Levine in several years. Specifically, the survey was updated and released by the World Bank in 2001, 2003, and 2007.[3]

This work provides evidence on the regulatory factors that influence banks' efficiency using the "The Bank Regulation and Supervision Survey" carried out by the World Bank (WB). With the help of this survey's questions, this work will examine the impact of several regulatory variables on banks' performance. These regulatory variables are:

(a) Capital Adequacy Requirements: Capital adequacy requirement is the amount of capital banks must hold as a cushion against losses and insolvency. In order to account for the risk profile of banks' assets in determining the required level of capital, banks have been made subject to risk-based capital requirements.
(b) Official Disciplinary Power: This variable stands for the ability of supervisors to have the authority to take specific actions to prevent and correct problems.
(c) Private Monitoring: This variable indicates the degree of information released to officials and the public, auditing-related requirements and whether credit ratings are required.

---

3 These surveys captured information as of 1998, 1999, 2000, 2001, 2003 and 2005. The 2007 survey was updated in 2008. The current 2012 survey (which is the fourth version of this survey covering the period 2008–2010) was not available at the time of writing this book. The first survey (2001) had 117 country respondents between 1998 and 2000. The 2003 survey characterised the regulatory situation at the end of 2002. It was updated in early 2004 with data from 2003. The third survey was posted on the World Bank website in the summer of 2007 with responses from 142 countries and it was updated in 2008.

(d) Deposit Insurance: This variable indicates whether a country has an explicit deposit insurance scheme or not.
(e) Entry Requirements: This regulation discusses the requirements to obtain a banking licence.

3. RESEARCH METHODOLOGY

This work analyses the impact of regulations on banks' performances in Turkey and Russia. The research is divided into three parts: theoretical, empirical, and policy analysis. To start, I discuss the theoretical rationales for banking regulation and the alternative predictions that theory generates on this basis.

The second part of the analysis is an empirical investigation of what implications banking regulation has on two comparable emerging economies (Turkey and Russia), using a two-stage regression analysis. In the first stage, the efficiency levels of both countries' banks will be estimated by applying Data Envelopment Analysis (DEA), which employs linear programming[4] to obtain the relative technical efficiency of both countries' banks. Data Envelopment Analysis (DEA) is one of the most popular linear programming methods examining the relationships between inputs and outputs of a production process. Since its introduction, the DEA model has been extensively applied in empirical studies to analyse both cross-section and panel data.[5] One advantage of DEA that attracts researchers is its ability to identify the potential improvement for inefficient units. In contrast to regression methods, DEA focuses on individual observations and optimises the performance measure of each unit.

At the second stage of the empirical analysis, Ordinary Least Squares (OLS) regression will be used for the identification of the regulatory variables that are significantly correlated with the Turkish and the Russian banks' efficiency conditional on other bank specific factors, market environment and economic conditions. Using regression analysis the efficiency scores from step one will be regressed on bank-specific and country-specific factors.

After having detected the regulatory variables that turn out to be significant on the empirical analysis, the third and last part of the book illustrates the empirical findings in a legal-economic perspective. The aim of this part is to tease out the policy implications of the empirical analysis. I will describe the regulatory variables that seem to make the difference between the two countries' banking sectors, from the legal perspective.

---

4 A linear programming problem is the problem of maximising or minimising a linear function subject to linear constraints. This is a typical problem for a firm that wants to maximise its profits.

5 In a panel data set, the behaviour of several entities is observed across several points in time.

The regulatory database used in this research, "The Bank Regulation and Supervision Survey" provides a dataset that allows the international comparison of various features of the bank regulatory environment. However, the authors of this survey (Barth, Caprio and Levine, 2008)[6] express some concern about the accuracy of the responses[7] obtained from the regulatory authorities. Even though the principal contacts to whom the survey was sent in each country should know the regulatory environment, the survey's scope is such that for any country a number of people usually are involved in its completion, and some or all of the members of this group might change over time. This circumstance raises the issue of differences in the interpretation of questions over time (in addition to changes in the wording). Hence Barth, Caprio and Levine (2008) make the remark that they did not always receive clear responses from the authorities and that the survey might suffer from a survey fatigue. Being aware of these problems, for the Turkish regulatory environment, I integrated the survey with information retrieved directly from an official at the national regulatory agency of Turkey. Regarding the regulatory data for the Russian banks, I used the database of the World Bank (WB) developed by Barth, Caprio and Levine over several years. To complete the missing years for the time period between 2008 and 2010, the survey was sent to the officials of the national regulatory agency of Russia and completed by them.[8]

4. STRUCTURE OF THE BOOK

This book is organised into three chapters.

Chapter 1 provides a theoretical discussion on the efficiency of certain solutions regarding banking regulations. It will first present the general features of banking and the theories of financial intermediation. This will be followed by the economic rationale of banking regulation and its role for financial stability. The final section of Chapter 1 will analyse the overall regulatory framework based on the objectives of different regulatory and policy measures. The aim of Chapter 1 is to explain the function of banking regulation in supporting financial stability. It presents the basic concepts necessary to understand the mechanism of banking regulation in dealing with market failures responsible for

6 James R. Barth, Gerard Caprio, Jr., and Ross Levine (2008): "Bank Regulations Are Changing: For Better or Worse?".

7 See Appendix A for the questions and other details of the survey.

8 This database is available at four points in time, specifically: 1998–2000; 2001, 2003 and 2007. Following Pasiouras (2011), I was able to use information from Version I for bank observations over the period 1998–2000, from Version II for bank observations over the period 2001–2003, and from Version III for bank observations for 2004–2005. Other studies using this database made the same assumption (Focarelli & Pozzolo, 2001; Demirgüç-Kunt & Detragiache 2002; Demirgüç-Kunt et al., 2004; Fernandez & Gonzalez, 2005; Beck et al., 2006), have implicitly made the same assumption. For more on this, see Pasiouras et al. (2007).

financial instability. Therefore, it will form the basis for the subsequent chapters' analyses. Very often the predictions of the theory regarding the impact of certain regulations on the efficiency of a banking system are ambiguous. This is particularly the case for emerging countries, justifying the analysis in the second chapter.

In order to understand the impact of certain banking regulations, whether a certain approach is more or less efficient in the context of two selected emerging countries – Turkey and Russia – will be presented as an empirical question in Chapter 2. The impact of regulations related to capital adequacy requirements, extent of power of regulatory bodies, information disclosure requirements, deposit insurance and entry regulations on banks' performances will be analysed. Chapter 2 will introduce the concept of technical efficiency as a performance indicator in order to establish the technical foundation for the methodology of this chapter. Data Envelopment Analysis (DEA) as a non-parametric measurement technique will be introduced as a performance measurement technique which will be used for calculating the efficiency scores of Turkish and Russian banks during 1999 and 2010. This chapter then explains the Ordinary Least Squares regression technique, which will be used to investigate the regulatory determinants of banks' efficiency scores. The chapter will end with a discussion of the empirical findings.

Chapter 3 analyses the regulatory variables that make the difference according to the empirical analysis of Chapter 2. Regulations will be described across the two dimensions of variability, Turkey and Russia from 1999 until 2010. The empirical findings will be analysed from a legal perspective, explaining in-depth how the regulatory frameworks in these two countries differ.

Finally, the main findings of this research will be summarised and some general policy implications will be drawn. Based on the findings of this study, policymakers can be informed about which regulations they can improve the banking performance in emerging countries. Recommendations and possible areas for future research will be also highlighted.

CHAPTER 1

THE ECONOMICS OF BANKING AND BANKING REGULATION

1. INTRODUCTION

A healthy and efficient banking system together with a well-managed macroeconomic policy is the key determinant of financial stability. The global financial crisis of 2007–2009 is one of the most dramatic crises in the current century. Its origins and causes have led many academics, practitioners and policy makers to seek an understanding of the deep roots of the new forms of banking. Secondly, and more importantly, the search for a new banking regulatory regime has been undertaken.

The aim of this chapter is to explain the function of banking regulation in supporting financial stability. It will present the basic concepts necessary to understand the mechanism of banking regulation in dealing with the market failures responsible for financial instability. Therefore, this chapter will form the basis for the subsequent chapters' analysis. Emphasis will be placed on the impact of banking regulation on banks' risk-taking attitudes, including the manner in which such behaviour adversely affects financial stability.

The literature is endowed with a vast amount of detailed analyses of how the 2007–2009 subprime[1] crisis that started in the US transformed into a global crisis.[2] It became obvious that financial crises are not confined to developing countries; developed countries' economies with relatively mature financial systems are also vulnerable to adverse shocks, systemic banking crises, cycles of booms and busts, and financial volatility.[3] Many developing countries experienced financial crises throughout the 1990s. Developing countries generally suffer larger exogenous shocks than advanced countries. Their domestic policies are a source of volatility and more importantly they have weaker macroeconomic and financial shock absorbers than developed countries

1 The term "subprime" refers to the credit characteristics of particular borrowers who have weak credit histories and a higher risk of loan default than do prime borrowers. These subprime borrowers are risky borrowers (Gorton, 2008).

2 The 2007–2009 global crisis is also called "the subprime crisis". See Hellwig (2008) and Calomiris, (2008).

3 For more on this, see Schmukler (2008).

(World Bank Development Research Group, 2008). The 1998 Russian crisis, the 1999 Brazil crisis, the 2000/2001 Turkey crises, the 2001 Argentina crisis, and the 1997–1998 Asian financial crises (which quickly spread to other emerging markets), are some well-known examples. However, especially after the 1997/1998 Asian financial crises, emerging market economies have been strengthened through various macroeconomic and financial reforms. Exposures to cross-border risks and risky sovereign debt have been limited. High-leverage strategies, heavy reliance on wholesale short-term funding and the risky expansion of off-balance sheet exposures, which are among the determinants of the global crisis, have been absent from banking in most emerging countries (Beltratti & Stulz, 2011; Boorman, 2009).

Given the lessons from the crises of the past 15 years, developing countries[4] have adopted measures to become less vulnerable to external shocks, isolating themselves from the turbulence in other parts of the world (World Bank, 2008). This time emerging markets were affected by the global crisis to some extent, but compared to their histories of previous crises, they displayed remarkable resilience and maintained robust growth rates. Although the financial institutions in emerging markets did not engage in the popular and complex financial practices seen in major industrial countries, transmission of the crisis from the US to Europe, and then from Europe to the rest of the world, came through several channels as a consequence of financial interconnectedness (BIS Study Group, 2011).[5] *The crucial starting point of this research is that the magnitude of contagion from developed economies has been smaller in emerging countries with stronger institutions and sounder policies.* The Bank for International Settlements (BIS) report of May 2011 on financial stability indicates that emerging markets have been more inclined than advanced countries to employ regulatory instruments for the stability of the financial system (BIS Study Group, 2011). Among the emerging markets that are members of the G-20,[6] only Turkey did not introduce any special stimulus package or require any rescue packages or other forms of government support. After the 2000/2001 crises,[7] the Turkish banking sector has developed a substantial amount of prudential and

4 Although some authors distinguish between developing countries and emerging countries, these terms are used interchangeably throughout this work.

5 For a detailed discussion on the transmission channels of the global crisis to emerging markets, see Boorman, 2009; and World Bank Policy Research Paper, 2008.

6 The Group of Twenty (G-20) is the premier forum for international cooperation on the most important aspects of the international economic and financial agenda. It brings together the world's major advanced and emerging economies. It includes Argentina, Australia, Brazil, Canada, China, France, Germany, India, Indonesia, Italy, Japan, Mexico, the Republic of Korea, Russia, Saudi Arabia, South Africa, Turkey, the United Kingdom, the United States, and the European Union.

7 In November 2000, the Turkish economy was hit by a severe liquidity crisis. The situation was normalised for a while by an IMF-led emergency package. However, Turkish currency came under heavy attack in February 2001 and this turned into the most serious financial and economic crisis Turkey has experienced in its post-war history (Özkan, 2003).

structural measures in banking regulations. The Russian banking system, on the other hand, has been strongly affected by the global financial crisis, resulting in major bank failures. In fact, *Russia was affected much more strongly by the global crisis than the majority of emerging economies* (Dreger & Fidrmuc, 2009; Fidrmuc & Süss, 2009). The Russian government and the Central Bank implemented a number of regulatory measures to support the Russian banking sector with liquidity in order to mitigate the effects of the financial crisis.

Regulatory intervention in financial markets, particularly banking, was in place all over the world when the global financial crisis began. This prompted a variety of proposals for reforming the banking system. There is still an on-going debate about the optimal structure of regulation. Regulation in the banking sector is more important than in other sectors because the externalities arising from an individual bank failure might lead to a systemic failure in the whole sector, hence affecting the economy and society as a whole.[8]

In order to place the subsequent analysis into an appropriate context, this chapter aims to provide the reader with a good grasp of the basics of banking and the behaviour of banks when they are subject to certain regulations.

Section 2 of this chapter sets out the general pattern for banking theory. To this end, general features of banking and theories of financial intermediation such as liquidity insurance, delegated monitoring, risk management and resource allocation will be highlighted as they appear in economic theory. These can be framed also as the services banks provide to the public.

Section 3 describes the changing nature of banks in the world due to financial innovation which began in the 1970s. Under the traditional model of banking, banks fund their operations primarily through deposits, which they transform into loans. However, through deregulation accompanied by financial innovation, banks began to rely on wholesale money markets rather than deposits for funding; and on securitisation which enabled them to change the structure of their asset portfolios and risk profiles. This part provides the basis for understanding the banking structures and operations taking place in two emerging markets: Turkey and Russia. The following chapter of this book will be concerned with these two countries.

Section 4 explains the economic rationale for banking regulation based on market failures, systemic risk factors and the concept of financial stability. Examination of economic theory may build a helpful basis for understanding the necessity of banking regulation. After identifying the sources of instability in the financial system and why these are a problem for the welfare of society, section 5 analyses the two main approaches to banking regulation that exist in the literature which deal with the role of government intervention. The role of regulation is explained in two dimensions: the public interest dimension and the private interest dimension of the regulatory process.

8 Systemic risk will be discussed in detail in section 4.2 of this chapter.

Section 6 discusses the structure of banking regulation. The overall regulatory framework is analysed based on the objectives of different regulatory and policy measures. The emphasis is on their impacts on financial stability. This section builds the basis for understanding the impact of regulations on Turkish and Russian banks' performance, which will be dealt with more specifically in Chapter 2. Section 7 concludes.

2. ECONOMICS OF BANKING

Financial intermediaries such as banks, insurance companies, finance companies, securities firms, mutual funds and pension funds have an important function in the economy. They take funds from firms and individuals that have surplus savings, and then allocate them to other firms and individuals who need to borrow. This is the basic meaning of financial intermediation. A well-functioning financial system contributes to the economic growth of a country. Various empirical and theoretical studies prove the positive relationship between a well-functioning financial system and economic growth.[9]

Whereas all the intermediaries mentioned above perform this function, banks have two other features that distinguish them from other types of intermediaries. Firstly, they commit to return the savers' funds at any time, on short notice or on demand. Secondly, banks issue money in terms of demand deposits, savings deposits and short-term deposits (Schooner & Taylor, 2009: 2–17; Dewatripont & Tirole, 1994: 13). Banks borrow money from their customers as deposits, and then invest (or lend out) that borrowed money in loans and other types of financial instruments. In simple terms, a bank intermediates its customer's investments into its loan portfolio. These two core activities of deposit-taking and lending form the traditional model of banking. Banks provide a link between creditors and borrowers, affecting the functioning of capital markets and financial markets and therefore the growth of economies.

Banks' liabilities, parts of which are in the form of deposits, constitute a large part of the supply of money in a country's economy. However, the rate of money supply that the banks can generate by making loans is limited by the reserve requirements that force banks to hold a portion of each deposit as a reserve, for instance in the form of deposits at a central bank. This maximum amount of money that banks are allowed to create (lend out) is determined by a measure called the money multiplier. If a bank receives a deposit, it is required to set aside a

---

9 For a detailed analysis of the relationship between finance and economic development, see: Gurely & Shaw (1955). For a literature review, see Levine (1997) and Gertler (1988). For empirical works on the relationship between financial development and economic growth, see: Demirgüç-Kunt & Maksimovic (1998), Levine & Zervos (1998), Rajan & Zingales (1998), Levine, Beck & Loayza (2000).

fraction of that deposit as a reserve.[10] It then lends out its excess reserves, creating new deposits in the banking system. As banks expand their depositing and lending activities, this multiplier process leads to an increase in the rate of reserves that banks are required to hold. Hence, the central banks have the power to control the amount of money that can be created by banks through the lending process (Keister & McAndrews, 2009; Platt, 2010). The proper functioning of financial intermediation is essential for the health of a country's economy because when this mechanism works well, it provides the most efficient allocation of resources between lenders and borrowers in a society (Merton, 1993). The importance of a healthy banking system for the economy is also stressed in the works of Gurley and Shaw (1955), and more recently by Bernanke and Gertler (1987) and Levine (1997).

However, economies are prone to banking crises as shown most recently by the global financial crisis of 2007–2009. This is due to the fragility of the banking system caused by short-term debt and interconnectedness.[11] When the banking system stops functioning, the ability of firms and individuals to obtain funds for their investments becomes constrained, hence curtailing economic growth (Gibson, 1995; Rosengreen & Peek 1995). Before starting with the analysis of banking regulation, it would first be useful to understand banks' unique features and functions, which will be discussed in detail in the next section.

The traditional theories of financial intermediation emphasise the role of banks as reducing asymmetric information and transaction costs. Asymmetric information refers to a transaction where one party has more relevant information than the other about the object being traded or the transaction itself. Banks transform deposits of lenders into credit portfolios demanded by the borrowers. Firms finance their projects with long-term credit whereas households prefer short-term and liquid deposits since they want to be able to withdraw their money whenever they want.[12] Hence, banks enable contact between these parties by arranging the transformation of each other's resources through issuing demand deposits or savings contracts. Banks help each party obtain information about the counterparty of the transaction. These kinds of debt contracts are complex agreements and preparing them in accordance with

10 Reserves are funds that are held by a bank in order to meet the bank's legal reserve requirement. These funds are held either as cash in the bank's vault or as balances on deposit at the central banks (Keister & McAndrews, 2009).

11 Banks produce liquidity by financing illiquid assets such as long-term investments with liquid and short-term liabilities. This maturity mismatch (borrowing short and lending long) in the operations of banks creates a fragile balance sheet since deposits have a shorter maturity than assets. If a bank is concerned about its counterparty's risk exposure, it will be reluctant to lend to other financial institutions. A temporary stop in the payment mechanism might distort banks' confidence in each other, namely the interbank trust market. Hence the failure of only one large participant can cause a big distortion in the system in terms of liquidity shortage.

12 Investors and depositors face an uncertain horizon in holding their assets because they do not know at which date they will need to consume (Diamond, 2007).

the best possible risk diversification method would increase transaction costs as well as search costs. It would be expensive for a firm to write these contracts; however, a bank can write and enforce these debt contracts in a less costly way (Tirole & Dewatripont, 1994).[13]

The contemporary theory of banking explains the existence of banks in terms of the valuable services they provide and justifies their existence on liquidity creation, risk transformation and acting as delegated monitors of depositors (Bhattacharya & Thakor 1993; Bouwman & Berger 2008).[14] The following sections explain these roles of banks in detail.

2.1. BALANCE SHEET AND INCOME STATEMENT OF BANKS

In order to describe the banking activities and performance of banks, it is useful to start with a presentation of a typical balance sheet and income statement. A typical balance sheet of a bank consists of the assets side and the liabilities side (see Table 1). Basically, a bank obtains funds by borrowing and by issuing (selling) liabilities such as deposits. Interbank deposits, retail and wholesale deposits (which are basically funds collected from households and companies), as well as subordinated debt[15] are on the liabilities side. Equity is the final category on the liabilities side of the balance sheet and is referred to as the banks' net worth or capital. It can be thought of as the difference between the value of the banks' assets and liabilities since total assets = total liabilities + equity. A bank may raise its own funds by selling new equity (stock) or from retained earnings which naturally increase the equity.

The funds that a bank has acquired by issuing liabilities are used to obtain income-earning assets (Mishkin, 2004: 201–205). On the assets side, banks have cash reserves, financial assets and non-financial assets. Financial assets include short-term assets (such as cash, interbank loans[16] and money market loans), credits in the form of loans or fixed income securities (financing both the public and the private sector), investment loans or real estate loans, and credit to households in the form of instalment loans or real estate loans (typically mortgages). Equipment and premises belong to non-financial assets. Banks may also hold stocks of other companies. Interbank operations normally take place in the form of short-term loans between banks on the money market (with maturities from overnight till three months) (Dewatripont & Tirole, 1994: 13–15).

13 For a more detailed discussion of transaction costs in financial intermediation theory, see Benston & Smith (1976).

14 Developed by Diamond (1984).

15 If a bank falls into liquidation or bankruptcy, the more senior debt-holders are reimbursed first. Holders of subordinated debt are then repaid if enough is left (Tirole, 2006: 76).

16 Banks finance each other through interbank operations.

Table 1. Balance sheet

Assets	Liabilities
Cash	Interbank deposits
Interbank loans	Retail and other whole-sale deposits (demands, savings and time deposits)
Credit to the public sector	
Credit to households	Subordinated debt
Credit to firms	**Equity (stock issues and retained earnings)**
Equity holdings	
Equipment and premises	

Source: Dewatripont & Tirole, 1994: 14.

Besides the balance sheet activities of banks, there are also off-balance sheet activities that may potentially affect bank profits (Tirole, 2006: 86; Mishkin, 2004: 223). They involve income from fees and loan sales,[17] financial guarantees such as standby letters of credit, bank loan commitments, and note issuance facilities; and also derivatives such as currency and interest rate swaps, over-the-counter options, futures, and forward contracts (Mishkin, 2004).

The income statement, presented below as Table 2, includes both the effects of on- and off-balance sheet activities. Interest income, commissions earned and dividends are the revenues of a bank. Operating expenses such as personnel, premises and equipment expenses together with loan loss provisions and depreciation are deducted from the revenue. The after-tax income is determined by the interest margin (which is the difference between interests earned and interest due) and by the income from equity holdings (Dewatripont & Tirole 1994). The income statement and the balance sheet together describe a bank's activities.

Table 2. Income statement

Debit	Credit
Interest and commissions paid	Interest and commissions earned
Operating expenses	Income from equity holdings
Depreciation	
Loan (and equity) loss provisions	
Taxes	
Profit after tax	

Source: Dewatripont & Tirole, 1994.

17 Loan sales are a recent innovation in banking where a bank makes a loan and then sells the cash stream coming from the loan without explicit guarantee, or insurance, to a third party (Gorton & Haubrich, 1989).

2.2. MATURITY TRANSFORMATION AND LIQUIDITY OF BANKS

The function of banks as liquidity creators is described as one of the major reasons for banks' existence in contemporary banking theory (Bouwman & Berger, 2008). Besides, financial crises and bank liquidity creation are often connected as evidenced in the latest global crisis (Berger & Bouwan 2008). Liquidity basically refers to a firm's ability to meet its payment obligations when they come due by having enough liquid assets that the payment of debt occurs without any losses. A liquid asset (or security) is an asset that is easily and cheaply turned into cash and short-term securities. Liquid assets are bought or sold with little or no impact on price.[18] The role of banks in liquidity management refers to the provision of sufficiently liquid assets to meet banks' obligations to depositors (Mishkin, 2004).

This basic function of banks is described in the famous model of Diamond-Dybvig (1983).[19] Banks provide financial intermediation between borrowers in need of funds and lenders that have surplus savings by transforming the credit portfolio demanded by the borrowers into a deposit portfolio desired by the lenders. In doing so, they create credit that allows the real economy to grow. In other words, banks produce liquidity by financing illiquid assets such as long-term investments with liquid and short-term liabilities. However, this maturity mismatch (borrowing short and lending long) in the operations of banks creates a fragile balance sheet for banks since deposits have a shorter maturity than the assets. That means that the illiquid loans cannot be sold quickly, because firms want to finance their projects with long-term credits. At the same time, households prefer short-term deposits for liquidity reasons since they want to be able to withdraw their funds whenever they want to accommodate their own spending needs. So, this liquidity mismatch subjects banks to runs which refer to situations when too many depositors try to withdraw (Freixas & Rochet, 1999).[20] On the other hand, the upside of banking fragility is liquidity generation which allows funds to flow to real investments, which, in turn, fuel economic growth (Diamond & Dybvig, 1983, 2000; Diamond, 2007).

The same mismatch in the operations of banks is reproduced by a new form of banking called *the shadow banking system*, or as Gorton and Metrick (2009) describe it, *securitised banking*. Much of the liquidity production by banks occurs today off the balance sheet in the form of loan commitments, credit lines

18 Cash, money in bank accounts, money market mutual funds, and treasury bills are examples of liquid assets.

19 D.W. Diamond and P.H. Dybvig (2000): "Bank Runs, Deposit Insurance, and Liquidity".

20 Gorton and Metrick (2009) describe the current global crisis as a system-wide bank run. Normally, in a traditional banking system a bank run occurs by the withdrawal of transaction deposits whereas a shadow banking run occurs by the withdrawal of repurchase agreements (Gorton & Metrick, 2009).

securitisation and syndicated lending rather than in the form of transaction deposits due to financial innovation (Strahan 2008; Gorton 2009).[21] Although the functioning mechanism of this new form of banking will be discussed in section 3.2, it is worth mentioning here in order to illustrate some of the implications of this system in terms of the liquidity concept.

First of all, there are several definitions of liquidity. The basic meaning refers to banking liquidity which is a bank's ability to fulfil its obligation towards depositors to transform their deposits into money. This function also includes maintaining a balance between in-coming and out-going cash flows that come from the management of payments made through using bank money (Gualandri et al., 2009). In order to meet its liquidity shortages, a bank can depend on funding liquidity and market liquidity (Brunnermeier & Pederson, 2005). Funding liquidity is defined by the ease and ability with which a bank can obtain cash from financiers. Market liquidity on the other hand is the ability to raise money by trading assets for cash without discount. With the emergence of a shadow banking system, the strategy of off-balance sheet vehicles exposed banks to funding liquidity risk. If funding liquidity is high, then it is easy to raise cash on demand. However, even a small and unexpected shock can cause the liquidity in the interbank market to dry up suddenly (Brunnermeier, 2009).

A liquidity crisis is defined as the sudden disappearance of both funding liquidity and market liquidity, which has a destabilising effect on financial stability and the real economy leading to a systemic crisis as evidenced by the 2007–2009 global financial crisis (Borio, 2009). In fact, the crisis of 2007–2009 was characterised by a massive illiquidity in the markets (Tirole, 2010). Since banks stopped lending to each other, liquidity in the market dried up (Berger & Bouwmann, 2008). This absence of liquidity has forced banks to restrict lending to households and businesses, thereby fuelling a recession.

The financial crisis that began in the US in 2007 spread to the rest of the world. It affected both financial systems and economic activity across the globe, including those of emerging markets. Especially in Russia, the drying-up of access to international capital markets hit some banks hard. There, the banking system was strongly influenced by the global financial crisis and experienced major bank failures. The disruption of lending caused the interbank liquidity crisis to transform into a more generalised liquidity crunch, where companies were forced to suspend investment projects due to a lack of financing. In addition, the depositors' lack of confidence in the Russian banking sector led them to withdraw their deposits, which caused a bank run and the resulting financial crisis (Dorbec, 2010). In Russia, many banks were transferred to the Deposit Insurance Agency (DIA), bailed out by the state, merged with other banks, or had their licenses revoked (see Appendix C). The Russian government

21 The new form of banking including the securitisation process will be described in the second part of this chapter.

and the Central Bank implemented a number of measures to support the Russian banking sector with liquidity in order to mitigate the effects of the 2008–2009 financial crisis. On the other hand, in Turkey, no banks had been transferred to the Savings Deposit Insurance Fund. There were no changes in the ownership of banks, no bank failures, no liquidation and thus no decrease in the number of banks. Besides, there was no dip in the profitability of banks (Uygur, 2010).

2.3. MONITORING AND INFORMATION SYSTEMS IN BANKS

In a lending relationship, asymmetric information on borrower exposes the lender to incentive problems, since the borrower has more information than the lender about the project for which he has been granted the loan (Bhattacharya & Thakor, 1992). Asymmetric information between borrower and lender causes moral hazard and adverse selection which reduce the efficiency of resource allocation. Banks can solve this problem by acting as delegated monitors of borrowers on behalf of the lenders (Matthews & Thompson, 2008).

Matthews and Thompson (2008) define monitoring as the collection of information about a firm, its investments and its behaviour before and after the loan application is made. Monitoring takes the form of screening loan applications in order to separate the risky applications from the good ones, investigating the borrower's creditworthiness and monitoring the borrower's adherence to the conditions of the agreement (Matthews & Thompson, 2008). The banks' role in overcoming this problem of asymmetric information is described by Diamond (1984) as "delegated monitoring". Processing private information about the borrower is costly for a lender. However, a bank that monitors learns the customers' account and payment histories and whether they had any business problems at a lower cost than the ultimate lenders (the depositors). By acting as delegated monitors, banks reduce the risk of the borrower running a different project than the one agreed upon in the loan agreement.[22] Besides, the routines designed for acquiring information about a customer can be used to process other customers. Hence, as a consequence of specialisation banks are able to achieve economies of scale (Benston & Smith, 1975).

2.4. RISK MANAGEMENT

Risk is inherent in the banking business because banks make profits by taking and managing risks. Risk management is the ability of a bank to isolate its

22 Allen et al. (1991) show in their empirical work how banks can use information produced through deposit accounts in designing future credit contracts.

returns against shocks which emerge out of the banks' control.[23] There are three major sources of risks that may affect banks' stability through their impact on banks' balance sheets: credit risk, liquidity risk and market risk.

(i) *Credit Risk:* The economic theory of asymmetric information provides a framework for understanding the importance of managing credit risk. Since there are differences in the information available to the participants in the market, markets might work imperfectly. Adverse selection is an asymmetric information problem in the financial markets which occurs when potentially bad credit risks are the ones who are most eager to obtain loans. Moral hazard is another asymmetric information problem in the loan markets. Once the borrower obtains the loan, the lender is subject to the risk of default, since the borrower might engage in risky activities that are undesirable from the lender's perspective.

Evaluating credit risk and estimating the risk return of a bank loan are some of the major functions of a bank (Pyle, 1997). A borrower may default on the principal or the interest payments of the loan. Credit risk is the possibility of failure of the counterparties to meet their contractual obligations (Matthews & Thompson, 2008). This type of risk is influenced by several factors such as borrower default ratings, credit ratings, estimates of loss in case of default on individual assets, measures of portfolio size and whether the amount of loans made to borrowers constitutes a large proportion of the portfolio (Carey, 2000). Lax credit standards for borrowers and counterparties are one of the major causes of serious banking problems such as the recent global crisis where relaxed credit standards caused an expansion of lending to risky borrowers (e.g. subprime mortgages) (Dell'Ariccia et al., 2008). Hence, the global crisis is also described as a credit crisis. Huge losses and numerous bankruptcies of subprime lenders showed that many financial institutions could not accurately assess the credit risk of borrowers.

There are several ways to minimise the credit risk that is reflected by the price of the loan in terms of its interest payment (the so-called risk premium). One way is putting credit limits on customers (Matthews & Thompson, 2008: 210–212). Collateral requirements,[24] effective screening of customers and information collections,[25] establishing long-term customer

23 J. Tirole (2010): "Illiquidity and All Its Friends" BIS Working Paper No: 303.

24 Collateral is the property promised to the lender as a compensation if the borrower defaults. If the borrower defaults on a loan, the lender can sell the collateral and use the proceeds to make up for the losses on the loan. That way, the losses of the lender will be reduced if the loan is not paid back.

25 When a bank provides a loan to a company, it collects information about the company's profits and losses and its assets and liabilities, future plans and sales figures in order to evaluate the likely future success of the business. By effectively collecting and screening

relationships,[26] and loan commitments,[27] are all tools used by banks for credit risk management (Mishkin, 2004: 217–220). However, with the changing structure of banking, a market for the efficient transfer of credit risk has developed. Credit derivatives and collateralised debt obligations (CDOs) were introduced to transfer credit risk. Credit derivatives allow the transfer of credit risk to another party without the sale of the loan. A CDO is a structured finance vehicle which buys a portfolio of fixed income assets and finances the purchase of the portfolio by issuing different tranches of securities (with different degrees of seniority and therefore different risk exposure) in the capital markets. Each tranche offers a different degree of risk and return to meet the investors' demand. In this way, the credit risk of a pool of assets is transferred from the originating bank to the investors (Fabozzi et al., 2007).

(ii) *Liquidity Risk:* The second type of risk is liquidity risk. Liquidity risk is basically the risk of not being able to immediately liquidate certain assets at current market prices (Berivas, 2006). When a bank funds its illiquid long-term assets with short-term liquid liabilities, it puts itself in a risky position. Hence, the bank might be unable to honour its liquid liabilities if faced with an unexpected and synchronised withdrawal of deposits by the customers. This uncertainty about the amount of deposit withdrawals increases especially when a bank is suspected of having solvency problems due to liquidity shortages or an adverse economic shock. Additionally, there is also some uncertainty on the asset side about the volume of new requests for loans, which might lead to the loss of profit opportunities. Furthermore, as recently experienced during the global crisis, off-balance sheet activities subject banks to liquidity risks due to their positions taken on derivative markets.

A final source of liquidity risk is the large volume of interbank payments. When a bank has concerns about a counterparty's risk exposure, it will be reluctant to lend to other financial institutions. A temporary stop in the payment mechanism might negatively affect the interbank trust market. Therefore the failure of only one large participant can create a large distortion of the system in terms of liquidity shortage (Rochet, 2008). If banks stop

---

information from prospective borrowers, the bank is able to distinguish between bad credit risks and good ones.

26 If a borrower has an account at a bank over a long period of time, a loan officer can learn much about the borrower by looking at his past activity on the accounts. The balances on these accounts reveal the borrower's suppliers and also how liquid he is, and hence whether he is a good or bad credit risk. That way, the costs of monitoring long-term customers are lowered through their previous records of the loan payments.

27 A loan commitment is the bank's commitment for a specified time period to provide a firm with a specified amount of loans at an interest rate that is tied to the market interest rate. The advantage for the firm is that it has a source of credit for when it is needed. The advantage for the bank is that this loan commitment provides a long-term relationship, making information collection easier for the bank and reducing the costs of screening and information collection.

lending to each other, liquidity in the market dries up, forcing banks to restrict credit to households and businesses. This is also what happened in the global crisis. The failure of Lehman Brothers in 2008 created fear in the interbank market about the risk exposure of other banks. Following that, once the liquidity crisis became systemic, even institutions with little fundamental risk exposure found themselves at risk, such as the two major investment banks in the US: Goldman Sachs and Morgan Stanley (Calomiris, 2008).

Cash reserves and government securities (used as collateral for borrowing liquidity) are instruments of liquidity management for banks (Rochet, 2008).[28]

(iii) *Market Risk:* The third type of risk banks are exposed to is market risk, which is the possibility of loss due to changes in asset value caused by possible changes in interest rates, exchange rates and equity prices (Freixas & Rochet, 1999). Interest rate risk is the main factor of market risk. It is caused by the volatility of interest rates and the mismatch in the maturity of assets and liabilities. Banks have long-term assets and short-term liabilities on their balance sheets. If the interest rates increase, then the market value of their assets will decrease more than the market value of their liabilities due to the shorter maturity of liabilities. Unexpected changes in interest rates subject banks to interest rate risks, which means that a rise in interest rates will reduce the net market value of banks (Matthews & Thompson, 2008: 211–213).

Banks are affected in terms of their net interest income, which is the difference between what banks obtain in interest receipts and what they pay in interest costs. In the 1980s, the US savings and loan industry was exposed to a massive interest rate risk because they provided mortgage loans at fixed rates with a long maturity whereas most of their deposits were paying short-term variable interest rates. When the Federal Reserve increased the interest rates as a monetary tool to decrease inflation, banks had to pay their depositors higher interest rates while at the same time the interest income on loan assets remained fixed. Over a period of time, this mismatch in the interest rates between the two sides of the banks' balance sheets resulted in huge losses for banks (Dewatripont & Tirole, 1999: 93–95; Schooner & Taylor, 2010: 178).

Interest rate risk was generally assumed to be a less important risk. Therefore, Basel I[29] primarily focused on credit risk and classified the assets

---

28 Under the assumption that the liquidity risk is policed by the market discipline, liquidity management was essentially unregulated before the crisis. But this is going to change with the overhaul of international banking regulation. The Basel Committee decided to establish a new set of standards, called Basel III, in response to the deficiencies in financial regulation that were revealed by the global crisis. This new set of measures not only strengthens capital adequacy ratios, but also introduces global liquidity requirements on banks. The Basel Accords and their evolution will be discussed in detail in section 6.1.1 of this chapter.

29 In 1988, the Basel Committee on Banking Supervision under the auspices of the Bank for International Settlements imposed a set of requirements to account for the different credit

of banks according to their credit risk. However, focusing only on credit risk provides an imperfect measure of a bank's riskiness. To account for this discrepancy, the Basel II Accord included the measurement of a bank's exposure to market risks (interest rate risk, exchange rate risk etc.) in the calculation of the regulatory capital that banks have to maintain (Dewatripont & Tirole, 1999: 93–95).[30]

One of the sources of banking crises in emerging markets is the exchange rate risk that occurs as a result of excessive currency mismatches. Due to their direct exposure to foreign exchange risk, when large devaluations occurred in the home country (weakening the ability of the banking sector to service foreign currency loans), banks were suddenly faced with huge credit risks (Hawkins & Mihaljek, 2001). In Turkey and in Russia, the pre-crisis environments were suffering from huge exposures to foreign exchange rate risk and liquidity risk.

3. FINANCIAL INNOVATION AND THE CHANGING STRUCTURE OF BANKING

3.1. INSTITUTIONAL SETTING OF THE TRADITIONAL BANKING SYSTEM

In traditional banking, banks simply provide the services of accepting deposits and making loans to individuals and small businesses. It is also called retail banking. Basically, the cash raised is lent out and these loans are held on balance sheets. Banks are required to hold a certain fraction of deposits in reserves at the central bank to promote bank liquidity. In cases of shortages, they can borrow from the central bank. Demand deposits are the main source of funds, and the interest rates on deposits can be raised to attract depositors when reserves are low. Demand deposits at banks are typically insured. Deposit insurance is an insurance mechanism designed by the government to pay depositors in the event of default (Gorton & Metrick, 2009). Under a deposit insurance system, depositors get their payments if the bank experiences a failure, in which case depositors are guaranteed to get at least the minimum insured amount of their deposits within a short time of the triggering event. The first formal national deposit insurance mechanism was introduced in the United States by the Federal Reserve in 1934 with the purpose of ending traditional bank runs.

---

risks of banks and also to establish the international harmonisation of banking regulation. The first and second versions of these reform measures are called Basel I and Basel II, respectively. These reforms will be explained in detail in section 6 of this chapter.

30 The Basel Accords and their evolutions will be discussed in detail in section 6.1.1 of this chapter.

After the post-War period and especially in the 1980s, many countries began to adopt this mechanism. In 1994, the European Union adopted deposit insurance as the standard for their banking system. Although it was mostly used in high-income countries until the mid-1990s, since 1995 lower-income countries also started to introduce deposit insurance to their banking systems.[31, 32]

The goal of deposit insurance is to protect banking systems from traditional bank runs (which supports the stability of the system) as well as to protect small, uninformed depositors (Laeven et al., 2005). It also shields bank depositors from losses in case a bank is unable to meet its obligations when they come due. However, the desirability of the implementation of this mechanism is a controversial issue. On one hand, as Diamond and Dybvig (1983) argue in their classic work, deposit insurance contributes to bank stability by preventing self-fulfilling depositor runs since depositors would have little incentive to withdraw their funds if they know that their deposits are insured by the government. On the other hand, deposit insurance might have a negative effect on bank stability by encouraging risk-taking on the part of banks. In the existence of such an insurance mechanism, depositors are not disciplining banks by requiring higher interests for risk-taking, because they know that any possible failure will be backed up by the deposit insurance and ultimately by the government. Banks thus have the incentive to engage in riskier activities for higher returns (Detragiache & Demirgüç-Kunt, 2002). This is known as the moral hazard problem in banking.

Before explaining the institutional setting of securitised banking, it would be useful to start with the basic differences between the two forms of banking systems. In securitised banking, repo haircuts play the role of reserves in traditional banking. A repo (= sale and repurchase agreement) is the sale of a security combined with an agreement to repurchase the same security at a specified price at the end of the contract. Effectively, a repo is a form of lending against the collateral being sold and repurchased. The "haircut" is a percentage that is deducted from the market value of the asset that is being used as collateral. The size of the haircut reflects the perceived risk associated with holding that asset. The repo haircut is the percentage difference between the market value of the pledged collateral (security) and the amount of funds the bank gets in exchange for that security. Repo haircuts force banks to limit their leverage when borrowing in repo markets. Although there are no official statistics on the size of the repo market worldwide, it is estimated to be around

31 Laeven, Karacaovali and Demirgüç-Kunt (2005) show that most countries provide deposit insurance. Furthermore, during the global crisis, there has been a surge in the number of countries such as Australia and New Zealand that are adopting deposit insurance for the first time while some other countries increased their insurance coverage (Laeven et al., 2005; Santos et al., 2010).

32 In Turkey, a deposit insurance scheme was introduced in 1983. In Russia, it was introduced in 2003.

$12 trillion, which is huge when compared to the total assets of the US banking system – $10 trillion (Gorton & Metrick, 2009).[33]

Repo agreements have a special status under the US Bankruptcy Code. They are exempted from the automatic stay.[34] According to the standard documentation, the non-defaulting party to a repo agreement is allowed to unilaterally enforce the termination provisions of the agreement as a result of a bankruptcy filing by the other party and keep the cash or the bond (Gorton & Metrick, 2009).[35] In securitised banking, creditors' rights are protected by the collateral used in repo markets, while in traditional banking creditors' rights are protected by deposit insurance. In traditional banking, the banks' cost of funding is covered by the interest rate at which depositors are rewarded, which increases with the intensity of competition. A bank in need of cash can increase the deposit rates to attract depositors whereas in securitised banking this is analogous to repo rates. Lastly, as opposed to loans that are held on a balance sheet in traditional banking, loans in securitised banking are repackaged and sold as securitised bonds (Gorton & Metrick, 2009). Table 3 below summarises these differences briefly.

According to Gorton (2010b), the two banking systems are intimately connected meaning that the traditional banking system wouldn't be able to function without the securitisation markets. Loans made to consumers and corporations correspond to the credit creation provided by the traditional banks. These traditional banks obtain the sources for lending to their customers by selling portfolios of loans as bonds to various securitisation vehicles such as the collateralised debt obligations (CDOs) which are in turn financed by the investors (Gorton, 2010b).[36]

Table 3. Traditional banking vs. securitised banking

Traditional banking	Securitised banking
Reserve rates	Repo haircuts
Deposit insurance	Collateral
Interest rates on deposits	Repo rates
Loans are held on balance sheet	Loans are packaged and sold = securitised

Source: Gorton & Metrick, 2009.

33 For more on the size of the repo market, see Gorton & Metrick (2009; 2010).

34 Automatic stay prevents creditors from seizing the assets of a firm in bankruptcy (Edwards & Morrison, 2004).

35 In fact, Gorton & Metrick (2010) argue that the evolution of a bankruptcy safe harbour for repo has been a key feature in the growth of shadow banking.

36 For details on how traditional banking funding works via the securitised banking system, see Gorton (2010b).

3.2. INSTITUTIONAL SETTING OF SECURITISED (SHADOW) BANKING SYSTEM

The Great Depression in the 1930s created a heavy-handed regulation environment for the banking sector characterised by deposit insurance, interest-rate regulations, entry restrictions, constraints on bank size and activities. The Banking Act of 1933 in the US – also called the Glass-Steagall Act – banned banks from engaging in non-banking activities such as securities activities. This created a stable banking sector even though it was accompanied by a gradual decline in efficiency and innovation (Tirole et al., 2010). However, within time, the financial environment in which the regulatory environment continues to exist has changed due to globalisation and technology. The 1970s and 1980s witnessed a trend towards deregulation. Especially in the 1980s, traditional banking started to become unprofitable since the commercial banks were faced with competition from other less- regulated financial institutions such as money market mutual funds, hedge funds and investment banks. Hence, the banking system started to change. Markets began to play a much bigger role in the financial system and deregulation contributed to the innovation in the supply of new financial products. This process reached its peak in the United States with the Gramm-Leach-Bliley Act in 1999, which allowed commercial banks to enter into trading of securities and insurance businesses (Schooner & Taylor, 2010). Basically, by the end of 1990s, a new model of banking emerged, based mainly on a European-style model of universal banking and the originate-to-distribute-model (OTD) rather than on the US model of strict sectorial separation between investment banking and commercial banking.[37] Adrian and Shin emphasise this transformation of banking as such: "*The rapid move toward a market-based financial system in recent years has accelerated the trend toward greater reliance on non-traditional, non-deposit based funding and toward greater use of the interbank market, the market for commercial paper, and asset-backed securities*" (Adrian & Shin, 2008).

This new model of banking can be characterised by three distinctive features. The first characteristic of this new form of banking is a greater reliance on wholesale money markets for funding. In the traditional model of banking, banks rely on deposits for funding which is considered a more stable form of funding. However, in the 1980s, with the emergence of money market mutual funds – a competitor to traditional bank deposits – banks started to fund themselves by borrowing funds from these funds. This wholesale funding provided banks with greater flexibility in borrowing because they could raise

[37] Some developed countries such as Germany and Japan have bank-dominated financial systems where firms rely primarily on bank loans as the source of funding for their operations. Other countries like the UK and the US have a market-dominated system where firms rely on securities markets to fund their operations.

funds quickly and easily. In case of sudden deposit withdrawals, a bank could easily fund itself in the money market, thereby reducing its exposure to a liquidity risk (Taylor & Schooner, 2010). However, the stability of this funding is questionable since during the global crisis of 2007–2009, banks that relied on wholesale funding became exposed to sudden losses of funding. Towards the end of 2007, when all banks tried to fund themselves from the markets to cope with their shortage in liquidity, they had difficulty accessing the funds they needed (*funding liquidity risk*) since the global interbank and other financial markets were frozen due to the fear of a system-wide bank run.[38]

Secondly, as the competition between commercial banks and investment banks for securities increased in the 1990s, a new mechanism called *securitisation* was developed as a product of financial innovation. Whereas the wholesale markets changed the way in which banks manage their liabilities, securitisation changed the way banks managed their assets (Taylor & Schooner, 2010). As mentioned before, traditional banking is the business of making and holding loans on the balance sheet while insured demand deposits are the main source of funds. However, as Gorton (2010b) argues, holding loans on the balance sheets is not profitable for banks. Securitisation is the process of transforming existing or predictable cash flows emerging from a pool of assets into a tradable security. In the first place, the assets (or receivables) originated by the banks are pooled together and sold to a bankruptcy-remote Special-Purpose Vehicle (SPV).[39] The SPV finances the purchase of these assets through the issuance of debt securities into capital markets. This pool of cash flows is tranched, meaning that securities with different seniorities are designed. These securities are called Asset-Backed-Securities (ABS) because payment to the investors depends on the cash flows coming from the underlying assets. Credit card receivables, auto loans, student loans, leases and any other kind of receivables are included in this set of securitised assets (Fabozzi et al., 2006).

There are several motivations for banks to securitise part of their balance sheets. As Fabozzi et al. (2006: 75–85) argue, the driving force behind securitisation has been the need for banks to realise value from the assets that existed on their balance sheets. Banks use securitisation to support asset growth. A bank can expand its loans faster through having access to the asset-backed securities (ABS) market than if it relied on traditional funding sources alone, since the market for ABS is large. If a bank were dependent on only a single or a few sources of funding, it could be risky if a market difficulty emerges. As a result, securitisation would help banks to optimise their funding through having

38 This was not a traditional run by the depositors, but rather a silent run by the wholesale investors who refused to roll over their lending positions.

39 A SPV is a specialised legal entity created by a firm (also known as the originator or sponsor) by transferring assets to the SPV in order to accomplish some specific transactions. They have no other purpose and they do not have any physical location.

access to a mix of retail, interbank and wholesale resources where securities are accepted as collateral.

Another advantage of securitisation is that, once the assets have been securitised, the credit risk exposure on these assets for the banks is reduced because the assets are sold to a SPV. By doing so, banks can also remove non-performing loans from their balance sheets, which would again decrease the credit risk exposure of the bank. Banks use securitisation also to improve their balance sheet capital management since it provides regulatory capital relief. According to the Basel Rules, banks must hold a minimum capital level for their assets in relation to the risk amount of these assets. Since a SPV is not a bank, it is not subject to these rules. It only needs to hold the amount of capital that is economically required to support the assets it contains. Hence, the regulatory capital relief for banks is significantly reduced after securitisation (Fabozzi et al., 2006: 76–77). The regulatory capital relief provided by the securitisation process helps the bank to improve its return-on-equity (ROE) since the amount of capital that has to be used to support the asset pool is reduced (Fabozzi et al., 2006: 78).

Thirdly, in the traditional model of banking, banks originated loans and owned them until maturity (*originate and hold*). The loan is funded with deposits and the bank itself is responsible for any borrower default. However, in the securitisation process, banks originate loans and then sell them to third party investors. This is called the *originate-to-distribute* (OTD) model.[40]

The early episodes of banking panics were prevented by way of deposit insurance which brought considerable stability to the financial system. The deposit insurance system works well in traditional banking since it protects retail investors. However, it is not useful for large financial institutions because the protection provided by deposit insurance is limited. On the contrary, institutional investors want to deposit large amounts of money in a safe place for a short period of time rather than depositing them as demand deposits where their money will not be insured. This need for saving large amounts of money for a short period in a safe place by large firms, hedge funds and so forth led to the growth of the repo market. With the development of securitisation (or securitised banking), sale and repurchase (repo) markets have developed where institutional investors can put their money.

A repo market is efficient in the sense that it provides the intermediation of funding where one side (= borrower/bank) needs to borrow money and the other side (lenders such as hedge funds, insurance companies, etc.) wants to save money by depositing it somewhere safe, collateralised with bonds. Repo financing is a very liquid form of financing, and it does not cause speculators to take

40 Goodhart (2009) defines this model as the "*originate and pretend to distribute*" model. Vehicles such as SPVs where banks were transferring their assets to were in fact closely related to these banks either by legal commitment or by reputational risk. Hence, whenever financial conditions became worse causing a shortage in the funding for these vehicles, banks had to support them (Goodhart, 2009).

advantage of the less-informed in the trade by having private information about the value of debt in comparison to an equity market. These features contributed to the increase in the demand for such debt, which in turn increased the demand for collateral in the repo market. This growing need for collateral led to the inclusion of securitised products for use in repo markets. Repos, like demand deposits, are also short-term and can be withdrawn at any time. However, contrary to insured deposits, repo markets are not insured and the resulting global crisis was a liquidity crisis caused by the run on the repo market. A traditional banking run happens by the withdrawal of demand deposits whereas a securitised banking run is driven by the withdrawal from repo agreements in the form of requesting higher haircuts and/or the termination of repo lending on some forms of collateral (Gorton & Metrick, 2009; Gorton, 2009).

3.3. BANKING IN EMERGING MARKETS

Banks are the dominant financial intermediaries in emerging markets (Caner et al., 2007). Whereas the structure of banking in developed countries has changed dramatically, the traditional role of banks remained key in emerging markets. Considering the fact that financial markets in emerging countries are less developed and asymmetric information problems are more acute, the traditional function of banks is essential for these countries (Vives, 2006).

The banking systems in emerging markets were traditionally a highly protected industry, based on depository banking and pervasive restrictions on domestic and foreign entry. However, with the changing environment in global markets accompanied by the developments in technology, macroeconomic pressures and the banking crises in the 1990s have forced the banking sector and the regulators of emerging countries to change the old ways of doing business as well as deregulate the banking industry. With this financial liberalisation, financial markets were opened up to foreign competition. As they became integrated into the global financial markets, their banking systems have been transformed by three major trends: privatisation of state-owned banks, mergers and consolidation and the entry of foreign banks on a large scale (Turner, 2006; Mihaljek & Hawkins, 2001).

The 1990s were a highly volatile period in developing countries, characterised by successive banking crises. Goldstein and Turner (1996) identify the origins of these crises as the following: (i) macroeconomic volatility, (ii) lending booms, (iii) increasing bank liabilities with large maturity mismatches, (iv) inadequate preparation with financial liberalisation, (v) heavy government intervention and loose control on connected lending,[41] and (vi) a weak legal framework. The

[41] Connected lending refers to the loans provided to banks' owners, managers and to their related businesses.

process of bank supervision was not being implemented properly and was lagging behind the pace of financial liberalisation. The Bank for International Settlements (BIS)[42] organised several meetings with the governors of developing countries starting in 1995 to focus on strengthening the banking systems and supervision in these countries. However, these attempts to establish more cautionary policies in bank lending proved inadequate. Accompanied by the persistent macroeconomic imbalances, the crisis in Thailand in 1997 set the stage for successive banking crises throughout emerging markets. This led to a contraction in bank intermediation, which lasted longer than expected. More importantly, this made bankers in these emerging market countries more risk-averse and caused them to tighten the supervisory oversight of the banking sector. Following these restructuring reforms, bank credit started to increase again in 2004. Furthermore, the international agreements on prudential regulation on banking supervisory regimes such as the *Core Principles for Effective Banking Supervision of 1997* published by the BIS and the *Financial Sector Assessment Program (FSAP)* of the International Monetary Fund (IMF) are intended not only for developed countries but also for emerging markets (Turner, 2006).

The reforms that had their roots in the late 1990s led to a significant overhaul of financial regulation in many emerging countries. Domestic financial markets have been further developed. Financial firms have become subject to market discipline and financial services and capital markets have become internationalised. This reform programme seems to have contributed to substantial structural strengthening of the banking system in emerging economies (BIS Monetary and Economic Department, August 2006). The financial crisis that began in the United States in 2007 and quickly spread to Europe has become a global crisis affecting the financial systems and economies across the world. Emerging market economies were also affected by this crisis. However, compared to their previous experiences in the 1990s and early 2000s, they showed remarkable resilience with robust rates of growth as the crisis was developing in advanced countries (BIS Monetary and Economic Department, December 2010) (see Table 4). The effects of stress of the Lehman Brothers bankruptcy have been limited in emerging markets, which started to recover immediately in the second quarter of 2009, showing improving signs of stability whereas the US and the European markets were trapped by recession and declining rates of growth followed by a sovereign debt crisis (BIS Monetary and Economic Department, December 2010).

42 The Bank for International Settlements (BIS) is an international organisation established in 1930 acting as the principal centre for international central bank cooperation. Its aim is to serve central banks in their pursuit of monetary and financial stability, to foster international cooperation in those areas and to act as a bank for central banks. (See: www.bis.org/).

Table 4. GDP growth projections (%)

	2008	2009	2010	2011
Advanced Economies	0.8	–3.8	0.01	2.6
US	1.1	–2.8	–0.05	3.5
EU	1.1	–4	–0.3	1.7
Japan	–0.6	–6.2	0.5	2.2
Emerging Market Economies	5.2	0.01	3.2	5.7
Emerging Asia	6.3	2.5	5	7.6
Emerging Europe	4	–4.8	0.7	3.6
Emerging Americas	4	–1.7	1.6	3.5
Developing Asia	7.7	4.8	6.1	8.3
China	9	6.5	7.5	10.2
India	7.3	4.5	5.6	6.9

Source: IMF World Economic Outlook (2009); Boorman (2009).

The resilience of real credit growth in emerging markets during the global crisis was closely related to prudential policies, measures and reforms implemented in the pre-crisis period (Montoro & Rojas-Suarez, 2012). The financial institutions in most emerging markets did not engage in the popular activities practised in advanced countries. Their balance sheets were not exposed to the "toxic assets" that dominated the financial positions of major institutions in developed countries. Derivatives were used less frequently and were mostly limited to the traditional instruments that are employed to hedge trade risks (such as currency risk). However, due to financial channels that connect countries worldwide, many developing countries are connected to the world economy. Any slowdown or recession in advanced countries may adversely affect developing countries' growth prospects. Besides, since crises are contagious, it is difficult to benefit from the opportunities of economic and financial integration without being exposed to the contagious effects of these integrations regarding trade (through declining demand for developing-country exports or a declining export process, including commodities), investment (as external finance contracts) and remittances (stemming from the recession in advanced economies) (World Bank Development Research Group, 2008).

Although the systemic weaknesses in the banking systems of emerging markets have been reduced compared to the 1990s, cautionary policies must be in place since the macroeconomic environment is more unstable in developing countries compared to the rest of the world. Additionally, they suffer larger exogenous shocks than developed countries, possess weaker financial shock absorbers and their domestic policies often represent an additional source of volatility (World Bank Development Research Group, 2008).

4. THE ECONOMIC RATIONALE FOR BANKING REGULATION

In the legal and economic literature, the term *regulation* has varying definitions (den Hertog, 1999). In general terms, regulation is the employment of legal instruments for the achievement of policy objectives. These legal instruments are compulsory, publicly enforced and also backed by criminal and administrative sanctions (Pacces & Van den Bergh, 2012). Through these legal rules, governments can force individuals and institutions to adhere to certain regulations under penalty of sanctions such as fines, imprisonment or closing down the business (den Hertog, 1999). There are two approaches investigating the theory of economic regulation. The *normative approach* explains regulation in terms of its economic justification. It is based on the assumption that efficient regulation is desirable for the well-being of a society. The other variant, the *positive approach*, discusses regulation based on its causes and effects, regardless of how it should be. Economic efficiency in providing resource allocation in society, including the costs of certain policies, is the normative criterion in analysing regulation (Pacces & Van den Bergh, 2012). Following this normative perspective of economic efficiency, regulation is justified due to the market failures which distort efficient resource allocation.

4.1. MARKET FAILURE IN FINANCIAL MARKETS

The theory of market failure forms the basis for understanding financial regulation. From the traditional perspective, the explanation of regulation is based on the welfare economics assumptions of neo-classic economic theory about the market system (Dragomir, 2010: 39). The central theorem of welfare economics asserts that under certain strong assumptions regarding technology, tastes and producers' motivations, the equilibrium conditions of competitive markets will provide a Pareto-efficient (economically efficient) allocation of resources (Bator, 1958). If there are no missing markets (including negative externalities and public goods), if producers and consumers behave competitively, and if there are no information problems in the market, then the allocation of resources will be efficient (Ogus, 1994: 23; Pacces & Van den Bergh, 2012). Market failure arises when the allocations achieved in markets are not efficient due to the lack of fulfilment of these assumptions. According to contemporary economic theory, financial markets are inherently imperfect (Heremans & Pacces, 2012). The global crisis is a good example of the fact that financial markets are not always functioning well. Market failure in finance depends on the existence of negative externalities and information asymmetries between buyers and sellers. These two fundamental problems inherent in financial markets form the justification for financial regulation since they may result in the failure of a competitive market to produce a socially optimal outcome (Taylor & Schooner, 2010). Market failures may be overcome by the financial intermediaries or they may require government intervention.

4.1.1. Asymmetric Information

Information problems refer to information asymmetries between buyers and sellers such as adverse selection and moral hazard. Any financial transaction in the market is prone to the asymmetric information problem. A financial contract starts with the transaction of money between the lender and borrower, followed by subsequent repayments. However, during this time interval, the borrower's conditions might change in terms of his ability to make the repayments. In the meantime, the lender might not be able to access information about the risk being transacted and thereby evaluate the progress of these repayments (Dragomir, 2010: 42). This would distort the functioning of the market in two ways. Firstly, due to incomplete information, the lender cannot distinguish between good borrowers and unreliable borrowers. The possible risk premium will increase the loan rate and adverse selection may occur where only risky projects would be funded (Heremans, 1999).[43] Secondly, a lender would be subject to moral hazard if the borrower has incentives to engage in risky activities after he receives the loan that is undesirable from the lender's point of view.

The role of financial intermediaries, particularly banks, in alleviating these information problems reveals their important role in the economy with regard to their competitive advantage in collecting and communicating information about the creditworthiness of borrowers. However, although economic theory explains the underlying reason for banks' existence as ameliorating these information problems in the market, the relationship of the bank itself with its customers is also subject to similar information problems. This problem might emerge from the depositors' side since they do not have information about a bank's riskiness, which would affect the bank's ability to get funding by attracting deposits. Before concluding a deposit contract, the depositor would not have enough information and understanding about the bank's creditworthiness since the proper evaluation of a bank's soundness requires sophisticated knowledge. The bank would best know its own risk characteristics, but not the depositor. In this case, the banks would be willing to risk offering high interest rates to attract depositors. In this case, adverse selection arises when the less risky banks find it difficult to attract funding from the depositors (Dragomir, 2010: 42).

Moral hazard occurs after a transaction takes place because each party might choose to behave opportunistically to maximise its own utility, thus placing the

---

43 This problem of the possibility of making the wrong choice of business opportunities where the good ones are ignored refers to the *lemon-market* problem introduced by Akerlof in 1970.

other party in a vulnerable position. Due to the profitable and risky opportunities provided by financial innovation, banks most probably will engage in sophisticated risky policies after the contract takes place. Depositors and other creditors cannot identify the deterioration of the quality of their funds in case the bank has engaged in a risky investment, which subjects the bank to a credit risk. Besides, they won't be able to distinguish between secure and risky banks. This will lead to a sub-optimal resource allocation in the economy (Baltensperger 1988: 56 in Dragomir, 2010: 43). This fact leads us to the other rationale for bank regulation, which is the need to represent small depositors by providing a *safety net* to protect them from the default risk of a bank (Freixas & Rochet 1999; Tirole & Dewatripont 1994). This argument is most famously formulated by Dewatripont & Tirole (1994) and Tirole et al. (2010) as *the representation hypothesis*. Due to the mere existence of the asymmetric information problems explained above, banks must be monitored. However, investors, depositors and other kinds of debt-holders do not have the sophisticated knowledge to be able to understand and evaluate the on- and off-balance sheet activities of banks. These activities are complex, time-consuming and expensive, and depositors do not have access to the necessary information. Hence, people have little incentive to monitor banks regularly since most of the depositors hold only a small amount of deposit. These depositors and other debt-holders therefore should be represented by a prudential supervisor that would replicate the control and monitoring function depositors would do if they could fulfil all the requirements mentioned above (Santos, 2000; Koehn & Santomero, 1980).[44]

Safety net mechanisms should protect depositors. Diamond-Dybvig (1983)[45] show in their model that deposit insurance is the optimal policy to protect depositors since banks are prone to runs caused by a depositor's self-fulfilling prophecy. The aim of this mechanism is to reassure depositors that in the face of a bank failure, they are guaranteed to receive back at least the minimum insured amount of their deposits, thus insuring that a negative event does not create a panic and turn into a bank run. However, this insurance exacerbates the moral hazard problem. Insurance exacerbates moral hazard because if the insured depositors know that the third party is going to pay the bill, they allow banks to incur greater losses. Knowing that the presence of a financial safety net is behind them in case of a failure, banks might tend to engage in riskier activities than they otherwise might do.

44 In addition to the asymmetric information problem between banks and their depositors, the other problem with depositors' presentation considers the corporate governance framework. Separation of ownership from management creates conflict of interest problems. Conflicts of interest are likely to arise between a bank's manager and its outside financiers, such as depositors. Managers may tend to choose risky projects which are not in the best interest of risk-averse depositors. Since depositors are unable to monitor a bank's management due to their limited knowledge, they need to be represented by a regulatory agency (Santos, 2000).

45 D.W. Diamond and P.H. Dybvig (1983): "Bank Runs, Deposit Insurance, and Liquidity."

There is much cross-country evidence suggesting that the more generous deposit insurance amounts are, the more likely banking crises are (Detragiache et al., 2002). In a study of the determinants of banking crises by Demirgüç-Kunt and Detragiache (1998), it is found that deposit insurance is positively correlated with the probability of a banking crisis. Another study conducted by the same authors in 2000 found again that this insurance scheme is detrimental to banking stability, especially when the coverage offered to depositors is extensive. Barth et al. (2006a) and Demirgüç-Kunt and Huizinga (1999) find that whereas deposit insurance contributes to depositors' safety, it reduces market discipline by the bank creditors. Barth et al. (2004) and Demirgüç-Kunt and Detragiache (2002) investigate the relationship between deposit insurance and banking stability and find that deposit insurance is detrimental to bank stability. In their earlier study conducted in 1999, they also found that deposit insurance increases banking system fragility in countries with weak institutions. A substantial amount of literature in economic theory supports the idea that the deposit insurance mechanism may increase banking stability by preventing a depositor run, but at the same time it may decrease bank stability by encouraging banks' risk-taking activities (moral hazard). Hence, to counteract these incentives caused by the existence of a financial safety net, governments introduce regulations to limit the moral hazard of banks.

To sum up, in the presence of these problems, regulation is needed firstly to the extent that banks cannot provide any solutions to information failures between borrowers and lenders. Secondly, although banks' existence is explained as correcting the market failures caused by these information problems, their own operation mechanisms create information problems, which call for government regulation and the supervision of banks (Dragomir, 2010: 45; Heremans & Pacces, 2011).

4.1.2. Negative Externalities

The second justification for financial regulation is the existence of negative externalities in financial markets. Negative externalities arise when the economic activity of some units generates cost to units for which the latter are not compensated (Schooner & Taylor, 2010). Banking is subject to systemic negative externalities. The nature of banks' operations caused by the maturity mismatch in intermediating funds between lenders and borrowers in the market subject them to fragility. The failure of one bank might raise concerns about the solvency of other banks. Depositors and other creditors of that bank may not be able to differentiate between solvent and insolvent banks. A run on deposits on one bank can cause a run on otherwise solvent banks and hence endanger the overall stability of the financial system (Heremans & Bosquet, 2011). The owners of that failed bank put the owners of otherwise well-run banks under distress and impose costs on them. This externality produced through the mismanagement of the failed banks might cause runs on otherwise solvent banks.

One of the ways this contagion arises is through information channels. Gorton and Penacchi (1990) argue that banks create a special kind of debt. Its specialty relies on the fact that it is immune to adverse selection caused by inside traders. Demand deposits of banks belong to this category of informationally-insensitive debt, as defined by Gorton (2009). Since the deposits are insured by the deposit insurance mechanism, the value of deposits is not sensitive to information and not subject to adverse selection, so speculation on the value of these deposits is not profitable (Gorton, 2009). However, in the new form of banking, banks obtain their funds in the form of repos on the money-market, which, like demand deposits, are short-term. However, unlike demand deposits, repos are not insured. This makes securities used in repo transactions vulnerable to private information in the market. Since repos are not insured, any suspicion about the value of the underlying collateral will cause investors to withdraw from the market. Followed by that, the overall lending in the market will stop functioning, and banks won't be able to refinance their short-term positions.

Brunnermeier et al. (2009) discuss that there have been two kinds of externalities that played a role in the global crisis. From a social welfare perspective, banks overexposed themselves to risk by holding highly leveraged positions with excessive maturity-mismatches. The first externality is called *fire-sales externality.* When banks cannot refinance their short-term positions, they have to sell their assets at fire-sale prices, meaning for less than the assets are worth. However, no bank takes into account the impact of its fire-sale on general asset prices. The losses of each bank worsen the funding liquidity for many other banks. Their balance sheets are adversely affected, which forces them to sell even more assets. This fire-sale of assets further depresses prices and increases losses. This loss spiral causes sharp fluctuations in asset prices, especially in times of crisis. This phenomenon was experienced in the global crisis (Brunnermeier et al., 2009).

The second externality is called the *interconnectedness externality.* If a bank fails, it does not care about how many others might also fail. The more globalised the financial system is, the more interconnected are the financial institutions. As a result, the failure of big and interconnected financial institutions in particular would spread these negative spill-over effects on others (Brunnermeier et al., 2009). A banking crisis causes a reduction in the money supply leading to a credit crunch for the real economy. Under conditions of uncertainty, investors hoard cash, which reduces the size of financial intermediation between savers and investors, causing a general slowdown in the economy (namely, a recession). The costs of the recession for society are, inter alia, reductions in consumption, investment and growth rate, as well an increase in the unemployment rate.

4.2. SYSTEMIC RISK FACTOR

The events of the 2007–2009 global crisis have caused regulators to put the phrase "*systemic risk*" into focus. Governments and international organisations were prompted to address systemic risk by regulation. Arner (2009) defines systemic risk as follows: "The risk that an event will trigger a loss of economic value or confidence in, and attendant increases in uncertainty about, a substantial portion of the financial system that is serious enough to quite probably have significant adverse effects on the economy. Systemic risk events can be sudden and unexpected, or the likelihood of their occurrence can build up through time in the absence of appropriate policy responses. The adverse real economic effects from systemic problems are generally seen as arising from disruptions to the payment system, to credit flows, and from the destruction of asset values" (Arner, 2009).

The failure of one bank can cause systemic disruption and negative externalities on others since doubts arising in the minds of depositors over the stability and soundness of other banks might lead to a depositors' run. If a large bank defaults, this will create uncertainty about the solvency of its counterparties leading to chaos in the system (Kashyap et al., 2008). Systemic risk also includes contagion risk (Dragomir, 2010: 45).

There are three stages of how a systemic risk occurs. The first stage occurs when the failure of one bank triggers the failure of other banks during a banking panic. In that context, banks are different from non-financial firms where the failure of one firm would benefit another since it means one less competitor. In banking, firms are more intertwined and interconnected. The failure of one bank may create a domino effect since the counterparties of that failed bank would be put under distress if the bank does not meet its obligations to them. This chain would then develop throughout the financial system (Tirole et al., 2010). The default of one institution would lead to the default of a second institution which would in turn lead to the default of the third one, and so on. At the second stage, through the contagion effect, banks' depositors would conclude from one bank's failure that other banks might also fail since depositors are unable to distinguish between solvent and insolvent banks.[46, 47] Hence, depositors would withdraw their funds from that bank and cause a run on funding. At the final stage, this

46 In early 2008, the nationalisation of Northern Rock – a medium-sized bank for residential mortgage loans – focused attention on British mortgage markets, which distressed other British banks. Another example is the bankruptcy of Lehman Brothers in the US followed by the crisis of the large insurance company AIG, the fire-sale of Bear Stearns to JP Morgan Chase, the failure of Merrill Lynch, Fannie Mae, Freddie Mac, Washington Mutual and Wachovia.

47 The same logic applies to wholesale lenders as happened in the global crisis. The 2010 European sovereign debt crisis is another example of the systemic risk inherent in the interconnected and globalised financial world. In 2010, the sovereign debt crisis of Greece spread to other European countries such as Ireland, Spain, Portugal, Iceland, Slovenia, Belgium, Latvia, Lithuania and Estonia.

contagion effect would lead to the fire sales of assets since the bank has to meet the withdrawals.

This chain (contagion) effect would distort interbank trust relationships so that the banks would stop lending to each other. In order to obtain liquid funds, a failed bank has to sell its assets even if that sale would depress the prices of these assets (fire sale). If there are too many assets that need to be sold, then the seller has to accept a lower price. This decline in asset prices would affect the solvency of all institutions that hold such assets.[48] Consequently, in a scenario where the bank cannot meet its obligations and where there are no other agents who would buy those banks' assets to recapitalise the bank, the bank becomes insolvent. Important segments of financial market stop functioning, which has significant effects on the real economy (Gorton, 2010a).[49]

Another form of safety net mechanism is provided by the government as a Lender of Last Resort, which also leads to a moral hazard problem like deposit insurance. This might take the form of liquidity injections to problematic banks by the central banks. The extent of providing unsubsidised support to illiquid but solvent banks by the central banks (as the Lender of Last Resort) might have an impact on market discipline. Central banks can abuse their power by providing open-ended support to banks in difficulties (Barth et al., 2006a: 57). Therefore, although this mechanism aims to overcome the systemic externalities described above, it induces risk-preferring behaviour by banks. This would then endanger the welfare of society since the scarce funds available for investment might be allocated into socially unproductive projects (Taylor & Schooner, 2010). Being confident in an implicit insurance provided by the central bank and ultimately the government, banks will be encouraged to invest in risky projects. This provides another rationale for bank regulation. Furthermore, the potential prospect of a government bail-out especially makes the institutions that are deemed to be "too big to fail" and "too interconnected to fail" more prone to taking excessive risk. Calomiris (2009) argues that this became very apparent in the behaviour of large investment banks in the US during 2008. After the rescue of Bear Stearns by the US government, other investment banks such as Lehman Brothers, Merrill Lynch, and Goldman Sachs did little to raise capital and improve their position. However, when the anticipated bailout of Lehman Brothers by the government did not materialise, those investment banks were either acquired or merged, or they transformed themselves into commercial bank holding companies to gain access to government support.

---

48 For a detailed analysis of the nature of systemic risk, see: CEPR Report 2009: "The Fundamental Principles of Financial Regulation", pp. 13–23.; and its role on the 2008 crisis see: Hellwig (2008): "Systemic Risk in the Financial Sector: An Analysis of the Subprime-Mortgage Financial Crisis".

49 For more on the costs of banking crises, see Rogoff & Reinhart (2009) and Hoggarth, Reis & Saporta (2001).

4.3. FINANCIAL STABILITY

The problems inherent in financial markets due to the information problems and negative externalities explained above reveals the fragility of the financial system. These problems have a detrimental effect on the social welfare of society, caused by the potentially inefficient resource allocation of financial resources in the economy. In the general theory of economic regulation, the goal of regulation is to protect consumers against market imperfections. In banking, this refers to the protection of depositors and other savers whose interest and well-being is threatened by banks' excessive risk-taking activities. In banking regulation, protecting depositors means preventing banks from engaging in unacceptably high risks (Heremans & Pacces, 2011). Overall, the big picture of this story of market failure and its consequences on society implies that prudential banking regulation and supervision mainly target banks' excessive risk-taking because excessive risk-taking is the ultimate source of instability.

Stability is the main concern of the financial sector. It can be defined as the condition in which the financial system – comprising financial intermediaries, markets and market infrastructure – is capable of withstanding shocks and the unravelling of financial imbalances, thereby mitigating the likelihood of disruptions in the financial intermediation process severe enough to significantly impair the allocation of savings to profitable investment opportunities (ECB, 2007). Goodhart (2006) defines a financial crisis as the sequence of events that would distort credit intermediation and capital allocation. Referring to this definition, he describes financial stability as the absence of financial crises.

Financial crises have been an intrinsic feature of the financial sector for hundreds of years. Usually, there is the existence of an asset price bubble accompanied by a credit boom and large capital inflows to the economy. However, the extent of their impacts on a country depends on that country's financial sector exposure to those conditions (Acharya et al., 2011). Emerging markets have been blamed for crisis episodes most of the time due to their macroeconomic imbalances, lending booms, exchange rate regimes, destabilising external factors, inadequate prudential supervision, and weaknesses in their legal and institutional frameworks (Eichengreen & Arteta, 2000). Goldstein and Turner (1996) argue that the banking crises in developing countries have been far more severe than the ones experienced in developed countries. However, the global crisis of 2007–2009 showed that not only emerging markets but also developed and sophisticated financial markets are exposed to financial crises (Pacces & Van den Bergh, 2012).

This global crisis showed also that, other than macroeconomic imbalances, financial innovation might also have a role in the emergence of a financial crisis. In fact, Vives (2006) argues that liberalisation, financial innovation and the integration of financial markets have been associated with increasing banking crises. As banks enter new and riskier segments of financial markets owing to the opportunities provided by globalisation and innovation, they would increase their risk appetite in the quest for more profit (Hoenig, 1998).

Regulation should address the above problems of asymmetric information and negative externalities by providing the banking and financial systems with stability to avoid the negative effects associated with failing institutions and systemic crises (Vives, 2006). Consumers should be protected against market imperfections. Other aims of banking regulation and supervision should therefore be to protect the interests of depositors by preventing banks from engaging in excessively risky activities. Financial regulation addresses market failures through the conduct of business rules in financial markets and through prudential regulation of the safety and soundness of financial intermediaries, mainly banks. Although regulation refers to the process of rulemaking, monitoring and sanctioning the application of these rules is also important to achieve the prudential objectives of ensuring the soundness of individual financial institutions as well as the stability of the whole financial system (Hereman & Bosquet, 2011).

To summarise, other than macroeconomic failures, financial instability increasingly arises from banks' excessive risk-taking activities because of moral hazard. The banking system suffers from market failures stemming from asymmetric information and negative externalities. However, the regulatory safety net mechanism designed to cope with these market failures gives rise to the problem of moral hazard by encouraging banks to take on greater risks than they otherwise would do. These risky activities expose banks to runs and contagion, which endanger the stability of the financial system as a whole. Besides, the losses of these bank failures are ultimately borne by the taxpayers, causing a reduction in the well-being of the society. Hence, the major goal of banking regulation and supervision is to prevent banks from engaging in unacceptably high risky activities so that the consumers (= depositors and other savers) are protected from market failures.

Having these theoretical foundations in mind, Chapter 2 will carry out an empirical investigation of which regulations had an impact on Turkish and Russian banks' performance in their post-crisis period. The regulatory variables that turn out be significant in this empirical analysis will be discussed in depth in Chapter 3.

5. APPROACHES TO BANK REGULATION

So far, I have identified the sources of financial instability and the market failures inherent in the banking sector. These problems explain the economic rationale of banking regulation and show the need for correction by way of public intervention. This section explains two conceptual foundations for bank regulation in terms of the role of government in correcting them. The first theory is called the *public interest view* according to which government regulation is the instrument for overcoming market failures. The second one is referred to as the *private interest view* which basically assumes that regulation will end up serving the benefits of certain interest groups such as regulators, financial lobbies or bankers.

5.1. PUBLIC INTEREST VIEW

According to the public interest view, governments regulate banks for the benefit and protection of the society at large (Domas, 2003). The aim is to provide socially efficient resource allocation to a society by correcting market failures (Barth et al., 2006a). In this context, the government's active role is related to the existence of market failures. According to the Coase Theorem (1960), in a world with zero transaction costs and well-defined property rights, market failures would be self-correcting and the efficient outcome would be achieved. In this case, government regulation of banks might have negative effects on society's welfare. However, the nature of the financial system reveals that markets are prone to failures because of substantial transaction costs. Hence, the government may have the ability to correct these market failures such as the disadvantages of imperfect competition, unbalanced market operation, missing markets and undesirable market results (den Hertog, 1999). A government with the social efficiency objective is able to overcome these failures, thereby protecting society through regulation (La Porta et al., 2002). Following these arguments, the role of government in banking regulation is justified mainly by the existence of market failures, which the government has the incentives and capabilities to correct. State intervention is necessary to reduce consumers' exposure to the risk of bank failure and insolvency (Dragomir, 2010: 49).

The consultative document "Microfinance Activities and the Core Principles for Effective Banking Supervision" of the Basel Committee on Banking Supervision issued on 7 May 2010 is based on the public interest view approach highlighting the importance of a powerful supervisory and regulatory agency (Barth et al., 2006a). These recommendations are based on three assumptions: there are market imperfections in financial markets, bank supervisors are able to solve these imperfections and their benevolent incentives aim at improving the operation of banks (Barth et al., 2006a). Central banks, which in some countries act as the bank regulator and supervisor and, in some cases, are a separate and independent regulatory agency, exercise the authority given to them by law over banks by subjecting them to certain rules and regulations. This theory, applied to banking, justifies official supervision of banks, limits on bank activities, restrictions on bank entry and deposit insurance mechanisms as appropriate policies that help to ameliorate market failures and enhance resource allocation

(Barth et al., 2001a). Since it takes market failures as given and asserts that the government can correct them, it assumes that stronger and stricter official supervision improves bank stability and performance (Barth et al., 2006a).

Applied to market failures, *the public interest theory seems to justify the existence of safety net mechanisms* (Dragomir, 2010: 49). However, both forms of state intervention in terms of "Lender of Last Resort" and "Too-Big-To-Fail"[50] suffer from moral hazard problem. Like all other forms of insurance, these two mechanisms imply that the bank is not allowed to fail and thus all of its creditors are fully protected.[51] In fact, Boyd et al. (2009) argue that the global crisis was largely due to the wrong incentives created by the US government's reluctance to allow large financial institutions to fail. The unwanted incentive effect of moral hazard in banking is inducing risk-preferring behaviour. Banks will be profitable on average but also vulnerable to suffering from bad luck and large losses due to their desire to take on higher risks and earn more money. Boyd et al. (2009) claim that this is exactly what happened to the banks in the US during the global crisis. By studying the performance of a sample of Too-Big-To-Fail firms over the last 23 years, they find that this group of banks grew much more rapidly than the rest of the industry and experienced high profits. This, however, was followed by great difficulties.

5.2. PRIVATE INTEREST VIEW

Although the externalities discussed in the previous section require government intervention to be in the form of regulations, the benefits of government intervention must be balanced against the costs since the process of regulation may impose substantial costs on the economy. More importantly, it is possible that the regulation will fail to promote socially desirable results and instead serve the special interests of certain groups. This underpins much of the analysis of regulation introduced by George Stigler in 1971 (further developed by Posner & Peltzman) called "the private interest theory of regulation". Stigler's theory is also known as "Capture Theory". According to Stigler, regulators are subject to pressure from regulated industries to modify regulations to suit their interests. He writes: "*Regulation is acquired by the industry and is designed and operated primarily for its benefit*", where he regards regulation as socially inefficient compared to public interest theory (Stigler, 1971: 3). Whereas the public interest theory of regulation supports the role of government and strict supervisory authority to correct market failures, the private interest view rather highlights

---

50 The failure of a very large bank increases the possibility that a major financial disruption will occur. Hence, bank regulators are reluctant to allow a big bank to fail and cause losses to its depositors (Mishkin, 2004: 263).

51 See previous section.

political failures based on the desire of politicians and government supervisors to maximise their own welfare instead of society's welfare. Governments would regulate banks only to serve the financing needs of government, or provide credit to interest groups (den Hertog, 1999; Barth et al., 2006a). Regulatory capture is defined as the possibility that the regulated institutions exercise influence on the regulator (Hardy, 2006). With time, regulation would end up serving the interests of the industry involved since a captured regulator would act in the interests of the regulatees (den Hertog, 1999; Hardy, 2006).

According to this approach, regulators have discretionary power in shaping banking policies where their private interests will dominate the public interest. Governments intervene in financial markets by subsidising or guaranteeing lending for specific sectors of the economy. Some government-sponsored banks provide home mortgages to borrowers or give cheap credits to particular sectors of the industry. In doing this, governments influence the choice of projects to be financed. However, this influence might lead to unsound borrowing or lending policies endangering financial stability. This was experienced in the US as the subprime mortgage crisis, the first stage of the global crisis (Heremans & Pacces, 2012).

Barth et al. (2006a) argue that politicians might also use banks through supervisory agencies for *connected lending*. If a bank supervisory agency can influence the banks` decisions, the government supervisors may put banks under pressure to provide credit to satisfy their own needs. At the same time, some powerful banks will induce regulators to act for the benefit of these banks' interests. In the end, these kinds of political failures (rather than market failures) will distort the efficiency of banks by causing connected lending and corruption. These two phenomena of connected-lending and corruption are two of the potential dangers, especially for banks in emerging economies. Politicians in these countries have a tendency to use banks either for easy financing of government or are directing credit to preferred ends such as their own political supporters (Barth et al., 2006a: 41).[52]

Dragomir (2010: 50) argues that in banking, it is possible that a group of banks will influence the outcome of regulation rather than the larger mass of small depositors. She points out the national options and discretions in the EU legislation reflect the fact that interests within a pluralistic banking market might not be aligned. Different groups might try to impose their views on the whole market such as national discretions in the EU legislation. This argument is supported by Hellwig (2010), who argues that the amendments made to the Basel capital accords[53] in the first half of the 1990s are the result of a regulatory

52 Connected-lending was a long-standing problem in the banking histories of both Russia and Turkey, both of which will be discussed in Chapter 3.

53 Basel Capital Accords refer to the set of rules formulated by the Basel Committee on Banking Supervision. These rules aim to improve the stability of the international banking system and prevent possible distortions arising from competition among countries.

capture process. In 1993, when the Basel Committee proposed a procedure to include market risks on the calculation of banks' capital requirements through a standard approach, large and internationally active banks opposed this approach. As a result of the intense lobbying by these prominent banking institutions, regulators allowed these banks to use their own quantitative risk models with the "1996 Amendment to the Basel Capital Accord to Incorporate Market Risks" rather than the standard approach for determining regulatory capital requirements (Hellwig, 2010).[54]

In the late 1990s Turkey suffered from a politicised regulatory structure and pervasive connected-lending practices, which played a role in the failure of banks during the 2000/2001 twin crises. One of the key changes in the regulatory system of the Turkish banking sector implemented after these twin crises was the introduction of new regulations which restricted this practice and at the same time increased the transparency of the practices that may result in connected-lending (Steinherr et al., 2004). Practices of connected lending and corruption have been a major problem for the Russian banking over a decade as well. However, Russia lacks legislation on connected-lending, which is still a pervasive practice in Russian banking (IMF, 2011c).

6. STRUCTURE OF BANKING REGULATION

The stability of the financial system and the protection of consumers are the main objectives of banking regulation. Following Heremans and Pacces (2011), regulations can be categorised into two groups. The first group refers to *protective measures,* which include the safety net mechanisms of lender of last resort, deposit insurance, liquidity injections and public bail-outs, discussed in detail in the previous section. These types of interventions focus on remedies to be implemented after a bank failure or crisis has occurred. The second group refers to *preventive measures* where the supervisory authorities aim to control the

---

54 Tirole et al. (2010) and Hardy (2006) argue that Basel II offers an arena of regulatory capture, too. The discussions on the design of these capital accords have been organised around consultations with banks. The complexity of these rules introduces a significant scope for discretion by supervisors. Furthermore, these consultations require banks and supervisors to be close contact. Hardy (2006) claims that since the supervisors are willing to work in regulated industries due to the high amount of salaries offered, they may be reluctant to antagonise bank management. Followed by that, they might rather choose to formulate regulations that are advantageous to its banks. Dragomir (2010) adds that the cases of crisis resolution processes of bail-outs and liquidity injections are another illustration of capture theory in banking. Referring to the global crisis, Kane (2009) suggests that the basis of the defects created by the incentive structure implied by the safety net is the corruption of supervisory incentives of poorly monitored safety-net subsidies in the US. By demonstrating the ratio of lobbying expenses for 2008 by selected large firms that received government help, he shows that during the initial stages of the crisis, financial institutions gained extraordinary benefits by trying to advise the federal officials on how to avoid crisis pressures.

amount of risk assumed by the banks and reduce the probability of illiquidity and insolvency. Preventive measures set the framework ex ante to prevent bank failures or crises from occurring. This can be implemented firstly by *prudential regulation*. By pursuing two objectives of financial stability and depositor protection, prudential regulation is designed to ensure the soundness and safety of the financial system (Dragomir, 2010). It is based on two rationales. The existence of information asymmetries between banks and their customers, and the moral hazard problem inherent in the safety net mechanisms underpin the micro-prudential rationale. The objective is to provide depositor protection and confidence by keeping the risk-taking behaviour of banks at reasonable levels so that it is ensured that the bank will meet its obligations to its customers. The macro-prudential rationale is laid down by the systemic risk concerns that may arise through spill-over effects and endanger the whole financial system (Allan & Herring, 2001; Dragomir, 2010: 42–48).

The second category of preventive measures is aimed at the structural limitations of competition and market forces, called *structural regulation* (Heremans & Pacces, 2011). It was mainly after the Great Depression that unrestricted competition was seen as a major threat to financial stability. Keeley (1990) argues that increased competition may reduce the charter value of a bank (which is defined as the bank's self-imposed risk discipline mechanism). It may reduce its incentives to behave prudently because the risk-taking incentives of a bank depend on its charter value (Gonzalez, 2005). Following this argument, it was considered necessary to introduce structural restrictions on the scope of permissible activities that banks could perform in order to limit competition and restrict the operation of market forces.

All these categories of regulations are designed to protect the financial stability and depositor protection. Fernandez and Gonzalez (2005) argue that banking regulations are complements to each other. This reveals the way in which they are interconnected. Protective measures alone are not enough to ensure stability and depositor protection since they suffer from the moral hazard problem by inducing risk-preferring behaviour. The global crisis revealed that banks engaged in transactions with unacceptably high risk levels. Hence, in order to maintain financial stability, ex ante measures of preventing risk-taking behaviours should be also in place.

6.1. PRUDENTIAL REGULATION

6.1.1. Capital Adequacy Requirements

One of the central instruments of prudential regulation is the capital adequacy requirement (CAR). Banks finance their operations with a mixture of debt and equity. Deposits – borrowings due to other banks and bonds issued by the bank in the capital markets – constitute a bank's debt. Equity is the difference between a bank's assets (such as loans and other investments) and its liabilities. Basically, a bank's equity is its own capital and it serves two important functions. The first function of capital is the *buffer effect*. Bank capital helps to prevent bank failures when the bank cannot meet its obligations to its depositors and other creditors (Freixas & Rochet, 1999). If a bank's assets lose value, this will lead to a corresponding decline in its capital.

An undercapitalised banking sector may experience serious defaults during times of adverse economic shocks. Equity capital works as a buffer protecting the depositors from the risk of asset returns. Hence, increasing equity would improve depositor protection (Blum & Hellwig, 1995). Bigger losses would cause a bank's capital to be wiped out, making the bank insolvent. Hence, if banks want to be able to absorb losses and meet the obligations of their creditors, they need to have an adequate capital amount (Taylor & Schooner, 2010). Basically, having excess capital serves as an insurance against the costs that can occur due to unexpected loan losses and difficulties in raising new capital (Lindquist, 2003). Additionally, a poorly capitalised bank is subject to lose its market confidence and reputation. Holding a substantial buffer of additional capital as financial slack would help banks to borrow additional funds quickly and cheaply in the event of unexpected profitable investment opportunities (Berger et al., 1995).

The second and more important effect of capital regulations is the *incentive effect* where the capital should give banks incentives for reducing risky activities that otherwise would end up burdening creditors or the taxpayer (Hellwig, 2010; Heremans & Bosquet, 2011).[55] Banks are subject to agency problems in raising external finance due to incentive problems between shareholders and creditors. Banks are highly leveraged[56] firms. Shareholders' return-on-equity (ROE)[57] increases with leverage, giving banks incentives to increase leverage. The imposition of capital requirements is necessary to limit the leverage ratios of banks. However, reducing leverage is costly to shareholders because it would transfer the value from them to debt-holders, creditors and taxpayers. Share prices decline through this value transfer, caused by the reduction in leverage (Admati et al., 2012). Hence, shareholders have an incentive to motivate the bank into risky activities since they earn all the upside potential and are subject only to a limited loss. The high leverage of banks allows for risk-shifting from shareholders to debt-holders. However, high leverage is a source of systemic risk

---

55 The incentive of shareholders to resist the reduction in leverage is explained in detail in Admati et al. (2012).

56 Leverage (= assets/equity) increases the expected rate of return on the equity because leveraged investments are riskier than unleveraged ones.

57 Return on Equity (ROE) is a basic measure of bank profitability. It is the net profit after taxes per dollar of the equity capital.

as it may encourage banks toward excessive risk-taking.[58] As explained before, excessive risk-taking is dangerous for financial stability and may lead to systemic failures. When a bank is highly leveraged, even a small decrease in its assets' value can create panic in the market and massive insolvency via contagion.

Even if a bank is not insolvent, any suspicion of its exposure would stop other banks from providing the funding it needs. The fear of contagion mechanisms or any suspicion about a bank's insolvency exacerbates the losses of leveraged institutions by collectively inducing more forced sales than necessary to absorb an initially small shock which further depresses the values of banks' assets. Due to the interconnectedness of the financial system, this can create negative spill-overs throughout the whole financial system, causing the market to freeze and leading to huge losses for the rest of the economy (Admati et al., 2011; Heremans & Pacces, 2011). This is also what happened in the global crisis. Banks and their special purpose vehicles (SPV) were highly leveraged in securitised transactions. When these securities became illiquid and lost value, banks became insolvent. This led to a contagion in the whole system. However, if these banks had been better capitalised, there would have been less risk of this kind of systemic failure (Admati et al., 2011).

Increased equity requirements would also have positive effects on the lending decisions of banks. Less-leveraged banks would have fewer incentives to provide too many risky loans and better-capitalised banks would make better lending decisions. Shareholders would only have incentives to monitor the financial soundness of banks that are well-capitalised because shareholders themselves are subject to losing their equities in the case of a failure. Hence, less leverage caused by higher equity requirements would reduce the conflicts of interest. Admati et al. (2011) add other benefits of imposing higher capital requirements. One of them refers to corrective measures after the failures. When the bank loses capital due to losses, it either has to recapitalise or deleverage by selling assets. Deleveraging might put the market under pressure as explained in the above paragraph. The extent of this process depends on the equity of the bank. The higher the equity of banks, the lower would be the possibilities of chain reactions caused by systemic failures. Concerning the social costs in terms of reducing the burden on taxpayers, equity cushions established by higher equity requirements would be able to absorb substantial losses in asset values without prompting a systemic default. This would reduce the probability of a bailout in the first place. Even if the bailout were inevitable, again the equity cushion would be able to absorb a large part of the losses so that the amount of support demanded from the government would be lower (Admati et al., 2011).[59]

---

58 The effects of leverage on the risk-taking behaviour of banks are analysed in detail in Admati et al. (2012).

59 See also Thakor (2013).

After the financial crisis of 2007–2009, capital regulation became more important for regulators. As financial innovation, globalisation of capital markets and developments in technology changed the structure of the banking sector; the focus of banking regulation has also changed from interest rates or asset diversification rules to capital regulation (Hellwig, 2010). Bank capital requirements can take different forms. A traditional one is the leverage ratio (gearing ratio), which is calculated as a fixed percentage of the assets. It aims to limit the leverage ratio by imposing an upper limit to a bank's debt to equity ratio.

However, the simplicity of this ratio causes some limitations on the overall risk profile of a bank. Since it ignores the risk level of a bank's assets by considering only the leverage component of a bank's risk profile, it ends up imposing a capital requirement that is too high for safe assets and too low for very risky assets (Koehn & Santomero, 1980). Banks will tend to shift to riskier assets due to their lower costs in terms of required capital. Besides, high-risk assets provide higher profits for banks. So, the overall effect of a leverage ratio on a bank's balance sheet is not clear. It reduces the probability of a failure by imposing a greater amount of capital as a buffer, but it also induces more risk-taking from banks.

Due to banking problems in the 1980s in the US, regulators became concerned about the amount of risky assets and off-balance sheet activities of banks. In order to account for the risk profile of banks' assets in determining the required level of capital, banks have been made subject to risk-based capital requirements. In 1988, the Basel Committee on Banking Supervision,[60] under the auspices of the Bank for International Settlements (BIS), imposed minimum capital requirements to account for the different credit risks of banks and also to establish the international harmonisation of banking regulation. This regulatory instrument is called the risk-weighted capital requirements.

With the emphasis on incorporating risk-adjusted assets to the measurement of capital, banks were required to hold at least 8% of capital against their risk-weighted assets. The objective of the first 1988 Basel Capital Accords (known as Basel I) was first to strengthen the stability of the international banking system

60 The Basel Committee was founded as the Committee on Banking Regulations and Supervisory Practices at the end of 1974 after several serious disturbances in the international banking markets. The committee members are the senior officials of central banks and supervisory agencies (the authority with formal responsibility for the prudential supervision of banking business not involving the central bank) of Argentina, Australia, Belgium, Brazil, Canada, China, France, Germany, Hong Kong SAR, India, Indonesia, Italy, Japan, Korea, Luxembourg, Mexico, the Netherlands, Russia, Saudi Arabia, Singapore, South Africa, Spain, Sweden, Switzerland, Turkey, the United Kingdom and the United States. The committee does not have any formal supranational supervisory authority. Its mission is instead to formulate the standards and guidelines for supervision and recommend the best practice statements. These recommendations and guidelines will be implemented by individual authorities in line with their own national systems. In this way, convergence towards common approaches and common standards of regulatory and supervisory techniques will be established. (However, the committee's conclusions do not have legal force.)

by encouraging banks to increase their capital positions and secondly, to eliminate competitive inequalities by providing a standard approach applicable to internationally active banks in different countries and to provide an adequate amount of capital for credit risks. The Basel Accords define capital as follows (Dewatripont & Tirole, 1994):[61]

(1) Tier 1 capital or core capital (equity tier one ratio): This includes stock issues and disclosed reserves without any limit. Stock issues include common stock and noncumulative perpetual preferred stock, which must be paid before any dividend distribution. Disclosed reserves are retained earnings, share premiums and other surplus.[62]
(2) Tier 2 capital or supplementary capital: This includes undisclosed reserves, general loan-loss provisions,[63] hybrid debt/equity capital instruments, subordinated term[64] debt and subordinated term debt with minimum maturity of 5 years. Tier 2 capital cannot exceed 100% of Tier 1 capital.[65]

The Basel Accords provide a harmonised and uniform definition of capital across countries. However, each country's regulator has some discretion in their choice of Tier 2 capital and also in their supervision of banks' accounting practices, especially regarding the level of provisions for loan losses.[66] According to the principles of Basel I, each bank is required to maintain a minimum of total capital equal to 8%. The assets and off-balance sheet activities are weighted by the coefficients designed to show the credit risk of these assets.[67]

6.1.2. *Shortcomings of the Basel Accords*

Although the introduction of the Basel Accords contributed to the recapitalisation of the sector,[68] it concentrated only on *credit risk* ignoring other

61 www.bis.org/publ/bcbsc111.pdf?noframes=1.

62 According to the Committee, equity capital and disclosed reserves are the key element of capital and are the only element of capital common to all countries' banking systems.

63 Provisions/Loan Loss Reserves ratio represents the amount of money set aside against presently unidentified losses that might materialise.

64 Subordinated debt has a lower priority than other firm debt and therefore, is paid after other claims.

65 For more details and explanations, see: BIS Publications, 06/1988: "International Convergence of Capital Measurement and Capital Standards."

66 BIS Publications, 06/1988: "International Convergence of Capital Measurement and Capital Standards" (page 4, article 14, article 19).

67 These risk-weighted assets measure the total credit risk taken by the bank. The weights were allocated into four categories: 0%, 25%, 50% and 100% depending on the nature of the borrower or the issuer of the security.

68 Following the introduction of the Basel Accords in 1988, an increase in the average ratio of capital to risk-weighted assets of G-10 banks has been observed (from 9.3% in 1988 to 11.2% in 1996); see Jackson (1999).

types of risk such as operational risks, market risks, risks on off-balance-sheet activities, etc. In 1993, the Committee proposed a procedure to incorporate *market risks* on banks' capital requirements through a standard approach that was also used for credit risks under the 1988 Basel Accord (Basel I). This approach was based on rigid capital ratios and was criticised by the banking industry as being a step back from the sophisticated risk management procedures that banks had started to develop. Hence, the 1996 Amendment to the Capital Accord to Incorporate Market Risks allowed banks to calculate their capital, held against market risks by using their *own internal quantitative models* (Hellwig, 2010).

However, this new amendment caused the amount of capital banks need to hold against any given asset to diminish (Hellwig, 2008). Banks misused the freedom given them through the risk-calibrated approach to determine the capital requirements in order to increase their activities supported by the equity they had. They presented themselves as sufficiently capitalised. The risk-weighting they used in their models was flawed and their leveraged positions were masked through accounting tricks (Hellwig, 2008, 2011).[69] The adverse effect of this new amendment was exacerbated with financial innovation and securitisation practices that further created opportunities for banks to mask their actual risk exposure. In that way, they could substantially reduce their regulatory capital amount with no actual corresponding reduction to their risk exposures. This regulatory arbitrage creates two consequences. It distorts competition between financial and non-financial institutions and more importantly, the reported capital ratios may disguise deteriorations in the balance sheets and the actual financial positions of banks. As a result, accompanied by the on-going financial innovations aimed at reducing the cost of regulatory arbitrage,[70] the function of capital regulations as a prudential policy tool is undermined (Jason, 2000).[71]

---

69 The first Basel Accord was also accused of causing a reduction in lending to individuals and firms since banks preferred to buy government bonds (whose capital requirement was zero) rather than making loans to households and firms (whose risk weight was 100%) (Benston, 2007; Blanchard et al., 2009; Buiter, 2007). This way banks could reduce their required capital ratios and increase their returns on assets. Besides, a risk weight of 100% (meaning 8% capital requirement) attached to a very safe loan given to an AAA-rated company was given to a very risky loan of a CCC-rated company. Hence, banks preferred choosing to substitute riskier assets in their portfolio for safer assets that have the same risk weight. This resulting regulatory arbitrage is a consequence of setting imperfect weights that are not able to differentiate between the risk profiles of different types of assets, encouraging banks to riskier activities rather than preventing them.

70 Regulatory arbitrage involves transferring risks through the Special Purpose Vehicles (SPV). Banks were able to invest in asset-backed securities through these vehicles. Since these were off-balance-sheet activities, banks were able to invest in these securities without putting up the equity that would otherwise be required if these investments were held on their trading books (Hellwig, 2010).

71 Banks see this capital requirement as a form of regulatory taxation since they have to hold equity cushions (that are higher than what they would otherwise hold) in order to meet the

With the recognition of these failures, the series of influential documents adopted by the Basel Committee[72] set the stage to the adoption of the second Basel Accords – Basel II (also known as the *International Convergence of Capital Measurement and Capital Standard*) – in June 2004. Basel II came into force in 2008. This document was embedded in the EU law through the Capital Requirements Directive (CRD) (Dragomir, 2010:83–97). The Basel II Capital Accord consists of three pillars.[73] The first pillar considers the methodology of determining the minimum capital requirements for credit, market and operational risks. The second pillar of Basel II addresses the supervisory review process and the third pillar deals with the effective use of market discipline.

Although the definition of capital and the 8% ratio for the minimum requirement remain the same in Basel II, there is one difference concerning the methodology for the measurement of capital requirement in the new Basel II Capital Accord. In order to prevent incentives for regulatory arbitrage, a more risk-sensitive approach for the calculation of capital requirements was introduced. This approach adds capital charges for *interest rate risks* and *operational risks*[74] through which a bank's actual risk position would be represented more clearly.

Another difference is that Basel II allows banks to use two different options to calculate credit risk. As an extended and modified version of Basel I, banks can use the standardised approach, which uses risk weightings based on the ratings assigned by external credit rating agencies. The other option for the calculation of credit risk is the Internal Ratings-Based Approach[75] that relies on banks' internal models for estimating the risk elements in determining the required capital. Incidentally, this option was already introduced by the 1996 Amendment to Basel I. So, basically banks were allowed to apply their own risk measurement methods and internal ratings with the permission of the regulatory authority (Hellwig, 2010).[76]

The second pillar of Basel II addresses the supervisory review process with a comprehensive assessment of capital adequacy, risk management processes and

---

required ratio. The reason why banks are unwilling to do this is that the cost of equity is higher than the cost of debt and deposits. When banks can substitute debt for equity, investors get greater returns because payments to the government are reduced. This is due to the fact that interest payments are tax deductible but dividends are not. For more on the issue of regulatory arbitrage caused within the Basel Accords, see: Jones (2000).

72 Such as the first Basel Accord (BCBS 1988), the Core Principles for Effective Banking Supervision (BCBS 1997), and their subsequent amendments.

73 Bank for International Settlements (BIS) Publications: www.bis.org/publ/bcbs107.pdf.

74 Operational risk is the risk of loss resulting from inadequate internal processes, systems and other external events.

75 It has two variants, called the foundation internal ratings-based (IRB) approach and the advanced internal ratings-based approach. In the Foundation IRB approach, risk weights are determined by supervisory authorities. In the advanced IRB approach, risk weights are determined through sophisticated risk models based on the history of credit defaults in loan portfolios.

76 www.bis.org/publ/bcbs107.pdf and Tirole et al. (2010:2).

risk profiles. Supervisors should ensure that a bank is sufficiently capitalised and consistent with its risk profile. It enables supervisors with early intervention to prevent capital from falling below prudent levels. According to the Principle 2 of Basel II, national regulatory authorities have regulatory discretion in tailoring regulatory capital levels where they can require banks to operate with capital in excess of the regulatory minimum to consider the risks not captured under Pillar 1[77] (Basel II, Article 745). Finally, the third pillar of Basel II deals with the effective use of market discipline via public disclosures of the capital structure, capital adequacy, risks covered in Pillar 1 and interest rate risk by banks. The aim is to encourage banks to disclose information in order to increase the role of market participants in monitoring banks (Basel II, Article 809).[78]

Basel II was developed due to some shortcomings from which Basel I was suffering. However, during the 2007–2008 crises it was also accused of several criticisms.[79] Firstly, the Basel II Accord allowed banks to use their internal rating methodologies for the assessment of credit risk. However, these models were too complex, which made it very hard for supervisors to verify the computations. Through these internal models banks could again show that their risks were limited.[80] These models were also blamed for failing to account for the dynamic aspects of a banking environment[81] and for neglecting the risk of illiquidity. Secondly, Basel II caused heavy reliance on credit rating agencies to assess the amount of regulatory capital a financial institution must hold. The quality and reliability of their rating methodologies, which were also subject to conflicts of interest, are seen as one of the causes of the financial crisis. Thirdly, these rating methodologies are blamed for being pro-cyclical (and providing insufficient capital during economic downturns) meaning that they have a tendency to reinforce business cycle fluctuations because of the interaction of fair value accounting with risk-sensitive capital requirements.[82]

---

77 BASEL II, Article 745: *Principle 2: Supervisors should review and evaluate banks' internal capital adequacy assessments and strategies, as well as their ability to monitor and ensure their compliance with regulatory capital ratios. Supervisors should take appropriate supervisory action if they are not satisfied with the result of this process.*

78 BASEL II, Article 809: *The purpose of Pillar 3 – market discipline is to complement the minimum capital requirements (Pillar 1) and the supervisory review process (Pillar 2). The Committee aims to encourage market discipline by developing a set of disclosure requirements which will allow market participants to assess key pieces of information on the scope of application, capital, risk exposures, risk assessment processes, and hence the capital adequacy of the institution. The Committee believes that such disclosures have particular relevance under the framework, where reliance on internal methodologies gives banks more discretion in assessing capital requirements.*

79 See also next paragraph.

80 For more on this issue see Tirole et al. (2010).

81 This was due to the VaR (Value at Risk) model: VaR is a widely used risk measure representing the potential loss of an investor regarding a specific portfolio of financial assets. It is estimated based on historical data.

82 Under fair value accounting, assets and liabilities are carried on the balance sheet at their market value, in other words at fair value or marked-to-market (Enria et al., 2004). When

Whether the shortcomings of Basel II may have contributed to the crisis is a controversial issue in the literature.[83] Furthermore, the fact that Basel II was not started to be implemented during the crisis, has not reached an agreement. The Basel II Accord came into force in 2008, which implies that it could not have had a direct impact on the global crisis that started in 2007 (Heremans & Pacces, 2011). On the other hand, Tirole et al. (2010) argue that although some countries, including the United States, had not implemented Basel II when the crisis started, it cannot be denied that all major international banks that have been affected by the crisis had mostly anticipated the principles of Basel II.[84] However, as Hellwig (2008) points out, it shouldn't be forgotten that although the regime change tends to be associated with the recent replacement of *Basel I* by *Basel II*, in fact the change of paradigm had already come with the *1996 Amendment to Basel I* which allowed banks to use their own risk models (Hellwig, 2008).

All these facts emphasise the shortcomings of Basel capital regulations up to this point in terms of underestimating significant risks and too much reliance on banks' ability to control them. This misunderstanding together with the belief that the securitisation mechanism of distributing risk would eliminate risk entirely from banks' balance sheets, led to inadequate regulatory capital

assets are accounted with fair value accounting, asset prices interact positively with leverage ratios as increases in asset prices raise the net worth of the equity in banks' balance sheets and create incentives to use that excess capital for taking on additional debt. Financial institutions will adjust their balance sheets according to changes in asset prices, so that leverage would be pro-cyclical. However, in bad times, the reverse happens and market illiquidity forces the use of distressed prices instead of more telling market prices. This is because banks' balance sheets became more vulnerable to fluctuations in asset prices, and then these losses in balance sheets forced banks to increase new capital because of minimum capital requirements, and reduce lending activities. This chain of events created an environment where there wouldn't be enough capital in times of bad economic conditions. Once the intermediaries realised the high amount of leverage, they tried to sell some of their assets, causing a reduction in the market prices of these assets and the amount of lending. The result of this kind of action on the side of intermediaries had a destabilising effect on the market where, at the same time, the pro-cyclicality of credit ratings affected the minimum amount of capital banks must hold. The interaction of marked-to-market accounting rules with the capital requirements worsened the situation leading to "fire sales" in the market because of difficulties in finding additional capital in such an economic environment. At the same time, a financial institution which is subject to a run stops giving credit to another institution (Blanchard, 2008). This had a big impact on the balance sheets of other institutions which held similar assets and that in turn caused further sales and, at the end, state intervention. The liquidity problem turned into a solvency problem.

83 See, Cannata & Quagliariello (2009).

84 Blundell-Wignall et al. (2008) and Blundell-Wignall and Atkinson (2008) support this argument by noting that these major international banks had obtained a guarantee from the committee that the application of Basel II would not involve an increase of average capital requirements for all banks. Besides, as an incentive to adopt the internal ratings-based approach, these banks in some cases benefited from a reduction of these requirements. They estimate a reduction of £220 billion in regulated capital for all American commercial banks in the transition to the internal ratings-based approach.

requirements (EU Commission, 2009). These kinds of activities erode prudential capital standards and undermine the regulatory discipline that is needed to contain systemic risk within the banking system. As a consequence of the inadequacies in the regulatory framework revealed by the global crisis, several amendments were made to Basel II in 2009.[85] In order to reflect the criticism of the risk-based approach in Basel II, and to prevent the regulatory arbitrage as a by-product of securitisation and sophisticated models, these amendments took a more restrictive prudential approach to prevent another systemic risk failure caused by excessive risk-taking (Dragomir, 2010: 149–152).

As an outcome of these reviews, the Basel Committee decided to establish a new set of standards called Basel III in response to the deficiencies in financial regulation revealed by the global crisis. This new set of measures not only strengthens capital adequacy ratios, but also introduces global liquidity requirements (Liquidity Coverage Ratio) on banks. It will increase the capital adequacy ratios and introduce new global regulatory requirements on bank liquidity and bank leverage.[86] Basel III will be ultimately phased in by 2018.[87]

The 1988 Basel Capital Accord was originally designed for the members of the Basel Committee. Although they were not intended to be included in the Basel I framework, other emerging market economies also started to adopt its recommendations from the mid-1990s including Turkey and Russia (Balin, 2008; Barrell & Gottschalk, 2006). Regarding the Turkish banking system, Turkey acted quickly and the capital adequacy standard ratio (Basel I) was put into effect gradually starting from 1989. Following the 2000/2001 crisis, the Turkish authorities started to work on strengthening the capital adequacy framework of the banking sector. The market risk regulations introduced by the Basel Committee were established in 2001 and 2002 (Asarkaya & Ozcan, 2007). The current regulation on the "Measurement and Evaluation of Banks Capital Adequacy" dated 2006 is compliant with the Basel II Provisions related to market risk. The current Capital Adequacy Regulation is also made compliant with Basel II, including operational market risk measurements as of July 2007 (Banking Regulation and Supervision Agency BRSA, Vice Chairman's Speech, 2011). As of July 2012, Turkey has fully implemented Basel II.[88]

The importance of maintaining a strong capital structure was emphasised in all policies carried out in the post-crisis period in Turkey. In 2005, the banking regulatory authority in Turkey required banks to hold a target capital adequacy ratio of 12% determined as a precondition to open a new branch. This ratio exceeds the capital adequacy ratio of many other emerging markets even in the global financial crisis years. In fact, one of the most important reasons for the

85 For the details of these amendments, see Dragomir (2010: Chapter 5).

86 For more details of Basel III arrangements, see: www.bis.org/press/p100912.pdf. See also Delimatsis, 2012.

87 The implementation will start in 2013.

88 www.bddk.org.tr/WebSitesi/turkce/Basel/11342ilerlemeraporu_06_12.pdf.

limited effect of the global crisis is the high capital adequacy ratio of the Turkish banking sector (Yorukoglu & Aysan, 2011; Atıcı & Gürsoy, 2011). Besides, regarding the liquidity ratio in Basel III, the ratio reported by all banks in the Turkish banking sector is parallel (even more conservative in some items) to the Liquidity Coverage Ratio of the Basel III Framework (BRSA Vice Chairman's Speech, 2011).[89]

In 1997, in order to co-ordinate its banking supervision, the Central Bank of Russia (CBR) signed a series of co-operation agreements with other countries' supervisory authorities to ensure its conformity with international standards in collaboration with the international financial organisations, such as the Basel Committee on Banking Regulation and Supervisory Practices. Russia implemented the Basel Accord in 1999 and established the 8% minimum capital adequacy requirement (Balin, 2008). Following the 1998 crisis, a banking reform was introduced in 2001 with the introduction of the new Banking Law. Pursuant to this new law, the CBR is authorised to introduce various capital adequacy requirements applicable to banks. In 2000, several Russian banks started to include market risk in the evaluation of capital adequacy.

In 2005, the CBR started to prepare for the introduction of Basel II by studying the nature and scale of the changes that would have to be made to laws and regulations in connection with the introduction of these standards. In 2009, in order to introduce the Pillar 1 of Basel II to its regulatory framework, the CBR issued a regulation[90] to implement Basel II simplified standardised approach to credit risk assessment. Amendments made to the CBR regulations on the procedure for the calculation of required ratios, market risks and operational risks became effective as of 1 July 2010. This allowed the Bank of Russia to use a simplified standardised approach to assess credit risk, and a basic indicator approach to calculate operational risk, in line with Basel II (CBR Annual Reports; 1999–2011). Although the capital adequacy rules in Russia generally meet the Basel II standards, the CBR is still in the process of its full implementation (IMF, 2011a).

The important question for this research is whether capital adequacy requirements are good or bad for an efficient banking system. The empirical literature on the impact of capital regulations is mixed. Some studies find that capital requirements increase risk-taking behaviour (Koehn & Santomero, 1980;

---

89 "Regulation on the Measurement and Evaluation of Liquidity Adequacy of Banks" has been in place since November 2006 (redrafted in June 2007 and January 2009). In Turkey, "Regulation on Measurement and Evaluation of Liquidity Adequacy of Banks" (November 2006, June 2007, January 2009), "Regulation on the Internal Systems of Banks (November 2006, June 2007, November 2008), "Regulation on Measurement and Evaluation of Capital Adequacy of Banks" (November 2006, October 2007, March 2008) have been implemented to bring the Turkish regulatory standards in line with the Basel standards.

90 "On Amending Bank of Russia Instruction No. 110 I" This regulation replaced the 2004 regulation on "Banks' Required Ratios" (CBR, 2009).

Besanko & Kanatas, 1996), while others argue that this happens depending on specific circumstances (Kendall, 1992; Beatty and Gron, 2001; Fernandez and Gonzalez, 2005). This work importantly contributes to the existing literature by providing evidence – which will be discussed in the following chapter – in favour of more stringent capital adequacy requirements. As the last chapter will discuss, such stringent requirements were introduced in Turkey at a certain point in time, but not in another comparable emerging economy, namely Russia.

6.1.3. Asset Holding Restrictions

Fernandez and Gonzalez (2005) argue that regulations are complements to each other, which reveals the way in which they are interconnected. Although a sound capital level in the financial system is important to deal with the moral hazard problems created by government safety net mechanisms, regulators face delays in taking appropriate actions. Hence, other regulatory tools are also necessary to support capital adequacy regulation (Heremans & Pacces, 2011).

The composition of asset portfolios is sometimes used as an instrument to control banks. The objective of restrictions on asset holdings is to reduce the proportion of risky assets such as real estate and common stocks in the portfolios of banks. Since depositors are not able to monitor banks by getting the information about the bank's risky activities, they cannot impose discipline on banks. Due to this asymmetric information problem between a depositor and a bank manager, a manager might tend to participate in overly risky transactions seeking higher returns. This regulation is thus justified by the goal of preventing a bank from taking excessive risks and increasing asset quality (Dewatripont & Tirole, 1994; Mishkin, 2000). Asset holding restrictions can take the form of requiring banks to have some minimum diversification of loans among sectors or setting some sectoral concentration limits on loans affecting the asset size of the balance sheet. This regulation additionally promotes diversification to reduce risk.[91]

As the last chapter will discuss in detail, low asset quality was a long-standing problem both in the Turkish and the Russian banking sector where banks overestimated their capital adequacy requirements for a long time. In that way, they were able to hide the actual risk-exposure in their balance sheets. Deteriorated asset quality caused the equity capital of both countries' banking sectors to melt down during their financial crises. Hence, the quality of capital is also important for a sound balance sheet.

---

91 Principle 10 under Large Exposure Limits of Basel Core Principles for Effective Banking Supervision (2006: 3) enforces this regulation as such: "Supervisors must be satisfied that banks have policies and processes that enable management to identify and manage concentrations within the portfolio, and supervisors must set prudential limits to restrict bank exposures to single counterparties or groups of connected counterparties".

6.1.4. Disclosure Requirements

The objective of disclosure requirements is to mitigate the asymmetric information problem in the banking industry. To ensure that depositors and other market participants have access to information about a bank's portfolio and degree of risk exposure, regulators can require banks to adhere to certain accounting principles and disclose a wide range of information about their financials such as certified audit reports for their financials, ratings from international rating agencies, consolidated information about banks' activities and risk management procedures. More public information about the risk profile and the quality of a bank's portfolio is likely to have a deterrent effect on banks' risk-taking behaviour through increased market discipline since depositors and other creditors will be able to monitor and evaluate banks' activities at a lower cost (Tchana, 2008; Mishkin, 2000).

The "Bank Regulation and Supervision Survey"[92] of the World Bank (WB) used in this book investigates the adherence of banks to information disclosure requirements mainly by looking at the presence of an independent assessment of the banks' financials by a certified audit, the percentage of top banks rated by an international credit rating agency, the disclosure of off-balance sheet items to the public, the disclosure of risk management procedures, the liability of directors for misleading information, the enforcement of penalties in case of presenting misleading or erroneous information, and the existence of consolidated accounts.[93] However, not all countries apply disclosure requirements. Furthermore, there might be differences in the extent of adherence to this regulation.

The results of the empirical chapter of this book regarding the impact of private monitoring on banks' efficiency indicate that information disclosure requirements may have a negative effect on banks' efficiency. The literature has mixed results about the impact of disclosure requirements on banks' performance. Barth et al. (2004) find that there is a positive relationship between accurate information disclosure and better banking performances such as greater bank development, better performance and increased stability. A theoretical study done by Vauhkonen (2011) about the impact of disclosure requirements on banks' safety shows that tightening disclosure requirements would improve the safety of the banking system. Cordella and Yeyati (2002) show that public disclosure mitigates banks risk-taking behaviour. On the other hand, Duarte et al. (2008) and Pasiouras et al. (2007) argue that increased disclosure requirements such as obtaining credit ratings from external agencies, disclosure of off-balance sheet items to supervisors and to the public,

92 See Introduction, section 2.

93 For details, see World Bank Survey III, June 2008, Survey on Accounting/Information Requirements.

disclosure of risk management procedures to the public as well as auditing by certified auditors, might all have a negative impact on banks' efficiency due to increased costs. Besides, Pasiouras et al. (2006) find a negative relationship between disclosure requirements and credit ratings. Girardone et al. (2012) find that private monitoring is associated with greater banking system inefficiency.

This work contributes to the existing literature by providing evidence – which will be discussed in the next chapter – on the negative impact of information disclosure requirements in Turkey and Russia. Both Turkey and Russia had a weak risk-management culture towards the end of the 1990s. Both countries' regulatory authorities took steps to develop their risk management practices, including disclosure requirements in their respective post-crisis periods. However, the qualitative analysis of the last chapter suggests that these practices have been implemented in Turkey more strictly than in Russia. On the other hand, the negative impact of this regulation suggests some limitations in the implementation of this regulation in these countries caused by the costs of ineffective implementation.

6.1.5. Bank Examination

Bank examination is also one of the regulations that aims to limit the moral hazard incentives of bank managers for excessive risk-taking. Other than establishing regulations, enforcement of these regulations is also very important. Bank examination is important for finding out whether banks are complying with these regulations. It also adds to the quality of the financial information disclosed to the public by bank owners and managers and to the strengthening of enforcement of existing regulations (Tchana, 2010). The Basel Core Principles for Effective Banking Supervision address bank examination under Principle 21.[94]

The purpose of bank examination is to provide safety and soundness for the banking system by information acquisition (Berger & Davies, 1998). Horvitz (1980) defines bank examination as the on-site evaluation of the assets, liabilities and the procedures of a bank conducted by a supervisory agency which has unlimited access to the records of the institution. Generally, the basic function is an evaluation of assets and particularly loan portfolios. The role of examination is not to prevent insolvency but rather the timely detection of insolvency. Gunther and Moore (2002) address the importance of bank examination in terms of imposing regulatory and market discipline on bank behaviour.

---

94 Principle 21 – *Supervisory reporting*: Supervisors must have a means of collecting, reviewing and analysing prudential reports and statistical returns from banks on both a solo and a consolidated basis, and a means of independent verification of these reports, through either on-site examinations or use of external experts.

As argued before, banks act as delegated monitors of customers and have a substantial amount of private information about them created over the course of time through bank–borrower relationships. This unique feature of banks implies their opaqueness. If regulators want to be able to impose discipline on them, they have to obtain information about banks' conditions through the examination process. The examination results convey auditing information, regulatory discipline information and private information to the market. Auditing information verifies the accuracy of banks' financial statements while regulatory information refers to the regulatory treatment of banks through ratings, and lastly private information is the data obtained after the examination process and conveyed to the market (Berger & Davies, 1998).

Swindle (1995) investigated the regulatory discipline effect of bank examinations. Considering the fact that it is costly for banks to raise capital, she found that supervisors had an influence on encouraging banks to increase their capital by giving a poor rating to their capital component. Gunther and Moore (2002) show also that supervisory examinations point to a significant auditing effect through revealing banks' financial problems. Given the central role of loan loss provisions and the allowances for loan losses in accounting that occur while determining asset quality – particularly loan quality – problems, they argue that banks have incentives to underreport provisions.[95] However, bank inspections contribute to the recognition of losses. This finding is also supported by Curry et al. (1999) who find that banks which have been poorly graded increase their provision expense.

In Turkey, following the 2001 crisis, the "Regulation on Internal Audit and Risk Management Systems of Banks" was published in 2001. Pursuant to this regulation regarding internal audit and risk management systems, banks were required to establish, manage and develop internal audit and risk management systems. During the restructuring process, the "Accounting Practice Regulation" (published in June 2002) played a significant role in resolving the crisis. In January 2002 the "Regulation on External Audit Procedures" was published to determine the procedures and principles of external audit to comply with the international standards.

In Russia, the CBR has the authority to establish accounting rules and procedures for banks. It also has the right to conduct full or selective audits of any bank at any time and inspect all books and records of the bank.[96] Regarding external audit, the Banking Law requires an independent auditor to certify banks' annual financial statements.

---

95 Banks have to add funds to allowances through provisions for loan losses. These provisions are an expense item and reduce the bank's net income. If the allowance for loan losses is found to be low, then the bank has to increase its provision expense and the allowance.

96 Under CBR Regulation No. 2332-U dated November 2009, routine reporting is performed by banks on a daily, five-day, ten-day, monthly, quarterly, half-yearly and yearly basis, and certain reporting is effected on an ad hoc basis.

6.2. STRUCTURAL REGULATION

6.2.1. Restrictions on Bank Entry

Entry restrictions are related to capital requirements. The first role of capital regulation considers the relationship of banks with the market. Banks need to have sufficient equity capital to obtain a license so that they can enter the market (Kashyap et al., 2008).

Entry restrictions have been an important issue in the history of the banking structure of many countries, especially in emerging countries. Brazil, Argentina, Chile, Mexico, Turkey, and Central and Eastern European countries (such as Bulgaria, the Slovak Republic, Estonia, Hungary, Latvia, Lithuania, Poland, the Czech Republic and Romania) experienced significant foreign entry into their banking systems. There are several types of restrictions on entry into the banking sector. They encompass the minimum capital entry requirements that the owner should provide to the regulatory agencies, restrictions on foreigners owning or investing in banks, qualification of founders, operating permissions, opening domestic branches etc.[97] Restrictions on foreign entry aims to protect banks from competition, reducing the exchange rate and the exposure to capital flight (Mishkin, 2000; Tchana, 2008).

Entry restrictions can contribute to the stability of the system by protecting the economy from the negative effects of bank failures since the entry of irresponsible or poorly-qualified bankers may expose the customers to the risk of fraud and bank failure (Hellmann, Murdoch, & Stiglitz 1999; Gorton, 2010a). Besides, easier entry could lead banks to behave imprudently in terms of granting overly risky loans. Overcrowding in the sector will create a scarcity of good quality credits, which will force banks to engage in risky loans. Due to excessive competition on deposit rates as explained above, banks will have to incur excessive free services for customers. They will again be tempted to take on risky activities to cover these costs (Alhadeff, 1962). Furthermore, Caprio and Summers (1996) and Keeley (1990) argue that since entry barriers would increase the franchise value of banks, bank managers would behave more prudently to maintain the successful state of their banks and prevent any insolvency. Hence, the private goals of bank owners will be aligned with the public goal of stability of the banking system (Gorton, 2010a).

On the other hand, since bankers may be tempted to opt for an entry restriction to limit competition, regulators may choose to help them for rent extraction (La Porta et al., 2000). Besides, the regulators and their supporters would gain a monopoly position. In contrast, a competitive banking sector would prevent such rent extraction or any kind of bribery. Credit would be allocated to a wider group (Barth et al., 2004). Demirgüç-Kunt, Levine and Min

97 For more on this issue, see: World Bank Survey, 3 June 2008, Survey on Entry Restrictions.

(1998) and Wang and Bayraktar (2006) support the view that the regulatory restrictions do have negative effects on competition in banking. Barth, Caprio, and Levine (2004) found that the percentage of entry applications denied is greater for low-income countries than for high-income countries and that developing countries place more limitations than developed countries on foreign bank ownership of domestic banks and foreign bank entry through branching. This work contributes to the existing literature by providing evidence – discussed in the next chapter – of the negative impact of entry restrictions on banks' efficiency in Turkey and Russia.

Starting in 2000, the establishment of a bank in Turkey or the opening of a branch in Turkey by a bank established abroad needs the permission of the BRSA, provided that the establishment conditions laid down in the Banking Law are fulfilled. The amount of legal submissions required to obtain a licence to operate as a bank increased with the 2005 Banking Law. In Russia, according to the Banking Law, the Central Bank of Russia is the licensing authority. Registration of banks and licensing of their activities is designated according to the Bank of Russia Instruction No. 75-I, dated 23 July 1998, "On the Procedure for Applying Federal Laws Regulating the Procedure for Registering Credit Institutions and Licensing Banking Activities". Regarding the amount of legal submissions required to obtain a licence to operate as a bank, there is no difference between Turkey and Russia.

7. CONCLUSION

This chapter has reviewed the basic concepts of banking, the economic rationale of banking regulation and their role in financial stability. The safety net mechanism aimed at preventing bank runs creates moral hazard and thus may increase instead of decrease financial instability by encouraging the risk-taking activities of banks. In order to counteract these incentives caused by the existence of a financial safety net, governments introduce regulations to limit the risk-taking behaviour of banks.

These risky activities expose banks to runs and contagion, which endanger financial stability. Due to their role as financial intermediaries in the economy, bank failures are viewed as the most serious failures compared to other industries. Contagion of these failures occurs fast, spreads more broadly within the industry, results in large losses to depositors of these banks and more importantly, a bank failure contagion spreads more beyond the banking industry and damages the whole financial system and ultimately, the real economy (Kaufman, 1994). Not only are the losses of these bank failures ultimately borne by taxpayers, causing a reduction in the welfare of the society, but also the deterioration of a country's economy is reflected in the reduction of real income, aggregate wealth and welfare of the society. Therefore, the major goal of banking regulation and supervision is to prevent banks from engaging in unacceptably high-risk activities so that the depositors and other savers are protected from market failures.

The main purpose of this chapter was to provide the basis for understanding the mechanism of banking regulation and its impact on financial stability. Very often the impact of certain regulations on the efficiency of a banking system is ambiguous. This is particularly the case for emerging countries. Based on this conclusion, we will now move to the empirical analysis of banking regulation in Turkey and Russia.

CHAPTER 2

EMPIRICAL ANALYSIS OF THE IMPACT OF REGULATIONS AND SUPERVISION OF BANKS' PERFORMANCES IN TURKEY AND RUSSIA

1. INTRODUCTION

The banking sector is the most highly regulated sector in the economy (Walter, 1985). Banking crises around the world over the last thirty years, especially the most recent 2007–2009 global financial crisis, have attracted the attention of policy makers on the construction of an appropriate regulatory and supervisory framework. However, as Demirgüç-Kunt et al. (2006) argue, this task is a complex and difficult process since there is no clear answer on what exactly is good regulation and supervision. Nor is it evident how specific regulations affect the performance and stability of the banking sector. Additionally, economic theory provides conflicting predictions about the impact of regulations and supervisory approaches on bank development, performance and stability (Barth et al., 2004).

The empirical research presented in this chapter investigates the impact of regulations and supervision on banks' performance at the international level. Most of the known studies such as Barth et al. (2004) and Demirgüç-Kunt et al. (2004) primarily use financial ratios as performance indicators. Instead, this study uses an efficient frontier technique called Data Envelopment Analysis (DEA). Berger and Humphrey (1997) highlight the superiority of frontier techniques compared to traditional performance measures such as return on assets, cost/revenue ratio etc., since they can account for the relevant inputs and outputs of a bank simultaneously and provide an objective numerical score, ranking and an efficiency score that is based on the criteria of economic optimisation.

Banks are the dominant financial intermediaries in emerging markets (Caner et al., 2007). In fact, Cläessens (2002) argues that the emerging markets differ from developed countries in terms of the relative importance of their banking, securities and insurance markets. As he point outs, banks are likely to be more important in developing countries whereas securities markets and insurance markets are much smaller (Cläessens, 2002; Demirgüç-Kunt & Levine, 2001). This is also true for Turkey and Russia, where the banking sector dominates the financial system: most of the transactions in the money market and in the capital markets generally are carried out by banks (Caner et al., 2007). The aim of this chapter is to analyse the impact of the regulatory/supervisory frameworks implemented in two emerging countries, namely Turkey and Russia, on the performance of their banks.

Turkey and Russia share a similar banking history where both of them experienced severe banking crises followed by major restructuring and recovery of the banking industry. Both countries have undergone major restructuring in terms of mergers, liquidations, and improvements in management and consolidation since 2000. In addition to the similar structural features of their banking sectors, a comparison of both countries' banking sectors' performances following their banking reforms would provide evidence to evaluate the regulatory policies implemented in both countries.

Specifically, the first consideration is how the efficiency of banks in both countries evolved over the 1999–2010 period. The reason for choosing this time period relies upon the fact that it encompasses the most important breaking points in both countries' banking history. In particular, Russia had experienced a banking crisis first in 1998 and again in 2004, both of which were followed by a structural banking reform implemented by the Central Bank of Russia.[1] However, this attempt at restructuring was not solid enough to prevent the emergence of another banking crisis in 2008–2009. The global crisis disrupted the rapid expansion of the Russian banking sector where many of the banks failed.[2] Profits started to decline due to bad loans. The ratio of non-performing loans to total loans was 9.5% in 2009, 8.2% in 2010 and 8% in 2011.[3] As sources of external finance dried up and interbank market trust declined, government support became necessary to stabilise the system.

Turkey, on the other hand, experienced twin banking crises in 2000 and 2001, resulting in serious damage to the financial system and especially to the banking sector. These crises were followed by a major Banking Sector Restructuring Program, changes in the Banking Law, implementation of several new regulations, and enhancement of the supervisory framework. Both countries experienced a similar banking history over the analysis period. However, the fact that Russia ended up with major bank failures in 2008 while the effects of the 2007–2009 global crisis on Turkish banks has been limited is an issue deserving attention about the role of regulation and supervision on banks' performance. Although the real economy has been affected mostly through international trade channels, the Turkish banking and financial sector has been quite robust whereas Turkish financial institutions, unlike those of many other

1 The Turkish economy was affected significantly by the 1998 banking crisis in Russia in terms of capital outflows and a slowdown in international trade, leading to a contraction in the Turkish economy in 1999 (Altunbas et al., 2009: 54).

2 See Appendix C for the list of failed banks in Russia during the global crisis.

3 This ratio in Turkey was 5.6% in 2009, 3.8% in 2010 and 3.1% in 2011.

economies, did not require any capital support. The average capital adequacy ratio of the Turkish banking sector has risen during the crisis, fluctuating around 20% – well above the target level of 12% and the legally required level of 8%. The profitability of Turkish banks also increased in 2008 and 2009. Moreover, Turkey is one of the few countries whose credit rating has improved during the crisis (Yorukoglu & Atasoy, 2010).

This chapter is structured as follows. Section 2 describes the banking sectors in Turkey and Russia underlining their structural commonalities. Section 3 provides a review of the production theory, and it introduces the concept of efficiency as the performance indicator. Since performance measurement is used in planning and controlling the activities of banks, it has been a primary concern of bank managers. Furthermore, the efficiency and productivity of companies are also a matter of concern for investors, lenders and shareholders. This section builds the technical foundation for the methodology of this chapter. Section 4 presents a literature overview of the empirical applications of DEA on Turkish and Russian banks, and includes other cross-country studies. This review assisted in identifying applicable methodologies and relevant variables for the purposes of the empirical analysis set out in this work. Section 5 explains the methodology applied in the empirical analysis of this chapter. It first introduces Data Envelopment Analysis (DEA) as a non-parametric[4] measurement technique which will be used for calculating the efficiency scores of Turkish and Russian banks between 1999 and 2010. This section then explains the Ordinary Least Squares regression technique which will be used to investigate the regulatory determinants of banks' efficiency scores which is the main aim of my research. Section 6 describes in detail the variables employed in the empirical analysis and presents the definition of the sample data and variables. Finally, a discussion of the empirical findings is presented in section 7.

My results indicate that there is a strong link between various forms of banking regulation/supervision and bank efficiency. The results suggest that strengthening capital adequacy requirements and the supervisory powers of regulatory/supervisory authorities can improve the efficiency of banks. On the contrary, increasing private monitoring and entry restrictions can adversely affect bank efficiency. The results also suggest the negative impact of deposit insurance scheme on efficiency. The results of this study are mostly in line with the findings of a paper by Girardone et al. (2012), who find that strengthening

4 Parametric and non-parametric methods differ in the assumptions imposed on random errors and the functional form of the cost frontier. They primarily differ in how much shape is imposed on the frontier and the distributional assumptions imposed on the random error and inefficiency. The DEA model is not able to distinguish between inefficiency and random errors. It presumes a particular functional form of the frontier. On the other hand, parametric approaches distinguish between random errors and inefficiency while imposing a particular functional form. However, if the form is wrongly specified, inefficiency levels would be overestimated (Berger & Humphrey, 1997; Hauner, 2005).

capital restrictions and official supervisory power can improve banks' efficiency, whereas policies such as private monitoring can impede efficiency. Section 8 concludes.

2. BANKING STRUCTURES IN TURKEY AND RUSSIA

As Caner et al. (2007) argue, the Turkish banking industry makes a good case for comparison with the Russian banking industry in terms of the relative importance of banks in the economy, aggregate financial ratios, the state-dominant structure and concentration levels. The Russian financial system is relatively small compared to the banking sector in developed countries. It is dominated by commercial banks. As of the end of 2010, total assets of the financial sector were around 80% of GDP and the share of banking sector's assets to total assets in the financial sector was over 90% in Russia (IMF, 2011b). As for Turkey, although its financial system deepened following the 2000–2001 crises, the system is also still dominated by the banking sector, with the banking sector having the greatest share in the Turkish financial system. The banking sector's share in the Turkish financial system is 77.2% as of the end of 2010 (BRSA,[5] 2010).

Table 5. Ratio of banking sector's assets to GDP in Turkey and Russia

	2003	2004	2005	2006	2007	2008	2009	2010
Turkey	69	72	83.5	86.7	67.9	78	87.4	91
Russia	42.3	42.1	45.1	52.4	61.4	67.5	75.3	75.2

Source: CBR Banking Supervision Reports (2003–2010). Central Bank of the Republic of Turkey (2003–2010), Banks Association of Turkey (2003–2010).

Table 5 shows the size of the transactions in the banking sector in both countries. As of 2010, the role of the banking sector in the economy is more than 70% in both countries. Banking industries in both countries have experienced continuous growth since 2001. The ratio of banking sector assets to GDP in Russia increased from 38.2% in 2002 to 75.2% in 2010 (CBR, 2002; 2010). Regarding Turkey, following the 2001 crisis, the asset size of the banking sector to GDP increased from 77% in 2002 to 91% in 2010. The asset to GDP ratio is much higher in Turkey. However, as Caner et al. (2007) explains, this is due to the longer period of asset accumulation in Turkey relative to the Russian banking sector.

5 Banking Regulation and Supervision Agency in Turkey.

In contrast to the banking industries in Central and Eastern European (CEE) countries where the banking industry became mainly foreign-owned, the Russian banking sector evolved in a different pattern. Its ownership structure of the banking sector differs from those in other emerging eastern European markets. In fact, both the Turkish and Russian banking sectors are characterised by the dominance of state-owned banks and the relatively small role of foreign banks (Caner et al., 2007). Although Russian state-owned banks have a bigger share of the banking industry than the state banks in Turkey, Table 6 reveals that state banks' involvement in banking is still very high compared to the presence of foreign-owned banks in both countries.

Table 6. Market structure of the banking sector*

	Presence of government-owned banks in %											
	1999	**2000**	**2001**	**2002**	**2003**	**2004**	**2005**	**2006**	**2007**	**2008**	**2009**	**2010**
Turkey	34.6	34.2	32.7	39.36	39.27	38.35	33.27	31	30.25	30.38	32.2	31.56
Russia	41.9	68	35.5	37.5	36	38.1	40.7	37.8	39.2	40.5	43.9	45.8
	Presence of foreign-owned banks in %											
	1999	**2000**	**2001**	**2002**	**2003**	**2004**	**2005**	**2006**	**2007**	**2008**	**2009**	**2010**
Turkey	5.3	5.2	3.1	3.29	3.01	3.47	6.32	13.07	13.93	16.96	15.72	16.48
Russia	10.6	9.5	8.8	8.1	7.4	7.6	8.3	12.1	17.2	18.7	18.3	18

* Presence of government-owned banks: the fraction of the banking system's assets in banks that is 50% or more government-owned. Presence of foreign-owned banks: the fraction of the banking system's assets in banks that is 50% or more foreign-owned.
Source: Banking Regulation and Supervision Agency of Turkey & Central Bank of Russia.

Table 7 presents the banking sector concentration levels, representing the percentage of assets held by the three largest commercial banks in both countries, which is high in both countries. The Russian banking market in 2010 is characterised by a high degree of concentration, as it has always been. The top 15 banks account for 50–60% of total liabilities and claims in the sector (CBR, Financial Stability Review 2010). Sberbank is the largest bank in the Russian banking sector and it is state-owned. It accounts for 26.9% of the aggregate Russian banking assets. As of January 2011, it accounted for 47.9% of retail deposits, 31% of consumer loans and 31% of corporate loans in Russia. The other two main players of the sectors, Vnehstorgbank (VTB) and Gazprombank, are government-owned, too. As of 2010, Sberbank, VTB and Gazprombank account for 44% of the total banking sector assets in Russia.

In Turkey, as of 2010, a government-owned bank, Ziraatbank, was the largest bank in Turkey. It accounted for 15.72% of the total banking sector assets and 21% of total deposits in the sector as at the end of 2010. It is followed by two privately-owned banks, IsBankası and Garanti Bank. As of 2010, these three banks accounted for 42.31% of the Turkish banking sector assets.

Table 7. Banking sector concentration levels*

	1999	2000	2001	2002	2003	2004	2005	2006	2007	2008	2009	2010
Turkey	33.39	33.49	37.07	40.38	49.92	42.56	45.63	42.15	40.86	41.21	42.98	42.31
Russia	47.39	40.35	37.71	35.6	35.95	37.97	41.95	40.44	40.27	43.84	42.33	43.99

* Concentration: Percentage of assets held by the three largest commercial banks in the country.
Source: Banking Association of Turkey; Bankscope.

These data support the fact that Turkish banks and Russian banks make a good case for comparison due to their similar structural features. Furthermore, Table 8, Table 9 and Table 10 measure the activity in the banking sector for both countries. Table 8 measures the banking sector activity by dividing the bank claims to the private sector with GDP. Table 9 shows domestic credit to private sector as of GDP. It refers to the financial resources provided to the private sector through loans, purchases of non-equity securities, trade credits and other accounts receivable that establish a claim for repayment. Finally, Table 10 presents the growing loan portfolios in the asset structure of both countries' banking sectors between 2001 and 2010 showing a similar trend for both countries.

Table 8. Activity in the banking sector

	1999	2000	2001	2002	2003	2004	2005	2006	2007	2008	2009	2010
Turkey	8.02	8.03	5.36	5.90	7.50	9.84	13.75	15.39	19.55	22.29	20.00	20.60
Russia	2.95	3.45	4.71	5.24	6.75	9.67	11.58	14.35	20.60	23.91	20.18	22.18

* Activity in the banking sector = Bank claims to the private sector / GDP.
Source: Global Market Information Database of Euromonitor International.

Table 9. Domestic credit to private sector (% of GDP)

	1999	2000	2001	2002	2003	2004	2005	2006	2007	2008	2009	2010
Turkey	16.6	17.8	15.4	14.5	14.5	17.3	22.2	25.9	29.5	32.6	36.5	44.2
Russia	13.1	13.6	16.8	18	21.2	24.3	27.5	32.5	38.8	42.2	46.2	44.9

Source: World Bank Data (1999–2010).[6]

6 http://data.worldbank.org/indicator/FS.AST.PRVT.GD.ZS/countries.

Table 10. Bank loans (% of GDP)

	2001	2002	2003	2004	2005	2006	2007	2008	2009	2010
Turkey	21	17.8	18.6	23.2	30.8	30	35.1	40.2	43	50
Russia	14.8	16.6	20.3	22.9	25.3	30	43.2	47.9	50.8	49.3

Source: CBR Banking Supervision Reports (2004–2010), Caner et al. (2007), Banks Association of Turkey (2005–2010).

In addition to these structural similarities, Turkey and Russia have a trade relationship based on natural gas and oil. Although the 2007–2009 global crisis led to a decline in trade, gas trade between the two countries reached its highest level in 2008 and was worth $35 billion.

3. THEORY OF PERFORMANCE MEASUREMENT

3.1. FUNDAMENTALS OF PRODUCTION THEORY

The production theory is based on a set of physical technological possibilities which are described by a production function. Economic theory regards the production function as a concept that describes the technological relationship between the outputs and inputs of factors of production. The aim is to explore the substitution possibilities among the factors of production, or in other words, among various amounts and combinations of inputs, in order to obtain a given level of output (Sato, 1977). Applied to banking, this concept means that the bank chooses inputs and outputs in its production structure.[7] A bank's output is defined as the bank's ability to solve asymmetric information problems between lenders and borrowers and manage risk. These are the most important components of a bank's production. These abilities affect the incentives of bank managers to produce financial services prudently and efficiently. In that sense, a bank is the financial intermediary that produces financial services and provides risk diversification combining the theory of financial intermediation with the microeconomics of bank production.[8] In order to provide the best level of output, banks must use their resources efficiently (Hughes & Mester, 2008).

Production functions are represented mostly by a mathematical function or by a graph. Although there are various functional forms, production relationships have been mostly analysed by the Cobb-Douglas production function which is a simple and non-linear functional form that assumes a

7 For example: a bank makes choices about its capital structure and the amount of risk to assume.

8 The theory of financial intermediation and the economics of banking are explained in detail in Chapter 1.

unitary elasticity of substitution (Sato, 1975; Arrow et al., 1961).[9] Graphically, a production frontier is employed to define the relationship between the input and output factors. The X-axis refers to inputs and the Y-axis refers to outputs. The production frontier, represented by the line 0F' in Figure 1, shows the maximum output that can be produced from each input level. In other words, it reflects the current state of technology in the industry (Coelli, Rao & Battese, 1998: 4).

Figure 1. Production frontiers and technical efficiency

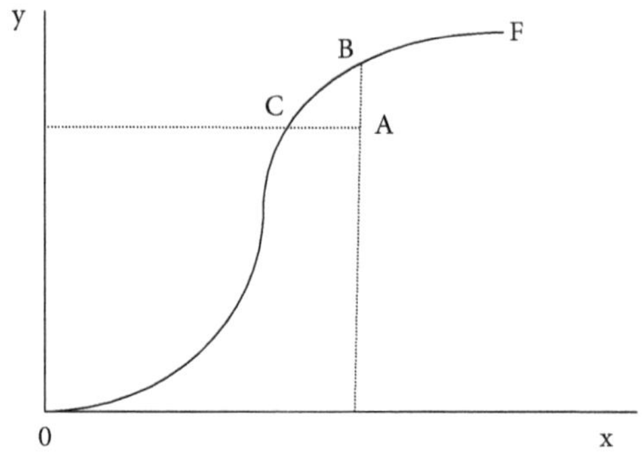

Source: Coelli et al. (1998).

The frontier line 0F' also shows the production possibility set (PPS) which is the set of all input-output combinations that are feasible. The PPS set includes all points between the production frontier 0F' and the X-axis, together with the bounds. The points along the frontier constitute the efficient subset of this production set. The distance of each individual unit from the frontier measures the efficiency differences of individual Decision Making Units (DMUs).[10]

Conventional microeconomic theory as well as theoretical production analysis is based on the assumption of optimising behaviour where the production activity is seen as an optimisation process (Färe et al., 1994: 1–3). According to this behavioural assumption, producers prefer to operate somewhere on the boundary of their production possibility sets, rather than on the interior, since cost minimisation requires producers to operate on rather than above their minimum cost frontiers for an efficient resource allocation. The DMUs possess the behavioural assumptions of cost minimisation or output maximisation since various combinations of inputs can produce the same level

9 The other widely accepted alternative is the Walras-Leontief-Harrod-Domar assumption of constant input coefficients. For a more detailed analysis of the application of different types of production functions see: Forsund & Hjalmarson (1979) and Kumbhakar, Ghosh & McGukin (1991).

10 The efficiency concept regarding decision making units (which are called *banks* in this work) will be discussed in the next section. For an in-depth analysis of input-output distance functions, see Faere & Primont, 1995.

of output. Hence, a firm (which is the DMU under consideration here) would want to choose an input vector that has the lowest costs and still produces the optimal output (Färe et al., 1994: 2). This cost minimisation technique – introduced by Samuelson and Swamy (1974) – claims that by changing the proportions of input factors, a firm can decrease the total costs without affecting total revenue, thereby increasing profits.

Another concept in cost minimisation regarding optimising behaviour is the returns to scale in performance measurement which shows the degree to which a proportional increase in all inputs increases output. A bank is said to be operating at constant returns to scale (CRS) when a proportional increase (a) in all inputs results in the same proportional increase in output. Increasing returns to scale (IRS) occurs when a proportional increase in outputs requires a less than proportionate increase in costs. Lastly, decreasing returns to scale (DRS) occurs when some restriction prevents some elements of production from increasing in optimal proportions (Morroni, 1992: 162).[11]

Table 11. Algebraic expression of economies of scale

Returns to Scale	Definition (α>1)
Constant	$f(\alpha x_1,\alpha x_2) = \alpha f(x_1,x_2)$
Increasing	$f(\alpha x_1,\alpha x_2) > \alpha f(x_1,x_2)$
Decreasing	$f(\alpha x_1,\alpha x_2) < \alpha f(x_1,x_2)$

Source: Coelli et al. (1998).

Figure 2. Graphical representation of economies of scale

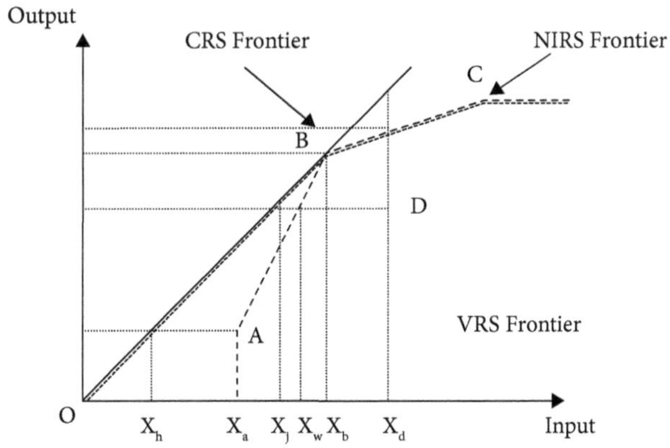

Source: Coelli et al. (1998).

11 See Table 11, which explains the algebraic expression of economies of scale. Figure 2 displays the graphical representation of economies of scale (Coelli et al., 1998: 18).

In Figure 2, the line from the origin through B is the frontier technology associated with the assumption of CRS, according to which only bank B would be considered technically efficient. The other banks A, C and D are considered inefficient. The efficient frontier, defined by the line X_a, A, B, and C, represents Variable Returns to Scale (VRS) under which banks of A, B and C are fully efficient but D is still inefficient.[12] Following these specifications, a measure of scale efficiency can be calculated from the ratio TE_{CRS}/TE_{VRS}. For example, bank B is CRS and VRS technically efficient whereas banks A and C are VRS efficient but CRS inefficient. Bank D is technically inefficient regarding both efficiency frontiers. One shortcoming of this procedure is that it is not able to show whether the DMU (the bank) operates under increasing or decreasing returns to scale. This problem can be solved by creating a linear programming model called Data Envelopment Analysis (DEA) (Murillo, 2004).[13]

3.2. PERFORMANCE INDICATOR: EFFICIENCY

As a performance indicator, efficiency is basically a component of productivity. The change in efficiency shows the change in how far an observation is from the frontier of technology and the technical change is the shifts in the production frontier (Fried, Lovell & Schmidt, 1993: 160).[14] Efficiency measures the success of a bank in converting inputs of the production process into outputs of the process according to the behavioural objectives of cost minimisation or output maximisation (Lovell, 1994).[15] Efficient usage of resources is the main idea in providing the maximum levels of output. Hence, efficiency indicators are also important in terms of providing information about a bank's behaviour.

Considering the Figure 1, the points along the frontier are defined as the efficient subset of the feasible production set. In Figure 3, Point A represents an inefficient point while B and C represent efficient points. By moving to B, A could increase its output to the level of B without requiring more input. On the other hand, by moving to C, it could produce the same level of output by using less input.

---

12 However, bank D's efficiency score has changed from the ratio X_j/X_d under CRS to X_w/X_d under VRS.

13 The objective can also be output maximisation. Here, the bank has a given level of budget; and the objective is to produce the maximum output possible by choosing the best combinations of input factors.

14 See Coelli et al. (1998: Chapter 1) for a graphical representation of technical change.

15 In other words: producing as much output as possible from a given set of inputs (Farrel, 1957).

Figure 3. Technical efficiency

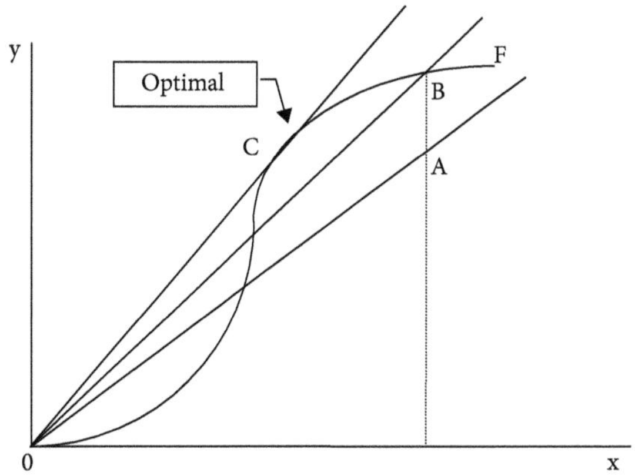

Source: Coelli et al. (1998).

The efficiency concept started with the analyses of Debreu (1951), Koopmans (1951), and Farrell (1957). The measurement of *technical efficiency* was introduced by Debreu (1951). Koopmans (1951)[16] provided a formal definition for technical efficiency: an input-output vector is technically efficient if, and only if, increasing any output or decreasing any input is possible only by decreasing some other output or increasing some other input (Cooper et al., 2006: 46; Färe et al., 1994: 7–8). Basically, *a DMU is technically efficient when it is not possible to generate more output with the same input level.* The assumption is that the inefficient management of a DMU explains its inability to produce the maximum possible amount of output (Segura & Braun, 2004).[17] The term "technical efficiency" is taken from the literature in economics, where it is used to distinguish the "technological aspects of production" from other aspects, generally referred to as the economic efficiency that is of interest to economists. The ability of banks to contribute to the welfare of society via cost minimisation or profit maximisation is called economic efficiency; technical efficiency is regarded as one component of this (Lovell, 1994).

A judgement of economic efficiency, however, requires information on prices and costs (Cooper et al., 2006: 11). Farrell (1957), drawing upon the work of Koopmans (1951) and Debreu (1951), suggested that economic efficiency has a second component called *allocative (price) efficiency.* This shows the ability of producers to choose the right technically efficient input-output vector given the input and output prices. It considers the information about prices in determining

16 Koopman efficiency was also called the Pareto-Koopman efficiency criterion.

17 Technical efficiency is the ability of a DMU to produce maximal output from a given set of inputs. A firm is technically efficient if an increase in any output requires a decrease in at least one other output or in at least one input.

the flow of resources to their best use. If the input prices are given, allocative efficiency in input selection involves selecting the combination of inputs that produce a given quantity of output at minimum cost. Allocative and technical efficiency together provide an overall economic efficiency measure (Coelli et al., 1998: 5).

Regarding the work of Farrell (1957), frontier estimation techniques were applied by the researchers to represent the technology by a bounding function, not by fitting a function through observed data. This bounding function may be based on production or input requirement and estimated by nonparametric or econometric methods. This methodology, which is also considered as a general standard for efficiency measures, is the best-practice production technology or frontier production technology of a product, defined as the maximum output attainable from given inputs. The technical inefficiency of a DMU is then measured by its deviation from the function (Forsund & Hjalmarsson, 1974; Paul-Morrison 1999: 211). Farrell measures efficiency by using graphs involving firms that use two inputs (x_1 and x_2) to produce a single output under CRS assumption. In Figure 4, the isoquant[18] SS' shows fully efficient banks. Bank P is inefficient. Its technical inefficiency is represented by the distance between P and the isoquant SS', which is the ratio 0Q/0P. The distance QP measures the technical inefficiency of P and this ratio can take a value between zero and one.[19]

Figure 4. Farrell's input-oriented model

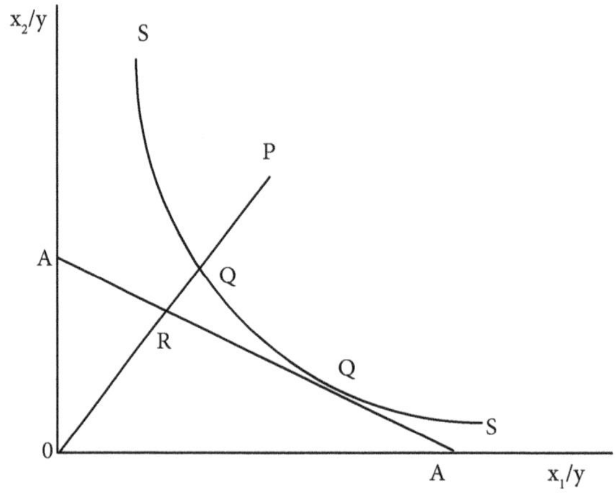

Source: Coelli et al. (1998: 135) adapted from Farrell (1957: 254).

18 An isoquant is the set of all possible combinations of input 1 and input 2 that are just sufficient to produce a given amount of output. Isoquants are similar to indifference curves with the difference that the isoquants are labelled with the amount of output they can produce, not with a utility level (Varian, 2002: 321).

19 If the ratio is one, then the bank is fully efficient. If it is smaller than 1, it is inefficient.

Figure 5. Farrell's output-oriented model

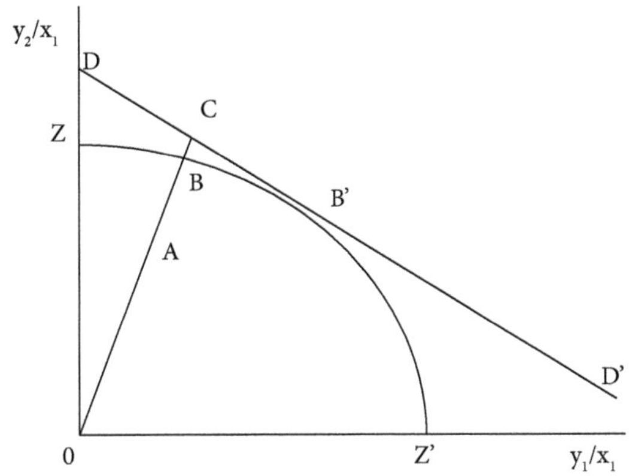

Source: Coelli et al. (1998: 138).

Figure 5 shows another representation and measurement of technical efficiency in terms of an output-oriented context. This approach answers how much output can be expanded given input use, rather than how much inputs can be contracted and still produce the observed output level (Morrison-Paul, 1999: 214). The line ZZ' is the production possibility curve and A represents an inefficient bank. Here, 0A/0B represents the technical efficiency of bank B and 0B/0C represents the allocative efficiency of bank B. The overall economic efficiency is 0A/0C. However, both input and output oriented models define the same efficiency frontiers and give the same solutions.

Other than graphical representations, efficiency measurements can also be obtained with empirical production functions and frontier estimations which are derived with the help of parametric and non-parametric techniques respectively. Parametric and non-parametric methods differ in the assumptions imposed on the data in terms of (1) the functional form of the best-practice frontier (a more restrictive parametric functional form versus a less restrictive nonparametric form) (2) whether or not account is taken of random error that may temporarily give some production units high or low outputs, inputs, costs, or profits. They primarily differ in how much shape is imposed on the frontier and the distributional assumptions imposed on the random error and inefficiency (Berger & Humphrey, 1997). The following section introduces one of the most widely used non-parametric approaches, called Data Envelopment Analysis (DEA) which I will use for the Turkish and Russian banks' efficiency estimations used in this study. In fact, since its introduction, the DEA model has been widely applied in empirical studies that analyse cross-section and panel data (Tavares, 2002).

4. LITERATURE REVIEW ON DEA BANKING APPLICATIONS

Various studies have applied DEA to the measurement of efficiency in banking. The empirical analysis conducted in this chapter runs a simple cross-section[20] regression with the DEA scores as the dependent variable after deriving the DEA efficiency scores.[21] This section will first provide a summary of the literature on several cross-country studies on bank efficiency that have used DEA. This will be followed by a short literature review on DEA applications on Turkish banks and Russian banks separately. The review will contribute to identifying the applicable methodologies and relevant variables for the purposes of the empirical analysis set out in this book. Each study presented below considers the following four points: types of banks analysed, types of input and output measures used, the results from the analysis, and conclusions in general relevant to the effects of financial reforms, financial crises and environmental variables on efficiency estimates.

4.1. CROSS-COUNTRY EFFICIENCY STUDIES

The first studies on comparisons of banking efficiencies across countries using DEA were conducted by Berg et al. (1993) and Bergendahl (1998) on Nordic countries. Berg et al. (1993) investigated how well banks of different sizes and from different countries perform to meet the intense competition of a common European banking market. This study measured the average productivity and the spread of efficiency levels of banks in Finland, Norway and Sweden in 1990. DEA was applied together with the Malmquist productivity index.[22] As the first step, separate frontiers were computed for each country to make pair-wise comparisons of the countries. A common frontier was then defined and hence, the results across countries were compared.[23] Their results indicated that the most efficient banks were found to be in Sweden. A similar study was conducted by Berg et al. (1995) for the same countries, but adding Denmark to the sample. They also found that Swedish banks were the most efficient. Bergendahl (1998)

---

20 A cross-sectional data set refers to a sample of individuals, households, firms, cities, states, countries, or a variety of other units taken at a given point in time (Wooldridge, 2000: 6).

21 See section 3.

22 The Malmquist index is used to identify the productivity differences between banks in different countries. See: S. Malmquist (1953): "Index numbers and indifference surfaces", *Trabajos de Estadistica 4*, pp. 209–242. For more on this, see Berg et al. (1992) and Mohammadi and Ranaei (2011). For details on the interpretation of the Malmquist Productivity Index, see: Berg et al. (1993), Grosskopf (1993) and Bjurek (1996).

23 They employed two inputs (labour and capital) and three outputs (total loans, total deposits and number of branches).

did another follow-up study on the same sample over the years 1992 and 1993, analysing banks in terms of their efficient risk management and service provision where he used credit risk in terms of credit losses (measured in terms of loss provisions), cost of personnel and cost of material as inputs. Outputs were defined as gross revenues, lending volumes and deposit volumes. Two Finnish, one Norwegian and one Swedish bank that were found to be efficient in 1992 remained again efficient in 1993. When they did the analysis under Variable Returns to Scale (VRS),[24] they found more banks became efficient.

After the introduction of the first applications of these cross-country studies, Pastor et al. (1997) also applied DEA together with the Malmquist productivity index to measure technical efficiency, productivity and differences in technology in the banking systems of the US and several European banking systems for the year 1992 following the intensive process of *financial European integration.* By using the valued-added approach,[25] non-interest expenses and personnel expenses were used as inputs; and loans, productive assets and deposits were used as outputs. The highest efficiency in the banking sector was found in France and the lowest efficiency level was found in the UK.

Another study conducted by Cockerill et al. (2004) applied DEA to examine the impact of *financial liberalisation* on the efficiency of commercial banks in India and Pakistan between 1988–1998 because this period was characterised by major changes in the banking industry, brought about by financial liberalisation.[26] Two models with two alternative input-output specifications were employed: a *loan-based model* where operating expenses and interest expenses were used as inputs to produce loans and advances, and investments; and an *income-based model* which used the same inputs to produce interest income and non-interest income. Cockerill et al. (2004) found that the overall technical efficiency of banks in both countries increased after the implementation of financial liberalisation.[27] Moreover, the efficiency results obtained in the loan-based model are greater than the ones obtained in the income-based model, meaning that banks are more efficient in generating earning assets than in generating income.

One other study done by Anayiotos et al. (2010) applied DEA to the emerging countries in Europe to investigate the relative efficiency of banks before and after the 2007–2009 global crisis focusing on the years 2004, 2007 and 2009 (before the pre-crisis boom, just before the crisis and after the crisis). This study

[24] See section 2.1 and Table 7.

[25] See section 4.1.3.

[26] Financial liberalisation refers to the lifting of restrictions on cross-border financial transactions, deregulation of interest rates and state-directed credit policies, the entry of non-bank financial institutions, reduced restrictions on entry and the privatisation of public sector banks (Cockerill et al., 2004).

[27] This increase in India was due to an increase both in pure technical efficiency and scale efficiency whereas in Pakistan this was only due to an increase in scale efficiency.

employed the intermediation approach[28] which will also be used in the DEA analysis in this book. Total capital, interest expense and operating expense were used as inputs while total loans, pre-tax profit and securities portfolio were chosen as outputs. After deriving the efficiency scores, a simple cross-section regression was run with the DEA scores as the dependent variable. The results suggested that the DEA efficiency scores were strongly linked to the countries' local banks' development level. Foreign-owned banks were found to be more efficient than domestic banks. The findings also suggested that as credit expanded before the crisis, bank efficiency suffered.[29] Bank efficiency increased during the pre-crisis boom, but fell during the crisis. In fact, the seeds of the 2007–2009 global crisis were sown in the credit boom in the period leading up to the crisis, which was followed by the failure of several banking systems (Scharfstein & Ivashina, 2008).

In the cross-country studies mentioned above, common frontiers were applied in order to explain the efficiency differences of banks by country-specific banking technologies. Performance differences among banks are attributed to differences in country-specific aspects of banking technology. However, cross-country disparities in environmental factors such as economic environment and regulatory structures should also be taken into account in doing performance comparisons.

One of the DEA studies that considers environmental factors during the estimation of efficiency is the one by Hauner (2005), who applied DEA to German and Austrian banks for the period between 1995 and 1999 to measure cost efficiency, scale efficiency and productivity change. These are estimated by DEA by using intermediation approach. At the second stage, cost-efficiency is regressed on explanatory variables which include the economic environment, the type of ownership, risk management, the structure of funding and the quality of staff. Inputs are given by the bank's aggregate funds (in terms of customer deposits, interbank deposits, and securitised liabilities) and labour. Interbank loans, customer loans and fixed-income securities are defined as outputs. Hauner (2005) found that Austrian banks are less cost-efficient than German banks. No significant differences between the cost-efficiency of privately-owned banks and cooperative banks were found. Furthermore, the study supports a further shift of funding towards interbank deposits and securitised liabilities. The methodology employed in this chapter is very similar to Hauner's (2005) empirical study since the efficiency scores of Turkish banks and Russian banks were also pooled in the regression analysis.

Casu and Molyneux (2003) also follow a two-stage DEA to measure the productive efficiency of European banks following the *process of EU legislative*

28 See section 4.1.2.

29 Other possible determinants of bank efficiency such as size, EU membership, being in a financial group with a presence in more than one country, credit market regulation, interest rate spreads, state ownership, asset quality and stock market size do not seem to have a statistically significant impact.

harmonisation[30] for the period between 1993 and 1997. Inputs are interest expenses, non-interest expenses, personnel expenses and total deposits whereas total loans and other earning assets comprise outputs. After deriving the efficiency measures obtained by the DEA estimations, they use them as the dependent variable in the Tobit regression[31] model to further investigate the determinants of European bank efficiency. Equity to total assets, return on average equity and the type of bank are the environmental variables. Their findings support the importance of country-specific factors in explaining the differences in bank efficiency levels across the EU. They interpret this finding as reflecting the legacy of different banking regulations.

The two-stage DEA is also applied by Grigoran and Manole (2002) to a wide range of transition countries (grouped as Central Europe, South-eastern Europe and the Baltic, and the Commonwealth of Independent States) for the period 1995–1998. Labour, fixed assets and interest expenditures are defined as inputs. Regarding outputs, they define two sets of outputs: (1) revenues (the sum of interest income and non-interest income), net loans and liquid assets as one set of outputs; and (2) deposits, net loans and liquid assets as the second set of outputs. At the second stage, they run the Tobit regression of these efficiency scores on variables related to the macroeconomic environment, the regulatory environment and bank-specific variables. One important finding is that the effects of prudential tightening on the efficiency of banks vary across different prudential norms due to the different objectives of regulatory authorities.

Although most of the above-mentioned studies incorporate environmental factors into the efficiency analysis, this literature is still in its infancy in defining the proxies for the regulatory environment and in incorporating the impact of regulatory and supervisory factors that influence a bank's technical efficiency. They mostly deal with the economic environment, examining the degree of concentration and industry average capital, profitability and intermediation ratios. Another approach is that the regulatory and supervisory variables are included in regression analyses, where performance is measured with financial ratios rather than with efficiency scores determined via a frontier analysis (Pasiouras, 2008).[32]

30 This process refers to the creation of the Single Internal Market. One of the major objectives of the European Union's Single Market Programme (SMP) in 1992 was to facilitate the free movement of goods and services across Member States and to improve economic efficiency. Harmonising regulations and improving competition in the banking sector formed an integral part of this programme. In January 1993, legislation was introduced in order to create a comprehensive framework for regulating all banking businesses in the EU. This legislation established the regulatory requirements across the European banking sectors (Casu & Molyneux, 2003).

31 See section 3.2.

32 Berger and Humphrey (1997), Berger et al. (1998) and Aysan and Ceyhan (2007) support the superiority of frontier approaches in measuring performance. For a more detailed discussion about a comparison of frontier efficiency methods, see Berger et al. (1998).

However, the empirical analysis presented in this book is most closely related to the study done by Pasiouras (2008), who, by using two-stage DEA, provides international evidence on the impact of regulations and supervision approaches on banks' efficiency with which he tries to fill the gap in the literature. First, by employing DEA, Pasiouras (2008) estimates technical and scale efficiency. At the second stage, in order to investigate the impact of regulations such as capital adequacy, private monitoring, banks' activities, deposit insurance schemes, disciplinary power of the authorities, and entry into banking on banks' technical efficiency, a regression is performed controlling for bank-specific attributes and country-level characteristics regarding macroeconomic conditions, financial development, market structure, overall institutional development, and access to banking services. The intermediation approach is adapted to a sample of 95 countries for the year 2003. Inputs are total deposits, interest expenses, non-interest expenses and equity. Outputs are loans, other earning assets and non-interest income. The results indicate that higher capital stringency increases banks' efficiency. Regulations that improve private monitoring also increase the technical efficiency of banks and finally, higher official disciplinary power is also positively associated with higher efficiency. However, only the existence of powerful supervisory agencies is significant in all Pasiouras' specifications.[33] The present study employs the same methodology with the difference that whereas Pasiouras (2008) applies the two-stage DEA analysis to a sample of 95 countries for the year 2003, this study applies this analysis to two countries (Turkey and Russia) over a period of twelve years (1999–2010).

4.2. EFFICIENCY IN TURKISH BANKING

There are several studies that applied DEA to the Turkish commercial banking industry. Yıldırım (2002) applied DEA to the Turkish banking sector during the period 1988–1998 analysing the technical and scale efficiencies of the banks. In 1980, Turkey began to transform itself with the financial liberalisation programme. However, this process was accompanied by an increase in macroeconomic instability. By employing the intermediation approach, Yıldırım (2002) uses total deposits, total interest expense and non-interest expense as inputs. Total loans, interest income and non-interest income are the outputs. She also investigates the relationships between profitability, asset quality, size and

33 Pasiouras (2008) runs several regressions and estimates several specifications of a Tobit model while controlling for bank-specific and country-level characteristics accounting for macroeconomic conditions, financial development, market structure, overall institutional development, and access to banking services. In several cases, the results provide evidence in favour of the adoption of strict capital adequacy standards, the development of powerful supervisory agencies, and the creation of market disciplining mechanisms. However, only the development of powerful supervisory agencies is significant in all of his specifications.

the two definitions of efficiency. The findings suggest that the Turkish banks did not achieve any sustained efficiency gains over the sample period. The performance levels over the period suggest that macroeconomic conditions had an important impact on the efficiency scores.

Zaim (1995) analyses the effects of post-1980 financial liberalisation policies on the efficiency of Turkish commercial banks for the years 1981 and 1990. By applying the intermediation approach, inputs are defined as number of employees, total interest expenditures, depreciation expenditures and expenditures on materials. Outputs are defined as the total balance of demand and time deposits, and the total balance of long-term and short-term loans. Contrary to Yıldırım's (2002) findings, Zaim (1995) reported that the Turkish banks experienced improved efficiency during the post-liberalisation era. Another study conducted by Denizer et al. (2007) also examines Turkey's post-1980 financial liberalisation experience, using data for 25 years from 1970 to 1994. A two-stage DEA analysis is conducted first with the production approach in the first stage and then with the intermediation approach in the second stage. Contrary to Zaim's (1995) findings, but in line with Yıldırım's (2002) findings, Denizer's et al. (2007) study suggests that the financial liberalisation process did not provide efficiency gains. Furthermore, considering the role of environmental factors in determining banks' efficiency, it is found that the unstable macroeconomic environment of high inflation and unstable growth patterns had a negative impact on banks' efficiency during that time period.

Aysan and Ceyhan (2007) analyse the productivity change and the technical efficiency in the Turkish banking sector between 1990 and 2006. The analysis particularly focuses on the period after the 2001 crisis, when the Turkish banking system underwent regulatory reform and a comprehensive restructuring process. The technical efficiency of banks is measured by using DEA and productivity change is measured by the Malmquist productivity index.[34] Inputs are loan, capital and loanable funds while credits, off-balance sheet items and other earning assets are used as outputs. The aim of this study was to understand how Turkish banks responded to the 2000 and 2001 crises as well as to the restructuring process. The results show that all banks experienced efficiency increases after 2001. Although this work follows a different methodology, the finding of the 2007 study is very much in line with my findings discussed below. This suggests that the steps taken in the regulatory/supervisory framework of the Turkish banking sector following the 2000/2001 crises had a positive impact on the performance of Turkish banks.

Jackson and Fethi (2000) apply DEA to Turkish banks for the year 1998. In estimating efficiency, they use the number of employees, and the sum of non-

34 The Malmquist productivity index is a distance function based technique used for measuring productivity scores introduced first by Malmquist in 1953 (del Gatto et al., 2009). For more on this, see Berg et al. (1992); Mohammadi and Ranaei (2011).

labour operating expenses, direct expenditure on buildings and amortisation expenses as inputs. Loans and deposits are defined as outputs. At the second stage, the determinants of efficiency are investigated with Tobit regression where a set of explanatory variables such as bank size, the number of branches, profitability, ownership and capital adequacy ratio are used. The study finds that the capital adequacy ratio has a statistically significant adverse impact on the performance of banks reflecting a risk-return trade-off in the sector.

Tektas and Ozkan-Gunay (2006) apply DEA to Turkish commercial banks during the period between 1990–2001 to assess the technical efficiency of commercial banks in the pre-crisis period and during the 2001 crisis period. Personnel expenses, administrative expenses, and interest expenses are defined as inputs while total deposits, total loans, total securities, total interest income, and total non-interest income are defined as outputs. The study shows that most of the banks that were taken over by the Savings Deposit Insurance Fund (SDIF) after the 2001 crisis were relatively inefficient in the period up to the 2001 crisis compared to banks that did not fail during the 2001 crisis.

4.3. EFFICIENCY IN RUSSIAN BANKING

There are only a few DEA applications to the Russian banking sector in the literature.[35] Although not directly, Grigorian and Manole (2002) apply two-stage DEA to a wide-range of transition countries, including Russia for the period between 1995–1998. Labour, fixed assets and interest expenditures are used as inputs. Interest income, non-interest income, net loans and liquid assets are used as one set of outputs; and deposits, net loans and liquid assets are used as the second set of outputs. At the second-stage, these efficiency scores are regressed on variables related to the macro-economic environment, regulatory environment and bank-specific variables. The findings are as follows: among the group of the Commonwealth of Independent States to which Russia belongs, Russia has the lowest efficiency scores in terms of revenue generating and the ability to provide services to their clients.

Ono (2004) investigates the impact of the 1998 Russian financial crisis on the technical and scale efficiency of the Russian banks during the period of 1997–2000 using DEA. Total interest expense and total non-interest expense are used as inputs. Total interest income and total non-interest income are defined as outputs. At the second stage, using regression analysis, Ono (2004) investigates the correlation of technical efficiency scores with the ratio of income and

35 Most of the efficiency studies applied to Russian banks employ the stochastic frontier approach, which is a parametric method in frontier analysis that considers the performance measurement.

expense items to the total income. It is found that the average overall technical efficiency score is highest in 1997, and then it falls following the 1998 crisis.

In order to understand how the transformation of banking has advanced in post-communist countries, Fries and Taci (2005) examine the efficiency of banks from 15 Eastern European countries over the years 1994–2001, including Russia. Russia is found to belong to the group of countries with the least efficient banks on average.

Golovan (2006, in Peteresetsky 2010) analyses the factors that contribute to the efficiency of Russian banks in issuing loans and attracting deposits. His findings show that the average bank efficiency increased over 2003–2005. Banks with a high capitalisation are the most efficient lenders. Besides, a high ratio of past due loans is negatively related to efficiency.

5. METHODOLOGY

Performance measurement is an important concept of the management process for banks since it provides them with valuable information for their operations. Considering the complex and rapidly changing structure of the financial services industry, it is of interest to measure the efficiency of financial institutions and then explain the variation in their efficiency measurements. Evaluating the performance of financial institutions requires first to separate the production units that by some standard perform well from those that perform poorly (Humphrey & Berger, 1997). Ratio analysis is one method to do this, where financial ratios are used as benchmarks in comparing several financial units. It calculates the ratio of an output variable to an input variable, where the unit with the highest output over input ratio or the lowest input over output ratio is evaluated as having the best performance level (Aysan & Ceyhan, 2008). However, this method is insufficient for application in banking industries since it uses multiple inputs and multiple outputs.[36]

The empirical estimation of the efficient frontier is useful for benchmarking the relative performance of production units, in other words, how close financial institutions are to a best-practice frontier (Humphrey & Berger, 1997).[37] In the non-parametric approach, no a priori assumptions are made regarding the form of the production function. A best-practice function is built empirically and solely from observed inputs and outputs (Norman & Stoker, 1991: 12). Hence, the possibility of mis-specification of the production technology is zero (Jemric & Vujcic, 2002). Additionally, it can easily deal with multiple outputs and variable

36 For an international survey of the methodologies used in the efficiency measurements of financial institutions, see Berger and Humphrey (1997).

37 The frontier is the boundary of the production possibility set. The best Decision Making Unit is the accepted benchmark bank.

returns to scale, and it provides meaningful scalar technical and scale efficiency levels without requiring data on input prices (Fukuyama, 1993; Favero & Papi, 1995).

On the other hand, one disadvantage of the non-parametric method is that the measurement error and statistical noise are assumed to be non-existent (Fukuyama, 1993; Fried et al., 1993: 34). As a result, it is necessary to control the sensitivity of results and eliminate the outliers so that they are stable and do not vary dramatically when some units are excluded from the sample (Resti, 1997). Fukuyama (1993) argues that the limitations of the non-parametric approach are usually the strengths of the econometric approach and the converse is also true. Resti (1997) indicates that (i) the econometric and linear programming results do not differ dramatically when based on the same data and conceptual framework; and (ii) when differences arise, they can be explained by going back to the intrinsic features of the models.[38, 39, 40]

5.1. DATA ENVELOPMENT ANALYSIS

One of the widely used non-parametric techniques is the Data Envelopment Analysis (DEA). Although the theoretical foundation of this method was proposed first by Debreu (1951), Koopman (1951) and Farrell (1957), the model was then developed by Charnes, Cooper and Rhodes (1978) named as the CCR (Charnes-Cooper-Rhodes) model. Since then, it has become a widely used methodology.[41] DEA is one of the most popular mathematical programming methods analysing the relationship between inputs and outputs of a production process by constructing empirical production frontiers and measuring the efficiency of decision making units (DMUs) relative to the constructed frontiers.[42] In this way, we are able to measure how much a bank departs from efficient management. By determining the efficient banks as benchmarks and then measuring the inefficiencies in input combinations (slack variables) of other

---

38 Resti (1997) also finds high correlations between the efficiency results derived by the application of the DEA technique and econometric estimation.

39 For more on the discussion of the differences that exist between econometric estimation and linear programming, see Berger and Humphrey (1997), and Fried et al. (1993: Chapter I).

40 Furthermore, regression analysis relies on central tendencies, and DEA is based on observations at the extremes. While the regression approach assumes that a single estimated regression equation applies to each observation vector, DEA analyses each vector (DMU) separately, producing individual efficiency measures relative to the entire set under evaluation (Jemric & Vujcic, 2002).

41 For a discussion of the evolution of DEA methodology, see Seiford (1996), Seiford and Thrall (1990), Lovell (1994) and Norman and Stoker (1991).

42 In this study, DMU is a bank. One of the most important features of DEA is that it can manage the multiple characteristics of a bank since it uses multiple inputs and outputs (Meryem-Fethi & Jackson, 2000).

banks relative to the benchmark, it enables us to compare the relative efficiency of banks (Jemric & Vujcic, 2002).

The technical efficiency of a bank refers to its success in producing a given set of outputs with minimal inputs, under the assumption of variable returns to scale. Allocative efficiency is the ability of a bank to use the inputs in optimal proportions, given their prices. These two measures together combine the total economic efficiency (Coelli, 1996; Hauner, 2005). The DEA frontier is constructed empirically from observed inputs and outputs as the piece-wise linear combination of the best-practice observations in the data set, thereby creating a convex Production Possibility Set (PPS). This set envelops the input-output combination of all the banks in the sample. DEA identifies reference points. In other words, relatively efficient DMUs (banks) and these reference points define the efficient frontier as the best practice production technology. The relative inefficiency of other banks situated at some interior points that are below that frontier will then be evaluated by these reference points.

The DEA, specifically the CCR model, allows each DMU to adopt its own set of weights that maximises its own efficiency level relative to other DMUs. Hence, efficiency is measured as the maximum of the ratio of weighted outputs to weighted inputs. Based on the work of Charnes, Cooper and Rhodes (1978), 100% efficiency is achieved by a decision-making-unit when comparisons with other units do not provide any evidence of inferior use of output or input (Charnes and Cooper, in Norman and Stoker 1991: 15). By generating the best units (most efficient), DEA forms a reference bank according to which other banks will be evaluated (Bergendahl, 1998).

5.1.1. The CCR Model (1978)

To measure the efficiency of a DMU (bank), Charnes, Cooper and Rhodes (1978) proposed the use of the maximum of the ratio of weighted outputs to weighted inputs for that DMU, subject to the condition that similar ratios for all other DMUs in the sample be less than or equal to 1.

Consider n number of decision-making units (banks in my case), each producing s number of outputs denoted as $y_{j,} j=1, \ldots, s$ using r number of inputs denoted as x_i where $i=1, \ldots, r$. The efficiency of a bank is then measured:

$$\text{Max } e_o = \frac{\sum_{j=1}^{s} w_j y_{jo}}{\sum_{i=1}^{r} v_i x_{io}}$$

Where: $_0$ is the specific bank to be evaluated
y_{j0} is the amount of the jth output produced by the bank$_0$
x_{i0} is the amount of the ith input used by the bank$_0$

w_j is the output weight
v_i is the input weight

So, the efficiency measure e_0 is maximised such that it is subject to:

$$\frac{\sum_{j=1}^{s} w_j y_{jm}}{\sum_{i=1}^{r} v_i x_{im}} \leq 1 \qquad m= 1,\ldots, n \tag{1}$$

$$w_j \geq 0 \qquad j= 1,\ldots, s \tag{2}$$

$$v_i \geq 0 \qquad i= 1,\ldots, r \tag{3}$$

Eq. (1) ensures that the efficiency ratios for other banks cannot exceed one.

Eq. (2) and Eq. (3) ensure that weights are positive.

These weights w_j and v_i are then determined, so that each bank maximises its own efficiency ratio.[43] The weights are selected to achieve Pareto optimality[44] for each DMU.

However, this fractional problem has an infinite number of solutions since if (w^*, v^*) is optimal then α $(\alpha w^*, \alpha v^*)$ is also optimal for each positive scalar. Therefore, it will be transformed into a linear program by setting $\sum_{i=1}^{r} v_i x_{io} = 1$, such that:[45]

$$\text{Max } e_0 = \sum_{j=1}^{s} w_j y_{j0} \tag{4}$$

$$\text{subject to } \sum_{i=1}^{r} v_i x_{im} - \sum_{j=1}^{s} w_j y_{jm} \geq 0$$

$$\sum_{i=1}^{r} v_i x_{io} = 1 \tag{5}$$

where $w_j \geq 0$ $j= 1,\ldots,s$ and
$v_i \geq 0$ $i= 1,\ldots,r.$

There are two approaches to estimate the efficient frontier for n observations in the DEA literature. Input-oriented models aim to identify technical inefficiency as a proportional reduction in input usage while output-oriented models identify technical inefficiency as the proportional increase in output production, given a

43 The resulting ratio must lie between zero and unity.

44 In a Pareto efficient economic allocation, no one can be made better off without making at least one individual worse off.

45 Theorem of the CCR Model: The fractional program (FP_0) is equivalent to LP_0 (Cooper et al., 2006: 23–24).

certain amount of input (Fethi & Jackson, 2000).[46] This maximising Linear Programming (LP)[47] model assumes constant returns to scale (CRS), which is the optimal scale in the long-run (Casu & Girardone, 2006). Since it constrains the weighted sum of the inputs to unity as defined by $\sum_{i=1}^{r} v_i x_{io} = 1$ and maximises outputs, it is an input-oriented efficiency measurement, meaning that given the output level, the bank minimises its inputs.

Another possible solution to the linear programming is the dual formulation which gives the same solution:

$$\text{Min } z_0 = \Theta_0$$

$$\text{subject to} \quad \sum_{j=1}^{n} \lambda y : \geq y_{r0}, \qquad r = 1, \ldots, s \tag{6}$$

$$\Theta_0 x_{i0} - \sum_{j=1}^{n} \lambda x \geq 0, \qquad i = 1, \ldots, m \tag{7}$$

$$\lambda_j \geq 0 \qquad j = 1, \ldots, n \tag{8}$$

Both linear problems give the same optimal solution Θ^* which is called the technical efficiency or the CCR efficiency for the particular DMU_0 and the efficiency scores for all of them are derived by repeating them for each DMU_j, $j=1, \ldots n$. The value of Θ_0 is less than or equal to unity. If the $\Theta^* < 1$ then the DMU is relatively inefficient; and if the $\Theta^* = 1$ then the DMU is relatively efficient and has its output-input combination points on the efficient frontier.

5.1.2. *The BCC Model (1984)*

The CCR model assumes CRS which is only appropriate if all DMUs are operating at an optimal scale. However, this is not realistic in real-life examples due to competition, constraints on finance etc. All of this may prevent a DMU from operating at the optimal scale (Ray & Desli, 1997; Coelli, 1996). Since the above dual formulation lacks the constraint for the weights λ, it implies constant returns to scale. Hence, if we add the constraint, $\sum_{j=1}^{n} \lambda j = 1$, the resulting DEA model will exhibit variable returns to scale. This model is called the BCC Model, named after Banker, Charnes and Cooper (1984). The scores obtained with the BCC model are called the pure technical efficiency scores because they are derived from a model that allows variable returns to scale eliminating the scale part of the efficiency from the analysis (Jemric & Vujcic, 2002; Cooper et. al., 2006: 92–93).

---

46 Alternatively, we can also constrain the sum of the weighted output to unity and minimise inputs. This would be an output-based efficiency measurement.

47 A linear programming problem is the problem of maximising or minimising a linear function subject to linear constraints. These constraints can be equalities or inequalities.

5.2. SECOND STAGE ORDINARY LEAST SQUARES REGRESSION[48]

It is a common practice to analyse efficiency in two stages. In the first stage, Data Envelopment Analysis (DEA) is used to calculate the efficiency of banks. In the second stage, regression is used to relate the efficiency scores to factors seen to *influence efficiency*. To this end, the efficiency scores from Step 1 are regressed on bank-specific and country-specific factors using regression analysis (McDonald, 2009).

There are different methods that incorporate the influence of efficiency factors in the DEA analysis,[49] but the two-stage procedure is very practical in terms of its simplicity and the way efficiency is described and interpreted (McDonald, 2009). Several studies examined the efficiency of banks using parametric or non-parametric efficient frontier techniques.[50] Many of these studies (e.g. Lozano-Vivas, et al., 2000; Dietsch & Lozano-Vivas, 2000) considered environmental factors during the estimation of efficiency. Pastor (2002) describes the advantages of this two-stage procedure as such: (i) easy implementation; (ii) possibility of considering many environmental variables simultaneously without increasing the number of efficient units; (iii) there is no need to know the orientation of the influence of each environmental variable; and (iv) the possibility of using of this process when some (or all) of the environmental variables are common to subsets of individuals. This study uses the banking regulatory environment during the estimation of banks' efficiency.

A simple regression model can be used to study the relationship between two variables. Linear regression is a method used to model the relationship between a dependent variable and one (or more) explanatory variables. Data is modelled with a linear function and the unknown parameters are estimated from these data. Hence, these models are called linear models. Ordinary Least Squares (OLS) is a method in econometrics and statistics used for estimating the unknown parameters in a linear regression model. This method minimises the sum of squared residuals which are the vertical distances between the observed data in the dataset and the data predicted by the linear approximation (Wooldridge, 2000: 27–40).

This method of OLS Regression will be used in the second-stage analysis of this chapter where I will investigate the determinants of the Turkish and Russian

---

48 Linear regression is a method used to model the relationship between a dependent variable and one (or more) explanatory variables. Data is modelled with a linear function and the unknown parameters are estimated from this data. Hence these models are called linear models. Ordinary Least Squares (OLS) is a method in econometrics and statistics used for estimating the unknown parameters in a linear regression model.

49 For other methods, see Cooper et al. (2000); Coelli et al. (1999).

50 See section 3.5.

banks' efficiency, conditional on other bank specific factors, market environment and economic conditions. Due to the limited nature of the dependent variable as the scores are bounded between zero and unity, the literature usually applies a censored[51] Tobit regression model.[52] However, contrary to the standard application of Tobit regression in the literature, the second-stage analysis of this study uses OLS regression as it is believed to provide unbiased results (Angrist & Pischke, 2008: 70–80).[53] Besides, one advantage of using OLS is that it increases the significance of results.[54]

6. DESCRIPTION OF DATA AND SELECTION CRITERIA

As discussed in the introduction of this chapter, the banking crises around the world attracted the attention of policy makers on the establishment of an appropriate regulatory and supervisory framework. At the global level, the better known examples are the 1988 Capital Accord (Basel I), Basel II and the new Basel III regulatory standards agreed upon by the members of the Basel Committee on Banking Supervision. Whereas Basel I focused on credit risk, the three pillars of Basel II, introduced in 2004, focused on minimum capital requirements, the disciplinary power of regulatory/supervisory authorities and market discipline (= information disclosure requirements). Following the latest 2007–2009 global crisis, the third of the Basel Accords (Basel III) was developed to strengthen bank capital requirements and to introduce new regulatory requirements on bank liquidity and bank leverage.

Regulations related to capital adequacy requirements, information disclosure requirements and the disciplinary power of authorities are the three main pillars of Basel II and are the central instruments of prudential banking regulation as was explained in detail in Chapter 1.[55] Other than these three standards, this

51 The Tobit model is applied to outcome variables that are continuous over positive values but have a positive probability of equalling zero. A model that has a similar statistical structure to the Tobit model is called the censored regression model. However, unlike the Tobit model, the censored regression model arises due to data censoring. Specifically, the underlying dependent variable is roughly continuous but it is censored below or above a certain value due to the way the data is collected or due to institutional constraints (Wooldridge, 2003: 551).

52 A limited dependent variable is defined as a dependent variable whose range of values is substantively restricted. In the DEA efficiency analysis, the efficiency scores are continuous and restricted between 0 and 100 (Wooldridge, 2000: 529–539).

53 The literature is divided between the use of Tobit regression and OLS regression. For more, see McDonald (2009).

54 Following the literature, Tobit regression was also performed in the second stage. The results were the same in terms of the direction of the coefficients; only the significance values decreased.

55 Section 6.1.

study also comments on two other measures that have an impact on banks' efficiency, namely deposit insurance[56] and entry requirements.[57] These have also been discussed in detail in Chapter 1.

Economic theory provides conflicting results about the effects of this regulatory and supervisory approach to banking (Barth et al., 2002). The traditional approach supports the fact that higher capital requirements would have a positive effect on the banking sector due to its buffer effect and incentive effect[58] whereas the empirical literature provides mixed results about this issue. Concerning the disciplinary power of supervisory authorities and market discipline, there is support for both the official supervision approach and the private monitoring approach to bank supervision. The public interest view supports strong official supervision of banks.[59] This approach claims that the supervisory authorities are capable of avoiding market failures by directly supervising, regulating and disciplining banks (Pasiouras et al., 2007). On the other hand, the private interest approach claims that the supervisory authorities might not have the incentives to fix market failures and instead try to maximise their own utility, which would lead to corruption and hence impede banks' performance (Levine, 2004).

Haselmann and Wachtel (2006) point out that banks behave differently under different institutional settings. This implies that the results obtained for two emerging markets (Turkey and Russia) may not apply to advanced countries. As Barth et al. (2004) and Demirgüç-Kunt et al. (2006) argue, there is no broad cross-country evidence and agreement on which of the different regulatory and supervisory theories used around the world would work best to enhance banks' performance. The empirical findings of this chapter will mainly have relevance for emerging markets. In addition, Pasiouras et al. (2011) argue that the regulatory efforts taken in emerging countries are qualitatively and quantitatively different from the ones of developed banking systems. Whereas developed countries aim to increase competition and enhance efficiency, developing countries' first concerns are stability and risk reduction. With this in mind, the aim of this study is to understand whether the different regulatory practices implemented in Turkey and Russia had any impact on their banking sectors' performance during 1999 and 2010. The results will provide general policy implications as to why regulations might be important for emerging countries.

---

[56] Chapter 1, section 3.1.

[57] Chapter 1, section 6.2.1.

[58] See Chapter 1, section 6.1.1.

[59] See Chapter 1, section 5.1.

6.1. VARIABLE SELECTION: MEASURING INPUTS AND OUTPUTS

Definition of the outputs and inputs produced by the DMUs[60] is critical for efficiency measurement (Yıldırım, 2002). The modelling of a bank's production process is still a controversial issue since there is no agreement in the banking literature regarding the proper definition of inputs and outputs (Lozano-Vivas et al., 2000; Grigorian & Manole, 2002). There are three main approaches in a bank's production process modelling: the production approach, the intermediation approach[61] and the value-added approach.[62]

6.1.1. Production Approach

The "Production Approach", developed by Sealey and Lindley (1977), accepts banks as primarily producing services to depositors and borrowers (Humphrey & Berger, 1997). Banks produce deposits and loans using inputs such as capital, labour and materials. The number of deposit and loan accounts is used to measure output. The production approach is generally used in studies of cost efficiency (Casu & Girardone, 2006). However, this approach fails to capture the role of banks as financial intermediaries. Bauer et al. (1993), Favero and Papi (1995), Swank (1996), Resti (1997), Berger and DeYoung (1997) are some of the most well-known studies that treated banks as firms transforming capital and labour into loans and deposits.

6.1.2. Intermediation Approach

The second approach is called the "Intermediation Approach", which was also originally developed by Sealey and Lindley (1977). In this approach, banks are regarded as intermediating funds between savers and investors (Berger & Humphrey, 1997). The objective of this approach is to examine the bank's ability to take in deposits and lend the money to worthy and profitable borrowers (i.e. banks collect funds, deposits and purchased funds, and intermediate these funds into loans and other assets). The intermediation approach is generally used when the aim is to analyse the total cost of the whole banking sector and the competitive power of banks (Aysan & Ceyhan, 2007). Berger and Humphrey (1997) argue that the intermediation approach may be more appropriate for evaluating entire financial institutions since it concerns the overall costs of

60 DMUs (decision making units) refer to banks in this work.

61 This study uses the intermediation approach.

62 For a detailed comparison of the modelling approaches, see: Berger and Humphrey (1997: 33–35).

banking. Besides, it is preferred when studying the economic viability of banks (Yıldırım, 2002).[63]

6.1.3. *Value-Added Approach*

The third approach in defining bank inputs and outputs is the "Value-Added Approach", developed by Humphrey and Berger (1992). According to this approach, loans and deposits should be regarded as outputs because they produce the largest share of value-added. This approach differs from the intermediation and production approaches in that it considers both liability and asset categories as having some output characteristics. However, only the categories that have substantial value added are treated as outputs. Others are treated as either inputs or intermediate products (Grigorian & Manole, 2002). Pastor et al. (2002) and Kumbhakar et al. (2001) are some of the studies which employed this approach for variable selection.

6.2. DATA AND THE SPECIFICATION OF VARIABLES USED IN DEA

In the banking literature, there is considerable disagreement on the proper specification of bank inputs and outputs (Grigorian & Manole, 2002). As mentioned above, there are three main approaches in banks' production process modelling: the production approach, the intermediation approach and the value-added approach. The intermediation approach[64] to banking behaviour was followed in this study since it is the most commonly used approach in cross-country studies (Pasiouras, 2008). The selection of variables is firstly guided by the objectives of the Turkish and Russian banking systems, where commercial banks dominate the financial system and act as intermediaries between savers and investors by collecting deposits and giving out loans (Caner et al., 2008; Fethi & Jackson, 2000). Investment and development banks are excluded from the sample because of their different structure, their different objective in the sector and also because of the different environment in which they operate.[65]

63 As Isık and Hasan (2003) claim, many studies on banking efficiency adopt this approach. Aly et al. (1990), Allen and Rai (1996), Kaparakis et al. (1994), Berger and Mester (1997), Altunbas et al. (1995), Barr et al. (1994), DeYoung and Hasan (1998), and Zaim (1995) presented empirical applications of the intermediation approach in their studies.

64 In the intermediation approach, banks perform as intermediaries between money holders and fund receivers.

65 Commercial banks deal with various deposit accounts such as savings and time deposits and provide loans to businesses and individuals. However, contrary to commercial banks, development and investment banks do not collect deposits. Instead, investment banks focus on corporate finance, foreign exchange, mergers and initial public offerings while

The sample includes a total of 869 observations corresponding to the period of 1999–2010. Panel data[66] over the period 1999–2010 is used rather than cross-section data at one point in time (e.g. 2009) as it is claimed that efficiency is better studied and modelled with panel data since it is able to account for time variations in efficiency (Pasiouras, 2007; Pasiouras et al., 2009; Baltagi & Griffin, 1988; Cornwell et al., 1990; Coelli et al., 2005). Besides, using panel data provides the opportunity for observing each bank more than once over the period of time under analysis which is especially important in a changing economic and financial environment (Isık & Hasan, 2002). An efficient bank in one period may not achieve the same performance over the following period. There may be also regulatory or environmental factors that affect the performance of banks over time (Pasiouras et al., 2009). Furthermore, Wheelock and Wilson (2000) indicate a direct link between inefficiency and the risk of bank failure.

The sample consists of state, private and foreign banks for which the data come from the yearly published, consolidated balance sheets and income statements. The primary source of data on Russian banks is the Bankscope database produced by the Bureau van Dijk. The Bankscope data are supplemented with data and information from the annual reports of banks and also from the Central Bank of Russia. Banks with any missing values or insufficient report of data were excluded from the sample. The data of Turkish banks in the sample are obtained from the Banks Association of Turkey (BAT). However, the number of Turkish banks in the sample varies between 2000 and 2003 due to the Banking Sector Restructuring Program. The national currency of Russia had to be converted into dollars by means of its official exchange rate presented in Bankscope. The balance sheet data of Turkish banks were already converted into dollars as they are presented in the BAT. The sample for Turkish banks covers all domestic and foreign commercial banks that operate in Turkey.[67] Considering the sample of Russian banks, although there are 969 active commercial banks in Russia, more than half of them are very small banks, called pocket banks. Hence, initially 50 Russian banks were considered in order to have a balanced sample of banks between two countries in terms of the number and the asset size. However, the final selection had to be based on the data available due to the following reasons: (i) some banks in Russia had no data prior to 2005; (ii) some of them had missing or negative values for the required input-output selection.

The choice of input and output variables is influenced by the selected concept of the banking firm, considerations from previous literature as well as by the

development banks provide medium-term finance to the industry and give government funds to the sectors with priority for the government (Etkin et al., 2000).

66 In a panel data set, the behaviour of several entities is observed across several points in time.

67 The sample excludes Adabank for missing values for some years. Arabic Turkish Bank, Bank Mellat and Habib Bank Limited are also excluded from the sample due to their different scope of operations.

availability of reliable information (Pastor et al., 1997). Following Sealey and Lindley (1977), Casu and Molyneux (2003), Pasiouras (2008), Casu, Girardone and Molyneux (2004), Casu and Girardone (2006) and Becalli et al. (2006) a variation of the intermediation approach is adopted where a model with three inputs and three outputs is estimated by using the Data Envelopment Analysis (Computer) Program.[68] Total customer deposits,[69] interest expenses and fixed assets are chosen to serve as inputs.[70] The output variables capture both the traditional lending activities (total loans, interest income) and the non-lending activities (other earning assets) of banks.

6.3. VARIABLES USED FOR THE SECOND STAGE OLS REGRESSION ANALYSIS

The banking sector is the most highly regulated sector in the economy (Walter, 1985). The objective of international comparisons of banks' efficiency is to understand the influence of different regulatory regimes. Dietsch and Lozano-Vivas (2000) found that ignoring country-specific regulatory characteristics can create biased efficiency results in international comparisons. In order to investigate the impact of the regulatory environment on banks' efficiency, the efficiency scores are regressed on the regulatory variables while controlling for other country-specific and bank-specific characteristics that are commonly used in the literature. The rest of this section outlines the set of regulatory and control variables used. Detailed explanations on their calculations and sources of information are provided in Appendix A at the end of this book. Firstly, the range of the proxies for regulations and supervision constructed on the basis of data from Barth et al. (2007)[71, 72] are presented and secondly, the control variables are explained.

---

68 DEAP Version 2.1. This program is developed by Tim Coelli to construct DEA frontiers for the calculation of technical and cost efficiencies (Center for Efficiency and Productivity Analysis – CEPA).

69 Deposits include time, demand and savings deposits.

70 Casu and Molyneux (2003) and Pasiouras (2008) use total costs = interest expenses + non-interest expenses. However, it was not possible to use this formulation in this research due to the fact that the non-interest expense variable was negative in several years for both countries.

71 Studies such as Pasiouras et al. (2007), Focarelli and Pozzolo (2001), Demirgüç-Kunt and Detragiache (2002), Demirgüç-Kunt et al. (2004), Buch and DeLong (2004), Fernandez and Gonzalez (2005), and Beck et al. (2006) that focus on banking regulation and supervision and use World Bank database, have implicitly made the assumption that the regulatory policies within each country remained constant over the time period of the analysis. As Pasiouras et al. (2007) argues, this does not seem unreasonable, since Barth et al. (2004) point out that such regulations change very little over time; and control of these influences in their study did not change their findings.

72 "The Bank Regulation and Supervision Survey" of Barth, Caprio and Levine includes the years 1998–2000, 2001, 2003 and 2007 (2007 survey was updated in 2008). In this work, to account for the missing years of 2009 and 2010 regarding Russian banks, the survey was sent to officials of the national regulatory agency of Russia, and completed by them.

6.3.1. *Regulatory Variables*

The broad range of regulatory variables used in the Ordinary Least Square (OLS) regression is collected from the Bank Supervision section of the World Bank database on Banking Regulation Survey carried out by Barth et al. (1998–2000; 2003; 2007). These variables represent the key aspects of the regulation and supervision framework (Pasiouras et al., 2007). The Banking Regulation and Supervision Survey has been carried out by the World Bank since 1998. It is a unique source of comparable world-wide data on how banks are regulated and supervised around the world.[73] The proxies for regulations and supervision are constructed following Pasiouras' (2008) methodology.[74] Specifically, several bank regulations such as capital adequacy requirements, the disciplinary power of authorities, private monitoring, deposit insurance scheme and entry regulations, all of which could have an impact on bank efficiency, are discussed. These regulatory variables are selected on the basis of data variability in both countries. Different authors use different combinations of these regulatory indexes. Pasiouras (2008) uses the above variables, including the regulatory variable on banks' activities. On the other hand, in one of his earlier studies (2007), he excludes the entry restriction variable. Beltratti and Stulz (2010)[75] choose to use only four regulatory variables which are official disciplinary power, capital requirements, activity restrictions and private monitoring.

This study covers five of the regulatory variables used in Pasiouras (2008).[76] These are the following: (1) capital adequacy requirements, (2) official disciplinary power, (3) private monitoring, (4) deposit insurance and (5) entry requirements. The indexes constructed with the use of answers from the survey questions are usually higher for Turkey than for Russia, which is also true for the regulatory quality indexes based on the World Bank governance database.[77] Since there is not much prior empirical evidence on the relationship of such regulations and efficiency, following Pasiouras (2008) the discussion is related to the studies that analyse risk-taking behaviour, banking sector stability and banks' performance as measured by financial ratios.

---

73 It provides information on bank regulation and supervision for 143 jurisdictions. http://econ.worldbank.org/.

74 See Appendix A.

75 As mentioned in Beltratti and Stulz (2010), it should be noted that these regulatory variables do not account for the stance of regulators. They argue that a country's regulations can give a lot of flexibility to banks, but regulators might prevent banks from using that flexibility. However, this discussion will be analysed in detail in the next chapter of this book.

76 The regulatory index on the restrictions on banks' activities is excluded since the survey answers obtained from the national regulatory agencies and the Word Bank data gave conflicting results.

77 The questions related to each of the regulatory variables are in Appendix A.

(1) CAPTRREQ is an index of capital requirements. It accounts for whether the source of funds counted as regulatory capital can include *assets other than cash or government securities and borrowed funds as well as whether the sources are verified by the regulatory or supervisory authorities.* It also stands for whether the risk elements and value losses are considered while calculating the regulatory capital. The first pillar of Basel II and Basel III promotes the adoption of strict capital adequacy standards.[78]

The capital adequacy requirement (CAR) is one of the central instruments of prudential regulation as explained before in Chapter 1 of this book.[79] It serves two functions: (1) buffer effect where bank capital helps in preventing bank failures when the bank cannot meet its obligations to its depositors and other creditors, and (2) incentive effect where the capital should give banks incentives for reducing risky activities which otherwise would end up burdening creditors or the taxpayer. In order to account for the risk profile of banks' assets in determining the required level of capital, banks have been made subject to risk-based capital requirements (Freixas & Rochet, 1999; Hellwig, 2010).

In Turkey, according to the Banks' Act No. 4389, the minimum capital adequacy requirement ratio was determined as 8% in 1999 in compliance with the Basel Accords. This Act was replaced by the Banking Law No. 5411 in 2005. Following this replacement, the banking regulatory authority in Turkey required banks to hold a target ratio of 12% determined as a precondition to open a new branch. This ratio exceeds the capital adequacy ratios of many other emerging markets even in the global financial crisis years. Russia implemented a banking reform in 2001 and introduced a new Banking Law. Following this reform, capital adequacy requirements were also brought in line with the Basel Accords. However, as the analysis will discuss in detail in Chapter 3, these requirements have been implemented in Turkey more strictly than in Russia. In fact, the Turkish banking sector utilises capital buffer as a precautionary measure against financial crises. The importance of maintaining strong capital structure was emphasised in all policies carried out during its post-crisis period (Atıcı & Gürsoy, 2011). Hence, I expect a positive impact of capital requirements on banks' efficiency.

The effect of this regulation on banks' risk-taking behaviour is a controversial issue in the literature. Some studies argue that capital regulation contributes to bank stability whereas others find that they make banks' balance sheets riskier than they would be in the absence of such requirements due to regulatory arbitrage. The empirical literature has mixed results on the effects of stricter capital regulations on banks' behaviour. Bolt and Tieman (2004) show in their theoretical framework that stricter capital adequacy requirements lead banks to set stricter acceptance criteria for providing new loans. Pasiouras (2008) finds

---

78 For the calculation of this index, see Appendix A.

79 Section 6.1.1.

that technical efficiency is positively related to stricter capital adequacy standards. A more recent study by Barth et al. (2010) found that greater capital regulation stringency is positively associated with banks' efficiency. Other recent studies conducted by Detragiache et al. (2010) and Beltratti and Stulz (2010) following the financial crisis of 2007–2009 found also that countries with better capitalised banks performed better during the crisis of 2007–2009. One comprehensive study by Barth et al. (2004) in a survey of 107 countries finds that capital requirements contribute to a decrease in the amount of non-performing loans.

On the other hand, some studies such as Calem and Robb (1999), Santomero and Koehn (1980), Blum (1999), and Kim and Santomero (1988) find that capital requirements increase the risk-taking behaviour of banks. This finding is supported by some other studies such as Fernandez and Gonzalez (2005), Kendall (1992), and Beatty and Gron (2001) only under specific circumstances.

(2) OFFDISCIPLINE stands for the *ability of supervisors to have the authority to take specific actions to prevent and correct problems* (Barth et al., 2001b). Disciplinary power is addressed in terms of the prompt corrective action, declaration of insolvency and restructuring power of regulatory authorities.[80] The second pillar of Basel II and Basel III focuses on enhancing the official supervisory practices of banks. As discussed in Barth et al. (2005) and Levine et al. (2005), in addition to the Basel Committee on Banking Supervision, the International Monetary Fund and the World Bank also emphasise the importance of strengthening official supervision of banks. Beck et al. (2006) and Levine (2003) discuss that a powerful supervisor could contribute to a bank's performance in terms of improving the corporate governance of banks, reducing the corruption in lending and enhancing the functioning of banks as financial intermediaries. Barth et al. (2004) stress the advantages of the disciplinary power of regulatory authorities in terms of preventing banks from engaging in excessive risk-taking activities and in terms of improving bank performance and stability. However, they also argue that granting too much power to supervisors may create incentives for corruption and have negative effects on bank performance. Followed by that, in one of their studies, Barth et al. find (2003) a negative relationship between supervisory indicators and bank performance. On the other hand, Fernandez and Gonzalez (2005) find that the greater disciplinary capacity of supervisors is useful in reducing risk-taking behaviour of banks. Pasiouras (2008, 2009) finds also that technical efficiency is positively influenced by more powerful supervisory agencies. A recent study by Barth et al. (2010) finds that stronger official supervision is positively associated with banks' efficiency, though only in countries with independent supervisory authorities.

80 These will be explained in detail in Chapter 3.

In Turkey, with the enactment of the Banks Act in 1999, an independent regulatory authority, the Banking Regulation and Supervision Agency (BRSA), was established. A new Banking Law, which abolished and replaced the previous Banks Act, became effective in 2005. This Banking Law strengthened the effectiveness of the BRSA. In Russia, the Central Bank of Russia (CBR) is the primary authority responsible for the regulation of the banking sector in Russia and also acts as Russia's central bank. However, as the analysis of this chapter as well as Chapter 3[81] will illustrate in detail later, the degree of disciplinary power in Russia is lower than that in Turkey. In Russia, the authority to enforce regulations is basically missing. Based on these differences regarding the extent of authority in enforcing regulations, I expect that this variable would have a positive impact on banks' efficiency.

(3) PRVTMONITOR stands for private monitoring index, which *indicates the degree of information released to officials and the public, the existence of auditing related requirements and whether credit ratings are required.* In addition to capital adequacy requirements and the disciplinary power of regulatory authorities, bank behaviour is also affected by private market forces (Barth et al., 2006a: 137). The private monitoring index takes values between 0 and 10, and higher values indicate higher degrees of private monitoring. Demirgüç-Kunt et al. (2008) and Levine et al. (2005) find that regulations that promote private monitoring contribute to bank development which is in line with the private monitoring approach. On the other hand, Barth et al. (2004) find no evidence that regulations which promote private monitoring decrease the possibility of the emergence of a banking crisis. Duarte et al. (2008) argue that increased disclosure requirements would have a negative impact on the efficiency of banks in terms of increasing the costs of making additional disclosures, not to mention the additional time and effort required to prepare the disclosure reports. This is supported by Pasiouras et al. (2007), who find that higher requirements related to private monitoring reduce cost efficiency.[82]

The questions of the World Bank survey regarding "Private Monitoring"[83] refer mainly to information disclosure requirements and bank examination which were explained in Chapter 1[84] as tools of prudential regulation. The objective of disclosure requirements is to mitigate the asymmetric information problem in the banking industry since depositors will not have the incentive to privately monitor the bank about the quality of its assets. Bank examination is also one of the regulations that aim to limit the moral hazard incentives of bank

---

81 Section 3.2.

82 Berger and Humphrey (1991) find that technical inefficiencies contain the vast majority of cost inefficiency in banks.

83 See Appendix A for the questions related to the "Private Monitoring" index.

84 Section 6.1.2.

managers for excessive risk-taking. Other than establishing regulations, enforcement of these regulations is also very important. Hence, bank examination is important to determine whether banks are complying with these regulations. It also adds to the quality of the financial information disclosed to the public by bank owners and managers and to the strengthening of the enforcement of existing regulations (Tchana, 2010).

Turkey had a weak risk-management culture towards the end of the 1990s. This became evident in the 2001 crisis when significant internal audit and risk management weaknesses emerged. The first steps were taken with the Restructuring Process after the crisis under the name of "Operational Restructuring of Public Banks". Several regulations were introduced regarding information disclosure requirements. With the introduction of the new Banking Law in 2005, the BRSA started to change its rule-based regulation and supervision in the direction of a more risk-based approach (Kaymak, 2009). Market discipline started to gain importance in providing financial stability in order to fully comply with the EU Directives.

In Russia, the CBR has the authority to establish rules and procedures for banks regarding information disclosure requirements. Following the Banking Sector Development Strategy introduced in 2002, the CBR started to work on bringing the existing procedures for disclosing information in line with the international standards. Although several important steps have been taken in Russia, risk management is still limited in Russia compared to Turkey (as will be discussed in the next chapter). My hypothesis regarding private monitoring effects on banks' efficiency is that it would have a positive effect on banks' efficiency.

(4) DEPOSITINSUR is a dummy variable[85] and indicates *whether the country has an explicit deposit insurance scheme or not.* According to Pasiouras (2008), the impact of other regulations should be examined by also considering the existence of deposit insurance schemes. Barth et al. (2006a) and Demirgüç-Kunt and Huizinga (1999) find that whereas deposit insurance contributes to depositors' safety, it reduces market discipline by the bank creditors. Furthermore, Barth et al. (2004) and Demirgüç-Kunt and Detragiache (2002) investigate the relationship between deposit insurance and banking stability and find that deposit insurance is detrimental to bank stability. In their earlier study conducted in 1999, they also found that deposit insurance increases banking system fragility in countries with weak institutions. Laeven (2002), Bhattacharya and Thakor (1993) and Hendrickson and Nichols (2001) also support the view

85 In econometrics, a dummy variable is a variable that takes the value of 0 or 1. Dummy variables are used to incorporate qualitative information into a regression analysis. In my analysis, it takes the value of 1 if the country has a deposit insurance scheme and takes the value of 0 if it does not have a deposit insurance scheme.

that deposit insurance creates moral hazard for banks and encourages risk-taking behaviour.

Deposit insurance is an insurance mechanism designed by the government to pay depositors in the event of default (Gorton & Metrick, 2009). On one hand, deposit insurance contributes to bank stability by preventing self-fulfilling depositor runs since depositors would have little incentive to withdraw their funds if they know that their deposits are insured by the government (Diamond & Dybvig, 1983). On the other hand, deposit insurance might have a negative effect on bank stability by encouraging risk-taking on the part of banks. In the existence of such an insurance mechanism, banks would have the incentive to engage in riskier activities for higher returns since they know that any possible failure will be bailed out by the government (Detragiache & Demirgüç-Kunt, 2002). Therefore, the implementation of the deposit insurance mechanism points to the moral hazard of banks.

In Turkey, the Savings Deposit Insurance Fund (SDIF) was established in 1983. In Russia, the Law on Deposit Insurance was introduced at the end of 2003. However, only by the end of 2005, the CBR had completely finalised all the evaluation procedures and hence March 2005 acceptances are referred to as "first round decisions" (Chernykh & Edmister, 2010; IMF, 2005). Due to the possibility of moral hazard of deposit insurance schemes, it is expected that this policy would have a negative impact on banks' efficiency.

(5) ENTRY stands for entry requirements. It shows *the number of requirements for a banking licence.*[86] The interaction of competition and financial stability is an important aspect in the banking sector and any competition policy should take this into account. Competition may be good for efficiency but it may have a negative impact on banks' stability (Allen & Gale, 2004). The competition-fragility view in the literature argues that competition encourages excessive risk-taking, which would lead to less stability (Allen & Gale, 2004). Hellmann, Murdoch, and Stiglitz (1999), and Gorton (2010a) argue that excessive competition caused by an overbanked[87] system would create instability. Furthermore, Caprio and Summers (1996) and Keeley (1990) argue that since entry barriers would increase the franchise value of banks, bank managers would behave more prudently to maintain the successful state of their banks and prevent any insolvency. On the other hand, since bankers may be tempted to opt for an entry restriction to limit competition, regulators may choose to help them for rent extraction (Schleifer, La-Porta et al., 2000). Demirgüç-Kunt, Levine and Min (1998) and Wang and Bayraktar (2006) support the view that the entry restrictions do have negative effects on competition in banking. This is supported

86 See Appendix A.

87 System with a high number of banks.

by Besanko and Thakor (1992), and Cordella and Yeyati (2002) where the relaxation of entry barriers is perceived as improving competition and hence contributing to efficiency and cost reduction.

Entry restrictions are one of the tools of structural regulations.[88] Literature provides different results on the impact of entry restrictions on banks. Keeley (1990) argues that banks with monopolistic power have greater franchise value, which would give them an incentive for prudent behaviour. On the other hand, by emphasising the positive effects of competition, Shleifer and Vishny (1998) do not support entry restrictions. Demirgüç-Kunt, Levine and Min (1998) and Wang and Bayraktar (2006) support the view that the regulatory restrictions indeed have negative effects on competition in banking. As the next chapter will discuss, the competition in both Russian and Turkish banking sectors is low. Hence, this regulation might be expected to have a negative impact on banks' efficiency due to its distorting effects on competition.

6.3.2. *Control Variables*

Control variables include four bank-specific and three country-specific factors which are selected on the basis of data availability and previous studies. The bank-specific variables are as follows: (1) EQAS is the equity to assets ratio which controls capital strength, (2) LOANTA corresponds to a bank's net loans to total assets ratio and is a measure for loan activity, (3) ROE is the pre-tax profit divided by equity, and (4) EXPTA is the non-interest expenses to assets ratio. Pasiouras (2006; 2008), Allen and Rai (1996), Isık and Hassan (2003) and Fries and Taci (2005) have used these variables to represent the relationship between bank-specific characteristics and efficiency.

Concerning country-specific characteristics, the annual growth in Gross Domestic Product (indicated as GDP) is used to control for the macroeconomic conditions within each country following Hauner (2005), Pasiouras (2008), Grigorian and Manole (2002), Pastor and Serrano (2005), and Pasiouras (2008). Yıldırım and Philippatos (2006) find a positive link between GDP growth and efficiency,[89] whereas Pasiouras (2008) illustrates that GDP growth can be negatively associated with banks' efficiency.

OFGOVBANKS indicates the fraction of the banking system's assets held by banks which are 50% or more owned by the government. Barth et al. (2002; 2005) argue that since government ownership may distort the application of different supervisory approaches, it is important to control for the degree of

---

88 See Chapter 2, section 6.2.1.

89 As argued by Grigorian and Manole (2002) and by Gadanecz and Jayaram (2008), controlling for crisis would not be easy due to the mere definition of it. Hence, following them, it is assumed that the regression will still account for the events of the crisis since relevant information is likely to be contained in the GDP growth rate.

state-owned banks. Hence, it is important to account for the degree of government ownership of banks while examining regulations and supervisory practices. Barth (2002, 2004), Fries and Taci (2005), Carvallo and Kasman (2005), Dietsch and Lozano-Vivas (2000) are some of the studies that controlled for cross-country differences in the national market structure when focusing on banks' performance.

Finally, according to La Porta et al. (1998), Pasiouras (2008), Levine (1998), Grigorian and Manole (2002), and Beltratti and Stulz (2010), it is also important to control for the institutional differences in order to understand the effects of different legal environments on the financial system. This work includes the institutional differences in the GOVNINTERV variable that stands for the government intervention in the economy.

The data for country-specific variables are collected from the Global Market Information Database (GMID) of Euromonitor International and the Heritage Foundation. The market structure data concerning the share of government-owned banks is obtained from the yearly banking supervision reports of both countries' national banking regulatory agencies and the EBRD Index of Banking Sector Reforms. Finally, the data for macroeconomic variables (GDP growth rate) are obtained from World Bank data and the Treasury of Turkey.

7. EMPIRICAL FINDINGS

7.1. FIRST-STAGE ANALYSIS: DEA RESULTS

In this section, an input-oriented DEA model is applied to a panel data[90] of 869 observations. In constructing the sample of banks for each country, both local and foreign commercial banks were considered.[91] The DEA efficiency computations are obtained by processing the Data Envelopment Analysis software[92] created by Coelli (1996). The focus on commercial banks permits an analysis of a more homogenous sample in terms of service, and hence inputs and outputs, improving the comparability among countries. Since the regulatory data of Barth et al. (2008) database are for commercial banks, this analysis only covers commercial banks following Pasiouras (2008) and Levine et al. (2004).

---

90 In a panel data set, the behaviour of several entities is observed across several points in time.

91 Applying the Wilcoxon-Mann-Whitney rank-sum test which is explained in Appendix B led to the conclusion that a common frontier approach can be used for both types of banks with the assumption that they use the same production technology. See Appendix B.

92 This program is developed by Tim Coelli to construct DEA frontiers for the calculation of technical and cost efficiencies.

Table 12 presents the distribution of sample banks by both countries for 1999–2010. The Russian banking sector had experienced a financial crisis in 1998, where many of the banks failed.[93] The sample starts with 1999 – the aftermath of the 1998 crisis in Russia – so that the effects of this crisis can also be shown in the analysis. Besides, there was no access to the balance sheets of failed banks in Russia during the 1998 crisis. This is also true for the aftermath of the banking crisis in 2004. However, as can be seen from the table, the number of banks changes remarkably during the analysis period in Turkey. In 1999, just one year before the twin crises of 2000/2001, there were 48 commercial banks in the sample of Turkish banks. During these two crises a lot of banks failed and some of them ceased their operations while others were taken over by the Savings Deposit and Insurance Fund (SDIF).

Table 12. Number of sample banks by countries 1999–2010

	1999	2000	2001	2002	2003	2004	2005	2006	2007	2008	2009	2010	Total
Turkey	48	48	35	33	31	30	29	28	28	27	27	27	**391**
Russia	40	41	41	41	41	41	39	39	39	39	39	38	**478**
Total	**88**	**89**	**76**	**74**	**72**	**71**	**68**	**67**	**67**	**66**	**66**	**65**	**869**

Table 13 introduces the DEA results under different scale assumptions (under CRS and VRS). The results are reported firstly for the Turkish banks indicated as Panel A, and secondly for the Russian banks in Panel B of Table 13. It shows the mean of technical efficiency scores (both under CRS and VRS)[94] and Scale Efficiency (SE) for each year. Technical efficiency under VRS is the focus of this study since it is the most frequently adopted assumption in recent studies (Pasiouras, 2008). Moreover, the employment of VRS can provide more realistic results in terms of real-life examples and in the presence of competition (Resti, 1997; Ray & Desli, 1997).[95]

---

93 The period of analysis covers the years between 1999 and 2010 (inclusive). Russia had experienced a financial crisis in 1998, 2004 and during 2008–2009. Turkey had a twin crisis in November 2000 and February 2001.

94 In constant returns to scale (CRS), an increase in inputs results in a proportional change in the outputs. In variable returns to scale (VRS), an increase in inputs does not result in a proportional change in the outputs.

95 Input-oriented DEA with Variable Returns to Scale (VRS) developed by Banker et al. (1984) allows for the possibility that the production technology of banks in the sample may exhibit increasing, decreasing or constant returns to scale (Girardone et al., 2012).

Panel A of Table 13 shows the mean technical efficiency results of Turkish banks. Following the 2000/2001 crises, there is a decrease in the efficiency scores of Turkish banks between 2000 and 2001, as expected. The reforms of the post-2001 Stabilisation Programme involved stronger capital structures, changes in the banking law, and better risk management and supervision. After the introduction of the Banking Restructuring Program in 2001, except between 2003 and 2004, there is a slight increase in the efficiency scores of banks until 2005. Following the introduction of the new Banking Law in 2005, there is a remarkable increase in the efficiency scores of Turkish banks that continues until 2010. The mean efficiency of 0.759 in 2007 is followed by 0.869 in 2008, 0.889 in 2009 and finally 0.878 in 2010.

Panel B of Table 13 presents the mean technical efficiency results of Russian banks. After the 1998 financial crisis, the Bank of Russia took steps towards restructuring the banking system. Looking at the efficiency results, it is observed that the Russian banks' performance increased between 1999 and 2005, with only a slight decrease between 2001 and 2002. Following the banking crisis experienced in Russia during 2004,[96] the Russian Government and the Bank of Russia adopted the Banking Sector Development Strategy in April 2005 for the 2005–2008 period. This reform aimed at the development of the banking sector and the enhancement of the banking sector's stability and efficiency in the medium term of 2005–2008. However, looking at the results, it is evident that the efficiency of Russian banks decreased after 2005. The mean efficiency of 0.821 in 2005 is followed by 0.802 in 2006, 0.763 in 2007, 0.688 in 2008, 0.640 in 2009 and 0.598 in 2010.

These results show that during the time period of 1999–2005, both countries exhibited predictable results following their banking restructuring programs. The legal analysis in Chapter 3 will explain in detail that the Turkish banking sector's restructuring efforts and regulatory reforms following the 2001 crisis were implemented very efficiently and strictly. None of the banks were affected during the 2007–2009 global crisis. Hence, although this analysis does not show causality, the increasing performance level of Turkish banks is not surprising. On the other hand, Chapter 3 will also argue in detail that the banking reform and restructuring process in Russia were not implemented as efficiently as in Turkey. Many Russian banks failed during the global crisis. Therefore, the decreasing trend in the efficiency levels of Russian banks is also not surprising. It can be claimed that the Turkish banks performed relatively better than the Russian banks after 2005, including the 2007–2009 global crisis, where the Turkish banks' efficiency increased as opposed to the efficiency of Russian banks, which decreased.

---

96 Steinherr and Klär (2005) argue that the main cause of the 2004 Russian banking crisis must be seen in the banking sector regulation.

7.2. SECOND-STAGE ANALYSIS: OLS RESULTS

In the second-stage analysis of this study, the determinants of efficiency are estimated by applying an econometric model using the VRS-technical efficiency score as the dependent variable. Due to the limited number of observations, following Hauner (2005), the technical efficiency scores of both countries for 12 years are merged in both estimations.

Two regressions were run (i) to see the impact of control variables on efficiency (specifically the country effect of TURKEY), and (ii) for the sake of robustness check. In the first specification presented in Table 14, when the regression was run without the regulatory variables, it was observed that the efficiency scores are positively and significantly related to the variable TURKEY. The positive coefficient on the dummy variable TURKEY indicates the fact that a bank being in Turkey has a positive and statistically significant impact on that bank's efficiency. In the second table, we see the negative coefficient on the dummy variable RUSSIA which indicates that a bank being in Russia has a negative and statistically significant impact on that bank's efficiency.

Table 13. DEA findings calculated on the basis of a common frontier

***Panel A*: Annual average DEA efficiency estimates of Turkish banks**

Years	CRSTE	VRSTE	SE
1999	0.325	0.606	0.559
2000	0.505	0.644	0.794
2001	0.498	0.629	0.816
2002	0.526	0.681	0.767
2003	0.662	0.741	0.878
2004	0.624	0.691	0.921
2005	0.526	0.691	0.794
2006	0.368	0.710	0.555
2007	0.719	0.759	0.951
2008	0.821	0.869	0.945
2009	0.818	0.889	0.922
2010	0.785	0.878	0.895
Average mean	**0.598**	**0.732**	**0.816**

***Panel B*: Annual average DEA efficiency estimates of Russian banks**

Years	CRSTE	VRSTE	SE
1999	0.594	0.653	0.905
2000	0.551	0.729	0.745
2001	0.716	0.804	0.892
2002	0.739	0.787	0.944
2003	0.735	0.805	0.925
2004	0.785	0.815	0.966
2005	0.810	0.821	0.988
2006	0.780	0.802	0.976
2007	0.713	0.763	0.936
2008	0.594	0.688	0.879
2009	0.561	0.640	0.895
2010	0.505	0.598	0.885
Average mean	**0.674**	**0.742**	**0.911**

Notes:
CRSTE: Technical Efficiency from Constant Returns to Scale
VRSTE: Technical Efficiency from Variable Returns to Scale
SE: Scale Efficiency = CRSTE/VRSTE

Figure 6. Graphical representation of DEA scores

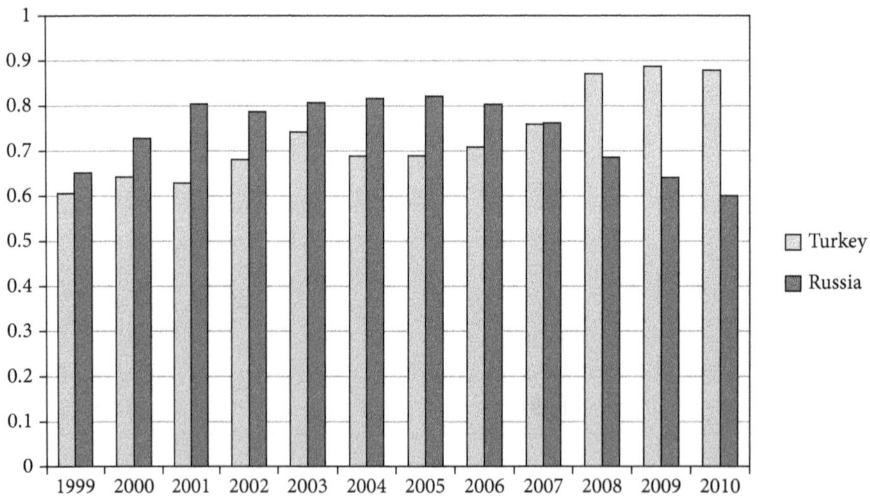

Table 14. Impact of control variables on technical efficiency

Variables	Coefficient	Robust Std. Error	t	P >|t|
ROE	0.0000186	0.0000507	0.37	0.715
EQAS	0.0029697	0.0008469	3.51	0.001*
LOANTA	0.0079086	0.0007313	10.81	0.000*
EXPTA	0.0009445	0.0015449	0.61	0.543
GDP	0.0024515	0.0015853	1.55	0.126
OFGOVBANKS	-0.0017184	0.0008687	-1.98	0.051**
GOVNTINTERV	-0.0024108	0.0124208	-0.19	0.847
TURKEY	**0.1889056**	**0.219252**	**8.62**	**0.000***
_cons	0.3523187	0.077009	4.58	0.000*

Variables	Coefficient	Robust Std. Error	t	P >|t|
ROE	0.0000186	0.0000507	0.37	0.715
EQAS	0.0029697	0.0008469	3.51	0.001*
LOANTA	0.0079086	0.0007313	10.81	0.000*
EXPTA	0.0009445	0.0015449	0.61	0.543
GDP	0.0024515	0.0015853	1.55	0.126
OFGOVBANKS	-0.0017184	0.0008687	-1.98	0.051**
GOVNTINTERV	-0.0024108	0.0124208	-0.19	0.847
RUSSIA	**-0.1889056**	**0.0219252**	**-8.62**	**0.000***
_cons	0.5412243	0.0768454	7.04	0.000*

Notes:
ROE: Return on Equity
EQAS: Equity/Assets
LOANTA: Net Loans/Total Assets
EXPTA: Non-interest Expenses/Total Assets
GDP: Annual growth in Gross Domestic Product
OFGOVBANKS: Presence of government-owned banks
GOVNINTERV: Government intervention in the economy
*Statistically significant at the 1% level

Since it is suspected that the regulations might be the cause of the difference between the two countries, a second regression was run. In order to test the impact of regulatory variables on the banks' efficiency, the dummy variable was excluded and the regression was run adding the regulatory variables of interest *(CAPTREQ, OFFDSCPLINE, PRVTMONITOR, DEPOSITINSUR, ENTRY)* by controlling for bank-specific (*ROE, EQAS, LOANTA, EXPTA)* and country-specific *(GDP, OFGOVBANKS, GOVNINTERV*) variables.

Regulations and constitutions in a country change very little over time (Barth et al., 2004). The impact of any change in the regulations may not be realised immediately by the bank's performance. In fact, Isık and Hasan (2003) indicate that a relatively long period is needed for developments in the regulatory environment to exert their influence upon banking technology. Following that, a 12-year time period is chosen since one cannot analyse the results independently of the past period. Increasing the size of the observation set provides more robust results. Furthermore, Barth et al. (2004), Fernandez and Gonzalez (2005), Pasiouras et al. (2007) and Pasiouras (2008) argue that since many regulations can be substitutes or complements, countries will probably not select these policies in isolation. Following this argument, all the regulatory policy variables are included in the regression. However, the degree of the included control variables is restricted since to include too many regressors would increase the potential for multi-collinearity.[97] Furthermore, each bank in the sample starts with a different baseline, so banks are clustered to account for the dependence. Table 15 presents the results.

Table 15. OLS regression results

Variables	Coefficient	Robust Std. Error	t	P >|t|
CAPTREQ	0.2329109	0.056166	4.15	0.000*
OFFDISCIPLINE	0.0578942	0.0114127	5.07	0.000*
PRVTMONITOR	−0.1770744	0.0394925	−4.48	0.000*
DEPOSITINSUR	−0.4754652	0.1092347	−4.35	0.000*
ENTRY	−0.1978618	0.0383493	−5.16	0.000*
ROE	−2.63E-06	0.0000468	−0.06	0.955
EQAS	0.0027487	0.000934	2.94	0.004*
LOANTA	0.0099268	0.0007869	12.61	0.000*
EXPTA	−0.0011137	0.0015121	−0.74	0.463
GDP	0.0009409	0.001244	0.76	0.451
OFGOVBANKS	−0.0020203	0.0011628	−1.74	0.086
GOVNTINTERV	0.0085346	0.0140041	0.61	0.544
cons_	1.065441	0.2014387	5.29	0.000*

Notes: The regression includes bank-fixed effects.
*** Statistically significant at the 10% level
** Statistically significant at the 5% level
* Statistically significant at the 1% level
CAPTREQ: Capital Requirements
PRVTMONITOR: Private Monitoring
OFFDISCPLINE: Official Disciplinary Power

97 High correlation between two or more of the independent variables is called multicollinearity (Wooldridge, 2003).

DEPOSITINSUR: Deposit Insurance
ENTRY: Entry Requirements
ROE: Return on Equity
EQAS: Equity/Assets
LOANTA: Net Loans/Total Assets
EXPTA: Non-interest expenses/Total Assets
GDP: Annual growth in Gross Domestic Product
OFGOVBANKS: Presence of government-owned banks
GOVNINTERV: Government intervention in the economy
REGQUALITY: Regulatory Quality

The results provide evidence *in favour of the regulations related to stricter capital adequacy standards (CAPTREQ) and official disciplinary power (OFFDSCPLINE).* Both variables are statistically significant. Higher capital stringency increases banks' efficiency, which provides support to the first pillar of Basel II and to its prospective enhancement through Basel III. Higher official disciplinary power (Pillar 2 of Basel II) is also positively associated with higher efficiency, providing evidence for the official supervision approach as well. Although not directly related to the performance of banks, the stabilising effect of capital regulations and supervisory power is supported by Pasiouras et al. (2011), who find that capital requirements and especially official disciplinary power provide a direct and effective mechanism in reducing both credit and solvency risks for banks. Their findings recommend improving the auditing of banks and imposing sanctions where appropriate. These findings support the theory of the official supervision approach, suggesting that powerful supervision can improve the corporate governance of banks and their functioning.

Regulations that enhance private monitoring – the variable *PRVTMONITOR* – (Pillar 3 of Basel II) are *negatively associated with banks' efficiency.* This is in line with Duarte et al. (2008) and Pasiouras et al. (2007), who argue that increased disclosure requirements such as obtaining credit ratings from external agencies, disclosure of off-balance sheet items to supervisors and to the public, disclosure of risk management procedures to the public as well as auditing by certified auditors might have a negative impact on banks' efficiency due to increased costs. Besides, Pasiouras et al. (2006) find a negative relationship between disclosure requirements and credit ratings. Another study by Barth et al. (2004) finds no evidence that regulations enhancing private monitoring would reduce the possibility of the occurrence of major banking crises. Girardone et al. (2012) find that private monitoring is associated with greater banking system inefficiency.

Regulations related to *deposit insurance (DEPOSITINSUR) and entry requirements (ENTRY) also have a negative impact on the efficiency of banks.* Demirgüç-Kunt and Detragiache (2002) show that safety nets such as deposit insurance and Lender of Last Resort (LLR) provided by the central banks are likely to increase the risk of bank instability.[98] Barth et al. (2006a) emphasise that subjecting bank liabilities to the risk of loss should be one of the key items of a prudential regulatory framework that aims to enhance market discipline and reduce risk-taking. Regarding the entry restrictions, Barth et al. (2004) found that the percentage of entry applications denied is greater for low-income countries than for high-income countries; and that developing countries place more limitations on foreign bank ownership of domestic banks and foreign bank entry through branching than developed countries.

From the control variables related to bank-specific characteristics, the variable EQAS measuring the capital strength, is statistically significant and positively associated with efficiency. LOANTA, a measure of loan activity, is also positively associated with efficiency, but it is statistically significant. Finally, expenses relative to assets (*EXPTA*) and profitability (*ROE*) do not have an impact on banks' technical efficiency which is in line with Pasiouras' (2008) findings. Controlling for macro-economic conditions, it is found that the GDP growth rate (*GDP*) has a positive impact on efficiency; however it is statistically insignificant.

The negative coefficient on *OFGOVBANKS* indicates that a lower number of government-owned banks would result in an increase in efficiency. This result is statistically significant and it is also in line with Barth et al. (2001a) and Pasiouras (2008) who find that greater government ownership is generally associated with less efficient financial systems. De Nicolo (2000) shows that banks in countries with a higher level of state ownership exhibit a higher insolvency risk. This is also supported by Caprio and Martinez (2000), whose results show that government ownership of banks is positively related with bank fragility. La Porta, Lopez-de-Silanes and Shleifer (2002) found also that countries with higher levels of government ownership of banks tend to have a lower level of financial development and slower economic growth rates.

The proxy used for the government intervention in the economy (GOVNINTERV) is meant to control for the differences in the overall institutional environment between Turkey and Russia. However, its impact is statistically insignificant.

8. CONCLUSION

This study applied a two-stage analysis in which the DEA empirical findings obtained in the first-stage analysis are regressed by OLS in the second stage in *order to examine the impact of regulation and supervision on banks' efficiency.*

[98] Unlimited access to deposit insurance and Lender of Last Resort functions of the central banks would induce banks to risk-taking behaviours, because the losses would be ultimately borne by the taxpayers (Pacces, 2010).

The variables describing the approach to regulation and supervision are as follows: capital adequacy, disciplinary power of the authorities, private monitoring, deposit insurance schemes, and entry regulations. The sample includes 88 commercial banks in total operating in Russia and Turkey over the 1999–2010 period. The results of DEA indicate that Turkish banks' performances in general show an increasing trend, firstly with the implementation of the Banking Restructuring Program in 2001 and then with the introduction of a new Banking Law in 2005, which is based on stricter regulations and supervision system. On the contrary, Russian banks' efficiency starts to decrease gradually from 2005 until 2010. Although Russia implemented a Banking Restructuring Program for the period 2005–2008, banks' performances deteriorated. This analysis is followed by the regression analysis to investigate the impact of regulations related to capital adequacy, private monitoring, disciplinary power of the authorities, entry into banking and deposit insurance on banks' technical efficiency while controlling for country-specific macro-economic factors, market structure, and overall institutional development.

The empirical analysis provides support for stricter capital adequacy standards and for the development of powerful supervisory agencies, but not for a private monitoring approach, deposit insurance schemes and entry regulations. This would imply that banking regulatory authorities in emerging markets should focus on maintaining high levels of capital adequacy requirements and developing powerful supervisory agencies for the sake of enforcement of regulations. With respect to the bank-specific characteristics, it was found that capital strength and higher loan activity result in higher technical efficiency. Expenses relative to assets and profitability do not have an impact on banks' technical efficiency. Finally, it was found that among the country-specific variables such as GDP, the presence of government-owned banks and the degree of government intervention in the economy, only the presence of government-owned banks has a significant impact on banks' efficiency, though in a negative way.

Looking at the regulatory indexes used in the regression analysis, it is observed that as most of the regulatory and supervisory indexes get a higher value in Turkey, Turkish banks' performance increases gradually, even during the 2007–2009 crisis. *This suggests that stricter regulations had a positive impact on Turkish banks across the years. On the other hand, most of the regulatory indexes in Russia get a lower value after 2005, which is accompanied by the decreasing efficiency scores of Russian banks after 2005.* These decreasing efficiency scores of Russian banks are even confirmed by the 2008–2009 banking crisis experienced in Russia where many banks were either wiped out or bailed out by the Central Bank of Russia whereas Turkish banks did not experience any other crisis after 2001.

Pasiouras et al. (2011) argue that new regulatory initiatives are not able to affect the risk-taking behaviour of banks immediately. If regulations have an impact on risk-taking of banks, then one should expect that there are lags between establishing new banking laws and taking new policy initiatives (which are reflected in the corresponding indices) and the time that these laws and initiatives are translated into more sound banking practices (Pasiouras et al., 2011). Hence, they suggest that the regulatory practices of the previous periods are expected to have an impact on the contemporaneous level of banks' risk-taking behaviour. The data here suggest that the important reforms implemented after the 2001 crisis in Turkey followed by the introduction of a stricter Banking Law in 2005 had a positive impact on the performance of Turkish banks in the earlier period. Following the argument by Pasiouras et al. (2011), mentioned above, although the empirical results of this chapter are based on earlier years, the solidity of this regulatory/supervisory framework might well have contributed to the good performance of Turkish banks during the 2007–2009 crisis. These results also suggest that regulation has a significant role in diminishing the effects of a financial crisis in emerging markets.

CHAPTER 3
BANKING REGULATION AND SUPERVISION IN TURKEY AND RUSSIA

1. INTRODUCTION

Banking crises in emerging markets during the 1990s were associated with major macroeconomic disruptions where the specific nature of banking and financial systems has played a crucial role (Özkan, 2003). As was explained in the first chapter of this book,[1] the existence of systemic risk and market failures constitutes the basis of the need for financial regulation. These problems tend to be more acute in emerging economies mainly due to institutional factors in terms of the indicators of the rule of law, enforcement, protection of property rights, supervision and accounting standards, all of which are poorly exercised in these countries. Furthermore, banks are the main drivers of economic development and their potential fragility may even exacerbate downturns (Vives, 2006). This was experienced in Turkey in the 2000/2001 crisis and in Russia in 1998, 2004 and 2008–2009.

The banking crises of both Turkey and Russia were followed by major restructuring and recovery of their banking industries.[2] The restructuring of the Turkish banking sector following the 2000/2001 crisis started immediately after the crisis whereas in Russia there was no serious banking restructuring programme for more than four years following the 1998 crisis. In fact, major reforms in banking were implemented in 2003–2005 (Barisitz, 2009). In the aftermath of the 1998 financial crisis, Russia's banking system has grown stronger and larger. However, despite important steps taken, the assessments of the progress made in banking supervision, in improving the legal and regulatory framework and in their enforcement suggest that the weaknesses in prudential supervision and regulation remained; and Russian banks continued to play a limited role in intermediating savings and investments (OECD, 2009; Thiessen,

1 Chapter 1, section 4.

2 The first Russian crisis mentioned in this work refers to the 1998 crisis. Russia experienced a crisis in 2004 and again in 2008–2009. Turkey had twin crises in November 2000 and February 2001.

2005). In fact, in 2004, Russian banks' stability proved weak again and the banking sector experienced a so called *mini-crisis* (Karas et al., 2008).[3] More importantly, the Russian banking sector succumbed to the global crisis in the second half of 2008 (Fungacova & Jakubik, 2012).

On the other hand, Turkish banks have been more resilient in terms of their ability to absorb shocks and maintain liquidity compared to Russian banks during the global crisis. The resilience of the financial markets in Turkey seems to be mainly attributable to the reforms and consolidation of the banking sector after the 2001 financial crisis (BRSA, 2010; Bredenkamp et al., 2009).

The aim of this chapter is to show that Turkey has implemented a stricter and more comprehensive banking reform than Russia in their respective post-crisis periods, that is, the post-2001 period for Turkey and the post-1998 period for Russia. Banking reforms implemented in Turkey involved stronger capital structures, stricter enforcement of the banking law (through supervision as well as numerous and detailed regulations intended to support the implementation of the law), more disciplinary power granted to the regulatory authority, and a better risk management policy compared to the reforms implemented in Russia.

Section 2 of this chapter describes the banking environment in both countries in their pre-crisis periods. Similarities in the problems of the banking sectors will be highlighted. Section 3 discusses the weaknesses and the strengths of the banking regulations which were implemented in both Turkey and Russia in their post-crisis period, taking also into account the impact of these regulations on banks' performances. The emphasis will be placed on the capital adequacy regulations and the official disciplinary power of the banking regulatory/supervisory bodies, since these variables seem to account for most of the differences in both countries, according to the qualitative analysis of this chapter. As found by the empirical analysis of the previous chapter,[4] these variables have a positive and significant effect on banks' efficiency. The qualitative analysis in this chapter suggests that the Turkish banking sector has a higher stringency in capital adequacy regulations and in the official disciplinary power of the regulatory authority compared to the Russian banking sector.

---

3 In 2004, the Russian banking sector experienced instability resulting in a crisis of confidence towards Russian banks by their customers. In May 2004, the Central Bank of Russia suspended the banking licence of a medium-sized bank that had been accused of breaches of the Russian anti-money laundering laws. This intervention of the CBR created uncertainty in the market and triggered panic, putting various banks under stress. Many banks stopped extending interbank loans. These developments provoked a widespread loss of confidence within the banking system. A deposit insurance system was not yet established. Hence, being concerned about their deposits, depositors began to withdraw their money from their banks. A number of banks had to sell securities and loans to meet their liquidity needs. However, the lack of trust among banks caused the drying up of liquidity in the interbank market. The volume of interbank lending on the domestic market contracted by 12.2% in May 2004 and 13.3% in June 2004 (CBR, 2004; Steinherr, 2006).

4 Chapter 2, section 6.2.

In addition to capital adequacy requirements and the disciplinary power of the regulatory authorities, bank behaviour is also affected by private market forces. Therefore, it is important to understand the extent of private monitoring that exists in a country (Barth et al., 2006a: 137). The empirical analysis in Chapter 2 showed that private monitoring[5] had a negative effect on efficiency. According to the qualitative analysis of this chapter, the Turkish banking sector has a higher stringency in private monitoring than the Russian banking sector. Regarding disclosure requirements, the public has more access to information about the overall condition of the banking industry. Besides, the risk management system in Turkish banks is implemented in a more disciplined way than it is implemented in Russian banks. However, increased disclosure requirements might have a negative impact on banks' efficiency due to increased costs (Duarte et al., 2008; Pasiouras et al., 2007).

The impact of regulations and supervisory practices on banks' performance may also depend on whether a country implements a deposit insurance scheme or not (Barth et al., 2006a: 133). It was found in Chapter 2 that deposit insurance has a negative impact on banks' efficiency. This system has been implemented in Turkey since 1983. In Russia, it was first introduced in December 2003. The qualitative analysis of this chapter suggests that the amount and duration of this insurance provided to banks is important in the sense that it might create a moral hazard for banks.

Entry requirements refer to the ability of banks to enter the banking industry in both Turkey and Russia. According to the qualitative analysis of this chapter, the number of barriers required as part of the licensing process is similar for both Turkish banks and Russian banks. Imposing basic requirements before a banking licence is accepted or rejected can enhance the overall performance of the banking sector, because in that way only the higher quality banks are allowed to enter the banking sector (Barth et al., 2006a: 111). In fact, considering both countries' banking histories, which are characterised by pervasive connected-lending and corruptive practices and abuses of banks' resources by their governments, imposing entry restrictions to better assure the quality of entrants gains a particular importance. On the other hand, the negative impact of this regulation on efficiency found in Chapter 2 suggests that its distorting effect on competition prevails.

Finally, the banking environment of both countries in terms of the share of government-owned banks will be discussed in section 4. This variable is found to have a negative impact on efficiency in Chapter 2. The qualitative analysis in

5 As was explained in Chapter 2, private monitoring mainly refers to the disclosure requirements such as obtaining credit ratings from external agencies, disclosure of off-balance sheet items to supervisors and to the public, disclosure of risk management procedures to the public as well as auditing by certified auditors.

this chapter will show that the ratio of government-owned banks in Turkey is lower than in Russia.

The suggestive results obtained by the empirical work of Chapter 2 combined with the qualitative analysis of this chapter can contribute to reforms that could be implemented in the long run to improve the efficiency and the resilience of both countries' banking sectors. After having understood the problems in the regulations in terms of their positive and negative impacts on banks' performances in both countries, policymakers can focus on these problems to improve the banking performances in these two emerging countries.

2. AN OVERVIEW OF THE FINANCIAL CRISES IN TURKEY AND RUSSIA

Both in Turkey and Russia, the economy relies primarily on the banking sector to promote its development and hence is highly vulnerable to the problems in the banking sector (Mahlberg et al., 2011; Caner et al., 2007). Both countries' banking sectors were exposed to connected and politicised lending for a long time. Politicised lending is rent-seeking political intervention in the allocation of bank credit (Bakır & Öniş, 2010). Private actors such as banking lobbies and politicians in both countries had a tendency to use private banks for government financing and to abuse the public banks, in order to maintain their electoral support through inefficient credit allocations instead of productive investments. These players even had a tendency to resist regulations that might have conflicted with their interests.[6]

The restructuring process and the regulatory/supervisory framework established after the 2001 crisis ended this practice in the Turkish banking sector. The legal component of the bank restructuring and reform process focused on the strengthening of prudential regulations, with special emphasis on connected-lending practices.[7] On the other hand, this is still a problem in

---

6 In Russia, in the period up to the 1998 crisis during the 1990s, the banking lobby opposed any steps to introduce stricter regulations based on the model of Western standards, if this meant lower earnings (Steinherr & Klär, 2005).

7 Following the 2001 crisis, the introduction of new regulations regarding connected lending practices replaced the narrow definition of the concept of a "risk group" which before the crisis led to much abuse of connected lending. The amount of a bank's exposure with each risk group was reduced from 75% of the bank's net worth to 25% in line with the EU standards. These limits are monitored regularly by the BRSA and the relevant information is included in the audited financial statements which are disclosed to the public (Steinherr et al., 2004). According to the Banking Law which came into force in 2005, violation of this regulation is punishable with imprisonment and compensation for the losses incurred by the bank (Banking Law (2005) – Article 160). Thanks to the regular supervision and control of

Russia where weak enforcement of regulations and delay of the restructuring process contributed to the existence of regulatory forbearance.[8] The aim of bank supervision and regulation is to give banks incentives to take fewer risks. However a policy of regulatory forbearance creates moral hazards for banks. Following the 1998 crisis, the Central Bank of Russia allowed for a high degree of forbearance towards large banks in financial difficulties.[9] As a result, only a few licences were cancelled creating a moral hazard problem (Ippolito, 2002). Tompson (2004) says: "*The CBR's long record of regulatory forbearance before and after the 1998 crisis led many banks to believe that they could violate prudential norms and default on obligations with impunity*" (Tompson, 2004).

This section will provide an overview of the reasons for the crises based on the weaknesses of both countries' banking sectors. The analysis shows that both countries' pre-crisis environment was suffering from the same problems such as macro-economic instability in terms of high and volatile inflation, fluctuations in growth rate and capital movements, high public-sector debt, exposure to foreign exchange rate risks and liquidity risks, a high proportion of state-owned banks in the system and their distorting effects, politicised lending to government-owned banks, poor capital adequacy, and weak accounting and auditing standards. More importantly, both countries suffered from a lack of a proper legal and institutional framework underpinning the prudential banking regulation and supervision. This created a very fragile banking system in both countries. The pre-crisis environments and the restructuring processes that the banking sectors of both countries underwent after their crisis periods are critical for an understanding of the context in which they both started their banking reform, and for an evaluation of the level of successes of these reforms.

---

the BRSA, connected lending became a less significant issue in the Turkish banking system (Bascı, 2006).

8 IMF Survey Online, (2010) Magazine: Interview with Poul Thomsen, 2 August 2010. Thiessen (2005) argues that the regulatory forbearance during and after the 1998 crisis was clearly further damaging the financial system. Causes of the crisis and its effects are explained in detail in Thiessen (2004) as well. It also provides evidence of the inadequate banking supervision in the aftermath of the crisis.

9 According to Instruction No. 1 of the CBR "On the Procedure for Regulating the Activities of Credit Organisations", Russian banks are not permitted to have an exposure to any single borrower or a group of related borrowers in excess of 25% of their capital (Article 64 of the Russian Federation Federal Law – On the Central Bank of the Russian Federation (Bank of Russia). However, poor monitoring of the CBR contributed to the incentives for connected lending which is still a problem in banking (IMF, 2010; 2013). The definition of connected borrowers and related parties in the legislation is still narrow and does not cover situations when influence and connection can be exerted by economic means. Besides, current limitations on the legislative framework also limit the CBR's powers to issue regulations or to impose supervisory restrictions to related parties' transaction. In addition, the CBR lacks the authority to sanction directors individually. The CBR's existing powers regarding related borrowers are not in the form of supporting laws or regulations (IMF, 2011a).

2.1. FINANCIAL CRISIS IN TURKEY (2000/2001)

In November 2000, the Turkish economy was hit by a severe liquidity crisis. The situation was normalised by an IMF-led emergency package for a while. However, the Turkish currency came under heavy attack in February 2001 and this turned into the most serious financial and economic crisis Turkey has experienced in its post-war history (Özkan, 2003).[10] While the economy was suffering from several macroeconomic problems including a weak external and fiscal position which were at the root of the crisis, the fragility of the banking sector increased the magnitude of the crisis (Penas & Tümer-Alkan, 2008; Akyürek, 2006). In fact, it is argued that the main cause of the 2000–2001 Turkish crises was the fragility of the banking sector, mainly as a result of the mechanism chosen to finance high public-sector deficits and hence heavy reliance on bank intermediation of government debt (Akyürek, 2006; Özatay & Sak, 2002). The poorly functioning and under-regulated banking system in Turkey contributed to the macroeconomic instability and the fragility of the financial system which characterised much of the 1990s in Turkey (Özkan, 2003).

2.1.1. Problems in the Economy and Financial Sector

The macroeconomic problems which have contributed to the 2001 crisis are long-standing conditions dating back to the 1990s (Özkan, 2003). The first source of vulnerability was the weak fiscal position due to high levels of public debt caused by record levels of interest payments on domestic borrowing. This caused a huge burden on public finances. Furthermore, fiscal imbalances were financed through inflation. This way of deficit financing increased the internal debt burden, leading to unsustainable public debt ratios. The second vulnerability was the weak external position of the balance of payments[11] due to excessive levels of debt repayment, which was aggravated by the unpredictable trend of the exchange rate (Özkan, 2003). A third source of vulnerability was the growth performance, which was showing a very unstable trend. It was mainly dependent on global capital inflows, which were constantly slowing down. In fact, the GDP growth in 1990–2000 oscillated between 9.3% and -5.5%. High domestic interest rates caused an increase in short-term capital inflows and hence, foreign direct investment (FDI) remained limited. The fact that these

---

10 Turkey also experienced financial crises in the 1980s and in 1994. However, they are not discussed here since the empirical analysis covers the period from 1999 onwards.

11 The balance of payments is a statistical statement that summarises the economic transactions of an economy with the rest of the world. Transactions (mostly between residents and non-residents) consist of those involving goods, services, and income; those involving financial claims on, and liabilities to, the rest of the world; and those classified as transfers (IMF, Balance of Payments Textbook, 1996).

capital inflows were not permanent affected the economic environment and the financial markets negatively. As a result, in 2000 monetary expansion became heavily dependent on capital inflows. However, political ambiguities taking place caused deterioration in investor confidence; and net capital entry started to decrease steadily (BRSA, 2010).

These structural problems caused inflation to follow a high and volatile trend distorting expectations and reducing the maturity for the funds within the economy. This situation, accompanied by the pressure on interest rates and exchange rates caused by the deterioration in public sector debt and the balance of payments, created an environment which was not appropriate for the proper functioning of banking activities (BRSA, 2010).

The weak banking sector basically prepared the ground for the liquidity squeeze[12] in November 2000 and aggravated the already distorted macro-economic environment (Altunbas et al., 2009: 26). Enforcement was very weak due to widespread regulatory forbearance and overly lenient prudential regulations. The high degree of politicisation of bank lending and heavy rent-seeking in the allocation of bank credit caused corruption in the banking sector. Towards the end of the 1990s, financial intermediation was not functioning properly. The banking sector was financing the government rather than the real sector. The government was incurring excessive public debt and misusing the public sector banks. Private banks were exposed to high levels of exchange rate and interest rate risk. Bank loans were not being allocated through market-based supply and demand mechanisms for credit and finance, but by political intervention. The result of this politicised bank lending was the inefficient allocation of bank credit for productive investments and the crowding out of the private sector (Bakir & Öniş, 2010; Bredenkamp et al., 2009; BRSA, 2010).

2.1.2. Build-Up of the 2000/2001 Crisis

The insufficiency of the scope and effectiveness of regulations in banking and the weak risk management applications made the banking system very sensitive to liquidity, interest and exchange rate risks. Lack of transparency caused by the deficiencies in the implementation of financial reporting and international accounting standards distorted the banking structure and reduced confidence in the sector. In the second half of November 2000, interest rates increased significantly, large capital flows went abroad, central bank reserves decreased rapidly, and a sharp decrease was observed in stock prices. Several banks became exposed to a liquidity shortage, resulting in their transfers to the Savings and Deposits Insurance Fund (SDIF) and/or termination of their operating licences. In order to prevent this first crisis of November 2000 from deepening, a series of measures were taken immediately in December 2000 with a relative recovery in

12 Liquidity crisis is explained in Chapter 1, section 2.2.

markets. However, at the end of December 2000 the average interest rates were four times higher than the levels at the beginning of November 2000. This unsustainable situation ended when the Prime Minister announced in 19 February 2001 that there was a severe political crisis which led to an equally serious economic crisis in highly sensitive markets. On that day, interest rates jumped to unprecedented levels and followed by these negative developments, a speculative attack started against the Turkish lira. Three days later the exchange rate system collapsed triggering a second financial crisis in February 2001 (BRSA, 2010; Özatay & Sak, 2003).

2.1.3. *The Impact of the 2007–2009 Global Crisis*

The Turkish economy was affected by the global crisis due to its interconnected relation with the world economy and hence, through international trade channels. Since Turkey is an open economy, the 2007–2009 global crisis transmitted itself to the Turkish economy in the sharp decline of world trade of goods and services.[13] Its economy was negatively affected by the deceleration of global economic growth and slowing international capital flows (Canakcı, 2009). The GDP growth rate of the Turkish economy dropped sharply from 8.5% in 2007 to –7.8% in 2009 (which had returned back to 4% in 2010). This was accompanied by a decline in external and domestic demand. External financing became limited. The unemployment rate and the current account deficit increased (Aras, 2010).

Regarding the effects of the global crisis on the banking sector, Turkish banks have been more resilient in terms of the ability of banks to absorb shocks and maintain liquidity compared to other emerging markets (including the Russian banks) during the global crisis. The asset quality of Turkish banks remained stable. Banks continued to provide their financial intermediation functions effectively. The average capital adequacy ratio (CAR) of the banking sector rose during the crisis, fluctuating around 20% – well above the target level of 12% and the legally required level of 8% (Yorukoglu & Atasoy, 2010). Although the stable growth environment created a rapid credit growth, excessive risk-taking of banks was prevented due to legal regulations.[14] Hence, the ratios of non-performing loans were rather low even in the period of the crisis (Aras, 2010). More importantly, there were no bank failures in Turkey. Unlike most of the other emerging markets, the Turkish banking system has not required any rescue packages from the government, nor any capital support or any other forms of government support. No banks have been transferred to the Savings Deposit Insurance Fund. There were no changes in the ownership of banks, no liquidation and thus no fall in the number of banks. There was also

[13] Foreign trade comprises more than 50% of GDP (Aras, 2010).
[14] Regulations will be explained in detail in section 3.

no fall in the profitability of banks. In fact, the profitability of Turkish banks increased in 2008 and 2009. Moreover, Turkey is one of the few countries whose credit rating has improved during the crisis (Uygur, 2010; Yorukoglu & Atasoy, 2010).

2.2. FINANCIAL CRISES IN RUSSIA (1998, 2004, 2008–2009)

2.2.1. Problems in the Economy and Financial Sector

Russia has a bank-based financial system. Banking in Russia is very young because most of the banks were established only in the 1990s. Until 1988, since Russia had a socialist economy, the banking sector was a mono-bank system which consisted of a state bank operating as both a central bank and a commercial bank. With the creation of a two-tier banking system in 1988, the banking sector consisted of the Central Bank of Russia (CBR) and five banks[15] that were designed to finance specific state programmes. When the government introduced "the 1988 Law on Cooperatives", banks were allowed to be formed with private capital. This was followed by the creation of the so-called "pocket" banks,[16] acting as agents for related companies. In 1992, the number of licensed banks in Russia was more than 1300. Lax entry conditions and close relations of former state bank officials with the CBR helped the bankers to accelerate their registrations. Besides, high inflation made it easy to satisfy the minimum capital requirements to establish a bank (Steinherr, 2006). In fact, the number of commercial banks registered by the CBR was 2552 in 1997 (CBR, 1997).

The CBR was responsible for supervising, regulating and licensing banks which exposed it to conflicts of interest: the regulatory agency (CBR) was in a close relationship with the commercial banks,[17] providing privileges to some of them. Although many of the Soviet era banks transformed themselves into private commercial banks, the largest banks were still state-owned through the CBR ownership. Besides, the CBR was the majority owner of the country's biggest bank, Sberbank. Due to its ownership status, Sberbank was able to enjoy

15 Agroprombank, Promstroibank, Sberbank, Vnesheconombank and Zhilsotsbank.

16 Pocket banks are best understood as tools of business groupings or state institutions rather than independent, profit-oriented businesses. Many larger Russian banks are closely affiliated with large financial industrial groupings and are oriented to serving the needs of those group members (OECD, 2004). Pocket-banks are also described as undercapitalised banks (Fidrmuc & Süss, 2009). Many banks in Russia were not operating as normal credit institutions. Instead of providing financial intermediation services to the public, they were rather privately used to allocate capital within industrial conglomerates and large corporations. These services were provided at a reduced cost and lower cost of capital (Ippolito, 2002).

17 This situation changed in July 2002. The law passed in 2002 limited the extent of bank ownership by the CBR. In 2003, it had only the right to control Sberbank and four banks abroad (Steinherr, 2006).

the privilege of a state guarantee of its deposits. Its privileged situation in attracting deposits at more favourable rates than its competitors had a distorting effect on the level playing field in the sector. More importantly, its dominance in the deposit market crowded out the private banks from the market. Due to these developments, banks were intended to extract rents from the state rather than to invest in improving financial intermediation between savers and investors (Steinherr, 2006).[18]

Most of the firms which were outside these industrial groups owning the banks did not have access to credit at all or they had to pay very high interest rates to get credit. These high rates exacerbated the adverse selection problem due to the asymmetric information in the market. The bankers had no incentives to move towards more transparent and clearer regulation. In fact, they strongly resisted the introduction of higher capital requirements. This situation was amplified by the high-inflationary environment where banks paid negative real deposit rates and made loans at very large spreads. In sum, the increasing size of private banks in this unregulated world, the governments' unusual relationship with banks, connected lending mechanisms between banks and the firms owning these banks provided an arena for rent extraction (Steinherr, 2006).

2.2.2. Build-Up of the 1998 Crisis

Russia had experienced a financial meltdown in 1998 caused by the capital movements all around the world following the Asian crisis in 1997.[19] The banking sector suffered from a liquidity shortage. Steinherr and Klär (2005), and Ippolito (2002) argue that the main cause of the banking crisis must be seen in the banking sector regulation, which was weak or, even absent in the sense that it encouraged banks to take big exchange rate risks on liabilities in foreign currencies, and also to lend with little risk diversification. Banks were allowed to borrow in foreign currency without matching foreign currency assets. Additionally, they were also free to open non-hedged positions in forward contracts in the foreign-exchange (FX) market, which was very risky. Hence, due to weak regulation and supervision, banks were able to provide risky loans that became non-performing in the 1998 crisis. Besides, the borrowing ability of banks from the capital markets was constrained since the domestic capital

18 Another problem concerning the playing field emerged when the government started to issue treasury bills (GKOs) to finance its deficit. The banking industry lobbied to exclude foreign investors from the market so that CBR sold these treasury bills only to a selected group of banks. During 1995 and 1996, banks earned a lot from their special relationships with government funds. As a result of this connected lending procedure, financial intermediation was disturbed (Steinherr, 2006).

19 The world financial and currency markets were hit by a wave of crises in the summer of 1997 that started in East Asia. It caused a big financial collapse with a crash in Asian foreign exchange and equity markets (Özkan, 2003).

market was under-developed.[20] Followed by that, Russian banks needed to borrow from external capital markets in foreign currency which exposed them to additional foreign currency risk (Steinherr, 2006).

During the four years preceding the crisis, Russia received foreign capital inflows taking advantage of the worldwide boom in capital flows into emerging markets. Besides, foreign investors were allowed to buy short-term treasury bills with high yields. These positive developments led to a rise in Russian stock markets, which however collapsed after the 1997 Asian crisis. After the collapse of the stock markets, foreign investors purchased futures on the USD/rouble exchange rate to hedge their portfolios against a depreciation of the rouble against the USD. However, their Russian counterparts had short positions on the same contracts and hence were subject to rouble devaluation. This prudent behaviour of investors increased concerns over Russia's reserve position and the sustainability of its exchange rate commitment. When investors started to reallocate their assets from risky countries to safer ones, the Russian government faced difficulties in rolling over its debt and defending its exchange rate. In August 1998, the government defaulted on its domestic public debt, declared a moratorium on private banks' liabilities, abandoned its exchange rate, and froze treasury bill operations. This meant a complete default by the government and by the banking system with a dramatic liquidity crisis and massive bank runs (Steinherr, 2006; Tompson, 2004; Perotti, 2001).

This crisis revealed the underlying structural flaws of the banking sector (Steinherr, 2006; Ippolito, 2002). First of all, there was a currency imbalance since foreign denominated currency assets were less than the foreign currency liabilities. Secondly, there was also maturity imbalance because banks borrowed foreign currency short-term to be rolled over and lent longer term. They financed their holdings via short-term foreign loans. A number of banks suffered from this maturity imbalance. The excessive risk taking behaviour of banks was exacerbated by inadequate risk and liquidity management at commercial banks, poor monitoring by the CBR and too much confidence in the CBR's ability to keep the rouble fixed (Steinherr, 2006).

2.2.3. *Build-Up of the 2004 Crisis*

The 1998 crisis revealed the vulnerability of the Russian banking sector. Regarding regulatory flaws, Perotti (2001) argues that the foundations of the Russian financial system with soft legal constraints were long undermined by perverse incentives before the 1998 crisis. When the banking system was newly developing in 1989, capital requirements for banking licence were very low. In the early 1990s, due to lax entry conditions, the number of banks increased from around 10 to 2,500. Legal rules were subject to arbitrary changes and were

---

[20] Banks can borrow from the government but this cannot be a regular funding source.

determined on a private bargaining process where rules were less important than the power of the parties involved. Similar to other economic and political activities such as privatisation or creation of a public debt market, the supervision of banks was implemented as part of a compromise with a powerful banking lobby. In that way, bankers were able to extract major opportunities and rents from the state without being exposed to any compulsory rules of conduct. Government was unable and more importantly, unwilling to control this process since it needed the support of special interest groups (such as the bankers' lobby) to remain in power (Perotti, 2001).

However, in the three years following the crisis, not much progress was made to restructure the banking system. Essential steps to strengthen the banking regulation were not taken (Steinherr, 2006). First of all, banks were still exposed to a significant amount of credit risk due to the rapid growth in credit caused mainly by the still-existent widespread practice of connected lending and insufficient transparency of borrowers. Banks were still lending money to borrowers that had economic links between them. Moreover, these connections were not easy to identify due to the continuing lack of transparency of borrowers. The Central Bank of Russia regarded the 1998 crisis as only a liquidity crisis and acted as a lender of last resort instead of following a clearly defined and transparent strategy. Secondly, there was a growing gap between the amount of loans provided to customers and deposits received from them. This maturity mismatch between banks' assets and liabilities exposed banks to further liquidity risk (ECB, 2005). Thirdly, Russian banks were still allowed to use accounting standards that did not represent the asset quality of their balance sheets correctly. Fourthly, the huge number of banks was an obstacle for efficient banking supervision (Komulainen et al., 2003).

At the beginning of 2003, Russia was still lacking a banking reform (Komulainen et al., 2003). Many flaws that affected the Russian banks before the 1998 crisis were still present in 2004. The government and the CBR had been unsuccessful in implementing a comprehensive banking restructuring programme and in establishing a banking reform, neglecting major flaws that affected the Russian banking sector before the 1998 crisis (Steinherr & Klär (2005); Ippolito, 2002). Compared to mid-1998, the weight of large credit risks in banks' portfolios has risen from 25.5% to 33% in mid-2003 given the emergence of a larger number of big borrowers. These portfolios were rated as very concentrated according to the OECD standards. Interestingly at the same time, thanks to the new legislation adapted in 2003 that simplified the procedures for lending to small firms, consumer credit had exploded between 2002 and 2004 (see Table 16). Besides, since Russian banks were dependent on a small number of clients to get funding, the liability side of the balance sheets was also highly concentrated. This implies that many banks could lose their liquidity overnight by the withdrawal of a single large depositor. This was the case in the 2004 crisis (Tompson, 2004).[21]

Table 16. Banking sector credit risks 2002–2003

	1.01.02	1.01.03	1.07.03
Volume of large credit risks in the banking sector (billion rouble)	982.3	1,329	1,607
Large credit risks as a share of total bank asset in %	31.1	32.1	33

Source: Tompson (2004). Tompson (2004) defines large credit risk as the exposure to a single borrower (or group of related borrowers) in excess of 5% of the capital.

The enduring vulnerability of the banking system became evident in the May–July 2004 crisis (Tompson, 2004). Like the 1998 crisis, the 2004 crisis also resulted in the collapse of the interbank market due to deteriorated liquidity situations (Vernikov, 2007). In fact, in April–July 2004 the Russian banking sector experienced its first serious turmoil since the financial crisis of August 1998. In early July, the liquidity crisis spread leading to a run on several banks (Steinherr, 2006; Tompson, 2004). The CBR revoked the banking licences of certain banks. Several small private banks failed while others experienced liquidity problems because they were unable to get funding from the interbank market or from their depositors. Several privately-owned Russian banks significantly limited their operations, collapsed or ceased to exist (CBR, 2004).

2.2.4. Build-Up of the 2008–2009 Crisis

Russia has been affected by the global crisis more strongly than the majority of emerging markets (Fidrmuc & Dreger, 2009).[22] Just as in the 1998 and 2004 crises, Russia's financial crisis in 2009 was due to liquidity shortage. Many Russian banks failed during the global crisis. The economy experienced a sharp fall in output in 2009. As a result, non-performing loans increased significantly (Jakobik & Fungacova, 2012).

Russian banks were not directly exposed to the financial instruments that triggered the crisis in the US and the EU. However, they were firstly affected through their dependence on foreign funding which reduced during the crisis due to the liquidity crisis experienced by the banking sectors in the EU and the US. Secondly, the global economic slowdown decreased the demand for commodities and this led to a decline in oil prices (Fidrmuc & Süss, 2009).

21 This crisis is described as a mini-crisis in most of the academic works since it was not considered as a systemic banking crisis.

22 In fact, Qu et al. (2012) argue that Russia is the most affected country among the BRIC countries.

Following the Lehman Brothers bankruptcy in September 2008, the confidence of international investors in the Russian market weakened. Like elsewhere, this resulted in a "flight to quality" of international investors.[23] There was a sharp decline in oil prices caused by the global economic slowdown, which decreased the demand for commodities. As more and more investors started to sell their assets, the Russian stock market became exposed to massive losses.[24] Increased counterparty risk and loss of confidence between banks caused a liquidity shortage in the interbank market (Fidrmuc & Süss, 2009).

Adrian and Shin (2008), Brunnermeier (2009), Gorton (2010a), and Diamond and Rajan (2009), and Beltratti and Stulz (2009) found in their analysis of crises that banks financed with short-term wholesale capital experienced a run on funding by investors and hence performed worse during the crisis. Fidrmuc and Süss (2009) argue that this trend resembles the high short-term repayment obligations of Russian banks where by mid-2008 Russia's external debt had increased to $527 billion. Banks actively participated in the stock markets, and they borrowed money on their own stocks as collateral. Hence, the decline in stock prices was directly connected to bad loans. When the crisis hit the banking sector directly, the low ratio of owner's equity and the long term loans using short-term borrowing triggered the crisis (Mizobata, 2009). The debt of the banking sector was 37% of overall debt (Bogetic, 2008; Fidrmuc & Süss, 2009). Small and medium-sized banks were dependent on short-term foreign borrowing as a funding source because deposit-based funding was weakened due to the dominant position of state banks.[25] This exposed those banks to sudden reversals in capital flows since their refinancing conditions for their foreign loans worsened (Fidrmuch & Süss, 2009). This foreign funding constraint caused a sharp slowdown in credit (Deutsche Bank Report, 2008).

The crisis occurred in two stages. In the first stage, banks started to face serious liquidity shortages and significant deposit withdrawals in the second half of 2008. The second stage occurred in 2009 in the form of rising credit risk, which is the key risk for banks as explained in the second chapter of this book (IMF, 2011b). Jorda et al. (2010) and Hume and Sentence (2009) found that credit growth is one of the pre-crisis dynamics followed by a slowdown in the post-crisis period. The role of credit in the Russian economy increased significantly during the 2000s. Bank lending to the private sector grew from 11.93% of GDP

23 The term "flight to quality" describes an environment where investors try to sell assets which they perceive as risky and purchase safe assets instead. This increases the risk premium and causes severe disruptions in the credit market and other financial markets. The US experienced a severe episode of this kind during the 2007–2009 global crises (Caballero & Kurlat, 2008).

24 In the fourth quarter of 2008, net capital outflows were $130.5 billion, of which $56.2 billion was from the banking sector and $74.3 billion was from the non-banking sector (Fidrmuc & Süss, 2009).

25 Beltratti and Stulz (2009) found also that banks that relied more on deposits for their financing performed better during the crisis.

in 1999 to around 42% at the end of 2008, and deposits rose from 15% to 30%. Between 2001 and 2008, credit grew by 50% per year. This increase in credit risk started to build up during the boom period just before the crisis when the lending standards were lowered. In fact, the credit expansion rates exceeded 40% before the crisis. It stopped in the second half of 2008, and then it collapsed to –2.5% during the crisis in 2009. As a result, credit to the private sector started to contract. This contraction in domestic lending shows a breakdown in bank intermediation. As the financial situation of borrowers deteriorated, they became unable to serve their obligations. The banking system was put under pressure from increasing overdue loans. Followed by that, growth in overdue debt increased significantly compared to 2007, by 129.2%. The share of the overdue debt of total loans extended in 2008 expanded from 1.3% to 2.1. In fact, due to weaknesses in supervision, regulators were unable to detect serious problems existing in important banks such as the Bank of Moscow (Fungacova & Jakubik, 2012).

The Russian government and the CBR responded by implementing measures to maintain the stability of the financial system. They provided liquidity to banks, a temporary decrease in reserve requirements, and guarantees for interbank lending to qualified banks. The limit of deposit insurance was increased and the deposit insurance agency assumed responsibility for restructuring individual troubled banks. State banks were recapitalised by the government in the form of capital support (IMF, 2011c).

2.3. POST-CRISIS PERIOD IN TURKEY AND RUSSIA

In the period after the crises in the late 1990s, the banking sectors in most emerging markets including Russia and Turkey underwent significant restructuring processes (Caner et al., 2007). Dziobek and Pazarbasıoglu (1997) explain that prompt corrective action (within about ten months after the crisis starts) is a key element of a successful reform and restructuring. In fact, they mention that countries making substantial progress all took action within a year of the emergence of their banking problems. These include identifying the reasons and extent of banking sector problems, identifying problem banks, starting the restructuring process and improving of accounting, regulatory and legal framework to restore the conditions of a sound banking system (Dziobek & Pazarbasıoglu, 1997).

Regarding Turkey and Russia, the banking industry in both countries experienced a reform process starting in 2001. However, interestingly there was no serious restructuring programme in Russia for more than four years following the 1998 crisis. Important steps started to be taken in Russia only towards 2002 revealing the slow response of Russian authorities to the crisis (Thiessen, 2004; 2005; Ippolito, 2002). Ippolito (2002) says: “We can therefore conclude that Russian authorities failed to exploit the unprecedented 'window of opportunity' offered by the crisis: a mistake that could have negative consequences for the future development not only of Russia's banking sector, but also of Russia's economy in a wider sense". On the contrary, Turkey adopted and implemented the restructuring process immediately after the twin crisis of 2000–2001.

2.3.1. *Post-Crisis Period in Russia*

Russia was not very successful in restructuring its banking sector after the crisis in 1998. The CBR and the government failed to promptly implement a restructuring programme, and improvement and enforcement of prudential regulation for banks (Thiessen, 2004). Thiessen (2000, 2004) argues that the requirements for a successful banking restructuring in Russia were not met. Only in mid-1999, ten months after the crisis, did the authorities started to develop a bank restructuring strategy.

In early 1999, the Agency for the Restructuring of Credit Organisations (ARCO) was established. However, this agency suffered from two problems: It was undercapitalised to effectively restructure the banking sector. Secondly, it did not have the right to close down insolvent banks (Thiessen, 2004; Steinherr, 2006). In fact, ARCO did not achieve much in restructuring the Russian banking sector. The majority of banks did not even start to restructure (Claeys & Schoors, 2007).[26]

In February 1999, the "Law on the Bankruptcy of Credit Institutions" was passed. The aim was to provide a definition for a "bankrupt bank" and establish the bankruptcy procedures. A bankruptcy law should protect creditors, impose financial discipline on managers, and induce restructuring (Lambert-Mogiliansky et al., 2003). However, the bankruptcy law in Russia was rather designed to protect the shareholders and not creditors. The law stipulated that creditors could only force banks into bankruptcy after the Central Bank of Russia had withdrawn its licence. However, the CBR was very reluctant to withdraw the licence of any big bank (Claeys & Schoors, 2007; Schoors, 1999). In fact, most of the bankrupt banks were not liquidated. They continued to accumulate liabilities instead of acting as a credit institution. After the introduction of the Law, many top-tier banks moved their businesses to the so-called "bridge" banks in violation of creditor rights (Steinherr, 2006). The failed banks were allowed to avoid repayment or liquidation without any legal consequences. Moreover, some bankrupt banks whose licences were withdrawn around the time of the 1998 crisis managed to get their licences back. The number of revoked licences for credit institutions even decreased significantly after the crisis. The number of institutions liquidated due to violation of

26 For more on the Bankruptcy Law of Russia, see Lambert-Mogiliansky et al. (2003).

legislation increased after the crisis but many banks were not liquidated despite having lost their licence, which resulted in the phenomenon of "phantom banks". These banks obtained their banking licences via court decisions after two years in bankruptcy proceedings, but without any new capital or restructuring plan (Thiessen, 2004) (see Table 17).

Table 17. Number of credit institutions and revoked licences in Russia 1998–2002

	1998	1999	2000	2001	2002
Number of credit institutions registered by the CBR	2,481	2,376	2,124	2,001	1,826
Revoked licences	229	130	33	12	10
Credit institutions liquidated due to revocation of licence for violation of the banking legislation	73	100	258	144	216

Source: CBR, Bulletin of Banking Statistics and Annual Reports 1997–2002; Steinherr (2004).

As the following analysis in this chapter will discuss, the weak accounting standards continued to hide the bad loans in banks' balance sheets. Excessive numbers of licensed banks, problems in banking legislation caused by the influence of the banking lobby over legislators, and poor legal enforcement continued to be the shortcomings in the Russian banking sector.

The legal framework for banking supervision in Russia consists of the *Federal Law on the Central Bank of the Russian Federation* of 2002 (in the course of time it was called the "Central Bank Law"/CBR Law)[27] and the *Federal Law on Banks and Banking Activity* promulgated in 1990, amended in 1996 (later on it referred to as the "Banking Law")[28] and the Federal Law on Insolvency (Bankruptcy) of Lending Institutions of 25 February 1999[29] (as amended). The Central Bank of Russia (CBR) is the primary authority responsible for the regulation of the banking sector in Russia[30] and also acts as Russia's central bank. Until 2002, the CBR had been operating under the general terms of the Federal Law on the Central Bank of the Russian Federation (the Bank of Russia) of 2 December 1990 (as amended on 26 April 1995). This law was superseded by the *Central Bank Law* in 2002. Two years after the 1998 crisis, at the end of 2001, the Government of the Russian Federation and the Central Bank of Russia issued a joint declaration called the "Strategy for the Development of the Banking Sector in the Russian Federation" (the Strategy) setting out the strategy for banking reform in Russia and calling for certain legislative steps and structural changes

27 The "Federal Law on the Central Bank of the Russian Federation (Bank of Russia)" No. 86-ФЗ of 10 July 2002 (CBRF Law).

28 The "Federal Law on Banks and Banking" No. 395–1 of 2 December 1990 (as amended by the Federal Law No. 17-ФЗ of 3 February 1996 and others) (Law on Banks).

29 No. 40-ФЗ.

30 Pursuant to Article 56 of the Banking Law.

to be taken during the following five years. In April 2005, the second Banking Sector Development Strategy was adopted for the period up to 2008 (CBR, 2005).

The Bank of Russia is led by the Basel Committee on Banking Supervision's Core Principles for Effective Banking Supervision in implementing its role as the regulator of the banking sector (ECB, 2005). However, according to the Olsen Report (ECB, 2005), in spite of some progress achieved after the 1998 crisis, the legal foundation of banking regulation and supervision in Russia is still far from perfect and requires further serious improvement, both in the form of statutory legislation and Bank of Russia regulations. The Report describes the Russian banking sector as insufficiently capitalised and strictly recommends the implementation of stricter requirements with regard to capital adequacy. Regarding private monitoring practices, further improvement was recommended in the legal framework for consolidated supervision, including the preparation of consolidated statements, the calculation of consolidated risks and management. Requirements should have been increased significantly concerning the owners and managers of banks since it was necessary to prevent the management of a bank from falling into the hands of managers and owners with a bad reputation and an unstable financial position (ECB, 2005).

2.3.2. Post-Crisis Period in Turkey

The main legislation regarding the Turkish banking industry is the Turkish Banking Law No. 5411 (the Banking Law), the Turkish Central Bank Law No. 1211 (the Central Bank Law), and Turkish Capital Markets Law No. 2499 (the Capital Markets Law), Law on the Protection of the Value of Turkish Currency No. 1567, Decree Law on Money Lending Transactions No. 90, and the regulations promulgated under these laws (Paksoy and Tiftikci, 2010).

Turkish banks today are governed by two primary bank regulatory authorities in Turkey: the Banking Regulation and Supervision Agency (BRSA) and the Central Bank (CB). The Banks' Act No. 4389 came into force in June 1999 and introduced major reforms into the banking system. The BRSA is established by the former Banks Act No. 4389 in 1999 as an independent agency to take over the supervisory and regulatory functions from the Treasury. It became operational on 31 August 2000. This was an important step because the regulatory framework needed improvement, especially regarding capital adequacy levels, connected-lending practices, transparency and consolidated accounts. However, as Steinherr et al. (2004) argue, the key problem was the lack of enforcement rather than the regulatory framework.

In the late 1990s, as explained before, the Turkish economy was suffering from several problems: a high degree of politicisation of bank lending and regulation, weak enforcement, state banks with inadequate amounts of cash, and inadequate capital for the risk exposure of most banks. In December 1999, the

Turkish government agreed on implementing an IMF-supported disinflation programme to address Turkey's macroeconomic instability. This programme also included a strategy for the banking sector. The institutional foundations of this banking sector programme included (i) rehabilitating insolvent banks through public money and their transfer to private players, and (ii) establishing the legal independence of the Central Bank. However, the most important step of this transformation was the enactment of a new Banking Act (1999) which provided the establishment of a new independent Banking Regulatory and Supervisory Agency (BRSA) to take over the regulatory and supervisory functions from the Treasury. The programme also aimed to promote the legal adaptation of this new Banking Act to Basel II- Banking Core Principles and banking norms of the EU (Steinherr et al., 2004; Bakır & Öniş, 2010).

However, due to the risks aggravated by the course of time, the programme came under heavy attack first in November 2000, then in February 2001 and it collapsed. Furthermore, it took more than one year to establish the board of the BRSA, so it was not able to commence its operations until 31 August 2000. On the other hand, the crisis provided a window of opportunity for banking sector restructuring in the sense that it revealed the structural weaknesses and the fragility of the banking sector and faced them with their eroded capital bases and deteriorated asset quality (Bakır & Öniş, 2010).

In May 2001 the BRSA formulated and executed the "Banking Restructuring and Rehabilitation Programme". During 2002 and 2003, fourteen banks were taken over by the Savings Deposit Insurance Fund (SDIF). The rehabilitation of banks involved recapitalisation and debt consolidation. The restructuring of banks included strengthening the management and reducing the number of personnel and branches.[31] In early 2004, 21 domestic private banks were taken over. Until the introduction of the new Banking Law in 2005, the Banking Act went through several amendments,[32] accompanied by several regulations to strengthen the power of the BRSA. Regulations of the BRSA focused on the following areas: capital adequacy, risk management, restrictions on loans and subsidiaries, loan provisions, compliance with international accounting standards, independent audit, and corporations with foreign supervisory authorities (BRSA Department of Strategy Development, 2006).

All banks in Turkey are subject to the 2005 Banking Law and its accompanying regulations as well as to the provisions of other laws regarding banks. Following the 2007–2009 global financial crisis, there was no serious deterioration in the financial structure of the Turkish banking sector. The impact of the global crisis on the Turkish banking system has remained limited, largely due to previous restructuring measures and comfortable prudential indicators

31 For details, see Bakır and Öniş, (2010); BRSA (2001, 2003). The BRSA kept the public informed about the restructuring process through regular reports.

32 A total of nine.

(European Commission, 2008). Accordingly, very tight limitations on the banking system were brought through high capital adequacy ratios, strong supervision and enforcement through the disciplinary power of the regulatory agency and proper risk management.[33]

3. REGULATORY VARIABLES

3.1. CAPITAL ADEQUACY REQUIREMENT

The importance of the regulatory requirements on the capital adequacy ratio has been explained in detail in the first chapter of this book.[34] The results of the empirical analysis in the second chapter also provided evidence in favour of the regulations imposing stricter capital adequacy standards. According to the consultative document of the Basel Committee on Banking Supervision (BCBS), banks entered the global crisis with too little capital and hence, the insufficiency of capital played an important role in the crisis (Hellwig, 2010).

The World Bank regulatory survey[35] conducted for both Turkey and Russia is based on the questions prepared by Barth et al. (2008) who compiled alternative quantitative measures of capital regulatory stringency categorised as *overall capital stringency* and *initial capital stringency. Overall capital stringency* refers to whether there are explicit regulatory requirements regarding the amount of capital that a bank must have relative to various guidelines.[36] These guidelines aim to understand the degree to which the leverage potential for capital is limited. *Initial capital stringency* refers to whether the source of funds counted as regulatory capital can include assets other than cash or government securities as well as whether the sources are verified by the regulatory or supervisory authorities (Barth et al., 2006a: 115–120).

The results of the survey reveal that there are three time periods that make the difference in the degree of capital stringency between two countries (see Table 18). In 1999, capital stringency was higher in Russia. However, starting in 2000, this degree became higher for Turkish banks compared to Russian banks. After that, once again there was a change in the stringency degrees of both countries, Turkey again having a higher ratio between 2004 and 2010. Looking at the capital adequacy ratios of both countries between 1999 and 2010 in Table 18, we observe that although Russian banks had a higher CAR in 1999 and 2000, starting in 2001 Turkish banks had a remarkably higher CAR than the Russian banks between 2001 and 2010.

---

33 Other tight limitations include liquidity ratios and foreign exchange positions.

34 Section 6.1.1.

35 See Appendix A.

36 These guidelines are explained in Appendix A.

Table 18. Indexes on capital requirements for Turkey and Russia*

	1999	2000	2001	2002	2003	2004	2005	2006	2007	2008	2009	2010
Turkey	5	7	7	7	7	7	9	9	9	9	9	9
Russia	6	6	6	6	6	6	6	8	8	8	8	8

* The index on capital requirements takes values between 0 and 9, with higher values indicating greater stringency.

Barth et al. (2006a: 118) argue that although most countries set minimum risk-weighted capital requirements in line with Basel I, in measuring the level of capital stringency the ability of banks in these countries to leverage capital may differ significantly. The reasoning of Barth et al. (2006: 118) is based on the fact that when calculating capital, countries differ both with respect to the types of losses that are deducted from the capital and the type of risk that is taken into account in setting the minimum capital requirement. With respect to *overall capital stringency*, there is no difference between Russia's and Turkey's CAR calculations. Regarding the *initial capital stringency*, Barth et al. (2006a: 119–120) expect substantial variation across countries in terms of to what constitutes initial capital and whether the sources of capital are verified by the authorities. They find that a high percentage of countries are not particularly stringent when it comes to the source of funds used to initially capitalise a bank. In fact, Turkey has a higher level of initial capital stringency than Russia. Overall, the survey results indicate greater capital stringency for Turkey since 2000. Russian banks' capital adequacy ratios are well below the CAR of Turkish banks during the period 2002–2010.

Table 19. Capital adequacy ratios (CAR) 1999–2010 in Turkey and Russia

	1999	2000	2001	2002	2003	2004	2005	2006	2007	2008	2009	2010
Turkey	8.24	9.29	20.78	25.34	30.93	28.24	23.73	21.91	18.94	17.98	20.50	19
Russia	26	24	24.4	22.2	19.1	17	16	14.9	15.5	16.8	20.9	18.1

Source: BRSA (1999–2010), CBR Annual Banking Supervision Reports (1999–2010).

3.1.1. Capital Adequacy Regulation in the Turkish Banking Sector

The global financial crisis had a limited impact on the Turkish banking industry.[37] One of the most important reasons of this limited effect is the *high capital adequacy ratio* of the Turkish banking sector (Yorukoglu & Atasoy, 2010; Atıcı & Gürsoy, 2011; BRSA Report 2010). In fact, Atıcı & Gürsoy (2011) argue

[37] Section 2.1.3. For more on this, see (Yorukoglu & Atasoy, 2010; Aras, 2010).

that the Turkish banking sector utilises capital buffer as a precautionary measure against the financial crises. The importance of maintaining a strong capital structure was emphasised in all policies carried out during this period. The average capital adequacy ratio which was 9.3% in 2000 increased to 23.7% in 2005 (BRSA, 2010). In fact, the levels of the capital adequacy ratio of Turkish banks have increased substantially after the 2000/2001 crises, well above the legally required ratio of 8% (see Table 19).

3.1.1.1. Developments after the 2000/2001 Crisis

Towards the end of the 1990s, the banking sector in Turkey was operating with low capital which was one of the factors that contributed to the emergence of the 2001 crisis. Although the minimum capital adequacy requirement ratio was determined as 8% in 1999 with the Banks' Act (1999) and brought in line with the Basel Accords, in the period up to the 2000–2001 crises, the already low level of own funds had further decreased. In addition to the negative effects of the crisis, the problems of private banks were aggravated due to the inadequate provisioning for non-performing loans[38] and the failure to meet the capital adequacy requirements (BRSA, 2010).

Following the 2000/2001 crises, the Banking Restructuring and Rehabilitation Programme was announced on 15 May 2001 in Turkey.[39] The priorities of the program were identified as *strengthening the capital structures of banks* that had eroded during the crises and *clearing the system of weak banks* in order to recover the banking sector from the deterioration caused by the 2000/2001 crises. The framework of the program of strengthening banks' capital was realised with two regulations under the "Regulation on Principles and Procedures of the Banking Sector Restructuring Program". The first Regulation dated 1 February 2002 framed the details of the capital support program to be realised under the scope of the restructuring program in order to increase the asset quality of the banking sector.[40] The second Regulation, published on

---

38 Loan loss provisions in accounting have a central role in determining the asset quality (particularly loan quality) problems. See Chapter 1, section 6.1.1 and 6.1.4.

39 The focus was on improving the intermediation function of banks and establishing an internationally competitive banking sector which would be resilient to internal and external shocks (BRSA, 2010).

40 In compliance with the Provisional Article 4 of the Banks Act (1999), the Regulation established the principles and procedures for the supervision of privately-owned deposit-taking banks founded in Turkey based on their financial statements and the investigation of their independent audit reports by a second independent audit institution determined by the BRSA. These procedures included the general assembly to be held by banks; increasing or decreasing banks' capital; measures that need to be taken based on the assessments of the BRSA; transfer period for shares which are subject to capital increase; issuance of convertible bonds and conversion of these bonds into shares; sale of banks' shares taken over by the Savings Deposit Insurance Fund; and conversion of subordinated debts to capital (BRSA, 2001).

27 March 2002, determined the principles and procedures of the investigation of the first independent audit institution by a second independent audit institution, which was to be selected by the BRSA. This regulation aimed at contributing to the quality of the supervision process which was crucial within the process of restructuring (BRSA, 2010).

The minimum capital adequacy requirements set by the regulators/ supervisors should reflect the risk that a bank undertakes and must also define the components of banks' capital. The quality of these components is important in the sense that it enables the bank to absorb losses.[41] For the reinforcement of the equity capital of private banks, a *three-party audit*[42] was made before extending capital support to banks whose asset quality had deteriorated and whose equity capital was diminished. The re-capitalisation of banks within the method of the triple-audit process was realised in 25 private banks (BRSA, 2010).

The second priority of the restructuring programme considered the problematic banks. In order to clear the system of weak banks, the operation licences of problematic banks with deteriorated financial structures were cancelled with the regulations of the BRSA. Their partnership rights and also their management and control were transferred to the SDIF. The aim was to rehabilitate these banks and make them active in the economy again. If there was no rehabilitation possible, then the banks were liquidated.[43] This settlement process of banks was very fast, lasting only 14 months. As a result, between 1999 and 2003, the Turkish banking sector went through a major consolidation process, with the number of banks decreasing from 81 to 50. This contributed to the improvement in the *quality of capital* of the banking sector (BRSA, 2010).

Another factor that distorted the asset quality of banks in the period up to the 2000/2001 crisis was the high inflation environment that encouraged banks to conduct their activities with foreign resources instead of own funds. In that sense, by tending towards risky activities, the incentive effect of the capital adequacy requirement was undermined.[44] As a result, the level and the quality of own funds were negatively affected. In 2002, the implementation of *inflation accounting* in the banking system was introduced, which enabled measurement of the real dimensions of own funds, making balance sheets more transparent.[45]

41 See Chapter 1, section 6.1.1.

42 The two audits were conducted by the banks' own auditors and an externally designated auditor for each bank. The final audit was essentially a judgment call by the BRSA (Steinherr et al., 2004).

43 Resolution instruments of the SDIF defined by the Law were: share sales, sales of insured deposit and loans (Asset and Liability Transfer) merger with a bank or transfer to another bank (BRSA, 2010).

44 The *incentive effect* of capital adequacy requirements is explained in Chapter 1, section 6.1.1.

45 "Regulation on Principles and Procedures of Independent Audit to Be Carried Out in Banks" – According to this regulation, audits were implemented based on the rules of inflation accounting, different from previous years (BRSA, 2010). Developments in the accounting procedures of Turkish banks in the post-crisis period will be explained in detail in section 3.3.1.

Banks' performances became assessable in a healthier way and capital quality improved (BRSA, 2009; 2010).

As explained above, the problems of private banks were aggravated due to the inadequate provisioning for non-performing loans. Loan loss provisions in accounting have a central role in determining asset quality (particularly loan quality) problems[46] and banks may have the incentives to underreport their provisions. In order to further improve the quality of capital, a regulation regarding *loan loss treatment and provisions* was published in June 2001.[47] The regulation[48] required a detailed classification of all loans (and other receivables) from borrowers categorised according to the borrowers' payment capabilities.[49] This regulation also provided a strong incentive for the connected-lending practices of the past (Steinherr et al., 2004; BRSA, 2010).[50]

Between 2000 and 2003, fourteen banks were taken over by the SDIF. During 1997 and 2003, the total number of banks taken over by the SDIF was 22 (SDIF, 2003). These banks were subjected to an intensive financial and restructuring process after their takeover.[51] Accordingly, the distorting impacts of problematic banks on the asset structure of the sector were removed from the sector (Steinherr et al., 2004).[52]

---

46 Chapter 1, section 6.1.1 and 6.1.4.

47 The Regulation on the Procedures and Principles for Determination of Qualifications of Loans and Other Receivables by Banks and Provisions to be Set Aside.

48 In November 2006, the regulation was amended by the BRSA and issued under the "Regulation on the Principles and Procedures Related to the Determination of the Loans and Other Receivables by Banks and Provisions to be Set Aside."

49 The regulation required the classification of loans into five categories: standard, closely-monitored, limited collection ability, remote collection ability and losses. Any loans that are subject to deterioration of credit or collateral quality, or in any case a non-payment of principal or interest on the due date should be moved out of the "standard category". If the non-payment period exceeds 180 days, the loan is progressively reclassified into the last three categories, which are considered "nonperforming" categories that prompt provisioning requirements. Loan provisioning starts at 20% and all loans with a non-payment period of one year must be fully provisioned. If a loan is classified as non-performing, then all other loans of the same borrower must be categorised as non-performing. These provisioning regulations outlined above were fully operational since January 2002 (Steinherr et al., 2004).

50 "Regulation on Establishment and Activities of Banks" was published in June 2001 to prevent the risk concentration in loans. Pursuant to this regulation, direct and indirect loans were taken into consideration in setting credit limits. This regulation aims to prevent the concentration of bank resources on specific groups. Besides, it ensures that banks consolidate their assets in line with security, liquidity and productivity principles (BRSA, 2010). If a bank's total credit amount given to a risk group exceeds the limitations in the Banking Law, it cannot extend new loans to natural persons and legal entities included in this risk group. With this regulation, it became obligatory for banks to remove the amounts exceeding the limitations until 2006 (BRSA, 2010).

51 Their short-term liabilities were liquidated, foreign currency open positions were reduced, deposit and foreign currency liabilities were transferred to other banks and a number of branches and personnel were cut down significantly (BRSA, 2010).

52 The cost of restructuring the banking sector was $53.6 billion, which was almost equivalent to one-third of the national income (BRSA, 2010).

Regarding the measurement of the capital adequacy ratio, in February 2001, the BRSA issued a regulation entitled the "Regulation on the Measurement and the Evaluation of Banks' Capital Adequacy"[53] to establish the methodology for the calculation of capital adequacy ratios of banks.[54] This regulation aimed to insure that banks maintain an adequate amount of capital against potential losses underlining the *buffer effect* of capital which protects banks against adverse shocks and enables them to absorb losses.[55] The minimum capital adequacy ratio threshold was determined as 8% in line with the Basel standards (BRSA, 2010; Bakır & Öniş, 2010).

In June 2001, with the amendments made to the 1999 Banks Act, the definition of "*consolidated own funds*" (*consolidated equity*) was introduced in compliance with the EU Directives. This definition became the basis for the calculation of credit limits to be applied to banks (BRSA, 2010). The same year, the BRSA, the Under-secretariat of the Treasury, CBRT and Ministry of Finance collaborated to incentivise the increase of own funds (equity) within the sector. Within this framework, regulations were introduced to provide tax incentives for corporate mergers and takeovers.[56] In addition to the incentives introduced with the legal framework, the banking sector voluntarily oriented itself towards a consolidation to increase their profit margins in an environment of high inflation rates and decreasing interest rates (BRSA, 2010).

Another attempt to bring the calculation of the capital adequacy ratio in line with these Basel standards[57] in Turkey, calculation was expanded to include capital charges for market risk[58] beginning January 2002 (BRSA, 2010). This new procedure had already been proposed by the Basel Committee in 1993. It introduced the incorporation of market risk on banks' capital requirements through a standard approach that was also used for credit risks under the 1988 Basel Accord (Basel I). Hence, the 1996 Amendment to the "Capital Accord to Incorporate Market Risks" by the Basel Committee allowed banks to calculate their capital to be held against market risks by using their own internal quantitative models.

---

53 Published in the Official Gazette dated 10 February 2001 (numbered 24314); The ratio is called the "Capital Base Divided By Risk-Bearing Assets, Non-cash Credits and Obligations Standard Ratio".

54 On both a consolidated and unconsolidated basis.

55 For the *buffer effect*, see Chapter 1, section 6.1.1.

56 The "Regulation on Mergers and Transfers of Banks" prepared by the BRSA defined the general principles and processes concerning the banks' mergers and transfers. It was published within the Official Gazette dated 27 June 2001. A legal regulation enabling the tax advantages given within the Act No. 4605 to be applied in the merger of banks' subsidiaries became effective on 3 July 2001 (BRSA, 2010).

57 Turkey is a member country of the Basel Committee on Banking Supervision.

58 Starting from July 2002
As was explained in Chapter 1, market risk includes interest rate risk, exchange rate risks and equity risk, see section 2.4.

In addition to the inclusion of capital charges for market risk in the calculation of CAR in 2002, the definition of own funds was changed,[59] and general loan-loss provisions were added to Tier 2 capital the same year.[60] As a result of these changes, a single own fund (equity) definition was established for the Turkish banking system, providing uniformity both in the calculation of credit limitations and in the application of financial ratios.[61]

Furthermore, this regulation increased the power of the BRSA in supervising banks' compliance with the capital adequacy requirement. It was decided that capital adequacy ratios would be monitored on a daily basis by the BRSA, and though the data were not public, the BRSA began informing the market with its banking sector reports. Since then, the capital adequacy ratios are calculated quarterly with on- and off-balance sheet risks incorporated in the calculation (BRSA, 2010).

Another regulation introduced in 2002[62] authorised the BRSA to establish a higher individual capital adequacy ratio for each bank and additions were made to the standards of risk measurement methods to be used by banks.[63] A provision regarding the publication of the capital adequacy ratio by banks in each March, June, September and December was added to increase transparency. During the 2000/2001 crises, banks' own funds had suffered from erosion due to interest rate volatilities caused by the crisis and capital shortage. Hence, a "Structural Position"[64] definition was introduced to prevent the erosion of banks'

59 Pursuant to the amendment made to the "Regulation on Establishment and Activities of Banks."

60 The Basel Accords define the capital of a bank as Tier 1 and Tier 2. Tier 1 is basically the core capital and Tier 2 is the supplementary capital. See Chapter 1, section 6.1.1.

61 The framework for the risk weights was also rearranged to comply with the inclusion of the repo transactions in the balance sheet (BRSA, 2010).

62 In January 2002, the BRSA cancelled the Regulation on the Measurement and the Evaluation of Banks' Capital Adequacy and replaced it with a new regulation under the same title which brought up additional regulations on capital adequacy. Under this regulation, the capital adequacy ratio was set at 8% both on a consolidated and unconsolidated basis by taking into account the market risks (BRSA, 2010).

63 Pursuant to the provisional article 1 of the Regulation, application of market risks in the calculation of capital adequacy was initiated beginning from 1 July 2002 (BRSA, 2010). Subordinated loans were included in the calculation of capital adequacy ratio in line with the EU Directives. Subordinated loans are listed as one of the items that constitute supplementary capital (i.e. Tier Two Capital) (Thompson, 2002). The subordinated debt has a market disciplining effect on banks risk-taking activities since it is unsecured by the government (Levonian, 2001). For more on the disciplining effect of subordinated debt on banking see Distinguin, 2008; Ashcraft, 2006.

64 "Structural Position" is basically a matched currency position to protect a bank's capital adequacy ratio. It protects against the possible losses from fluctuations in exchange rates. If a bank has its capital denominated in its domestic currency and has a portfolio of foreign currency assets and liabilities that are completely matched, its capital to asset ratio will fall if the domestic currency depreciates. The bank can protect its capital adequacy ratio by running a short position in the domestic currency. However, the position would lead to a loss if the domestic currency were to appreciate (BIS, 2005).

equities from these kinds of price movements and foreign exchange rate movements (BRSA, 2010).[65]

As a result of these positive developments, the balance sheet of the banking sector grew stable after 2002. Thanks to the policies on capital quality, the composition of the banks' balance sheets was improved. The high growth experienced in the banking sector increased financial deepening and the banking sector became able to support the real economy again. During 2002 and 2005, the ratio of loans to GDP reached from 17.8% to 30.8% (See Table 20). Total assets of the sector increased by 24% and total loans grew by 45% on average. The deposit/loan ratio rose from 35.5% in 2002 to 62.2% in 2005. The ratio of non-performing loans (NPLs) to gross loans decreased from 17.6% in 2002 to 4.8% in 2005 sharply revealing the sound growth in loans (BRSA, 2010).

Table 20. Turkish banking sector 2001–2005

	Assets/GDP	Capital/GDP	Loans/GDP	Deposits/GDP
2001	95.9	8.6	21	66.1
2002	77.3	9.3	17.8	50.2
2003	70	10	18.6	43.5
2004	71.4	10.7	23.2	44.6
2005	81.6	11	30.8	50

Source: Caner et al. (2007).

3.1.1.2. Developments after 2005

Since 2004, the BRSA has been working on the implementation of Basel II in Turkey. In 2005, the 1999 Banks Act was abolished and replaced by the Banking Law No. 5411, which came into effect on 1 November 2005. The new Banking Law (2005) was an important step in terms of the implementation of Basel II. One amendment made was the incorporation of the banks' operational risk (in addition to credit risk and market risk) in the calculation of the capital adequacy ratio in order to bring it in line with the EU standards. As of June 2007, capital adequacy regulation in Turkey has been made compliant with Basel II by including the operational risk component in the capital adequacy calculation. Currently, Turkish banks' capital adequacy is calculated on the basis of the "Regulation on Measurement and Evaluation of Banks' Capital Adequacy",[66] which is compliant with the Basel-II Provisions (BRSA, 2010).

65 Principles and procedures regarding the structural positions to be taken into consideration in the calculation of CAR were published on 8 May 2002.

66 Published in the Official Gazette dated 1 November 2006.

The new Banking Law basically maintained the same provisions regarding capital adequacy. The minimum CAR ratio required by the BRSA remained at 8% (or greater). The BRSA kept its right to set and monitor the capital requirement ratios for all banks. It maintained its power to increase the minimum capital adequacy ratios, set different ratios for each bank and revise the risk-weighting of assets, taking into account banks' internal systems, as well as their asset and financial structures.

Additionally, since November 2006, the BRSA requires banks to hold a CAR target ratio of 12% which is determined as a precondition to open a new branch. This ratio exceeds the CAR of many other emerging markets even in the global financial crisis years.[67] This policy is considered a variation of the *capital buffer* in excess of what is required by the regulations recognising the fact that more capital is required in good times if a bank tends to exploit favourable market conditions by opening new branches. On the other hand, during periods of adverse economic conditions, this prerequisite becomes a slack condition since banks will have less incentive to open a new branch. Besides, banks will be protected against negative shocks with a cushion (Yorukoğlu & Atasoy, 2010). One of the most important lessons gained from the 2000/2001 crisis was the significance of maintaining a strong capital structure in the banking system. Therefore, the importance of maintaining a strong capital structure was emphasised in all policies carried out since the *May 2001 Rehabilitation Programme*. Since the beginning of the restructuring period, the capital adequacy ratio of Turkish banks was increased well above the legal requirement. In fact, the CAR, which was 9.3% in 2000, increased to 23.7% in 2005 (BRSA, 2010).[68]

In order to control the credit supply for credit cards, the risk weights assigned to assets were adjusted. The risk weights for credit card limit commitments were increased from 50% to 100%, which pushed down the capital adequacy ratio, hence encouraging banks to decrease the limits they assigned to credit cards (Yorukoğlu & Atasoy, 2010).

As a result of these developments in restructuring and reforming the banking sector, performance of the banking sector improved greatly between 2002 and 2008. The total assets increased to $465 billion from $130 billion, and the total asset to GDP ratio increased from 57% to 77%. Banks' shareholders' equity increased to $54 billion from $16 billion (Gursoy & Atıcı, 2011).

---

67 The CAR declined from 25.3% in 2002 to 17.9% in 2008. The recent decline in the CAR was due to increased bank loans and increased weights for letters of guarantee and letters of credit imposed in January 2008. It should be noted that the CAR will fall further with the full application of the Basel II standard depending on the size of foreign currency Turkish government securities holdings, which will be the 100 per cent risk weight (Bakır, 2009).

68 It increased to 20.78% in 2001, to 25.34% in 2002 and 30.93% in 2003. The decrease to 23.7% in 2005 is due to the adoption of International Financial Reporting Standards (IFRS) in 2005 where banks suffered a temporary reduction in capitalisation due to mark-to-market valuation losses on their holdings of government securities (IMF, 2007).

3.1.1.3. Measures Taken during the Global Crisis

During the 2008 global crisis, the Banking Regulation and Supervision Agency (BRSA) adopted measures to preserve the financial strength of banks and contain the effects of abrupt changes in the financial asset prices on banks' capital adequacy. For this purpose, BRSA made the distribution of banks' 2008 and 2009 earnings subject to permission in order to contribute to the strengthening of banks' capital structure (BRSA, 2010). Yorukoglu and Atasoy (2010) evaluate this measure as a tool for increasing banks' resilience to vulnerabilities. In 2008, 20% of the profit and in 2009, 15% of the profit was distributed.

Although there was a considerable credit growth in the sector, banks were prevented from taking excessive risks through the regulations applied and as a result, the non-performing loans ratio remained low even during the global crisis. One of the measures that the BRSA took during the global crisis was to restrict loan to value ratios for certain segments of bank credits, and also to increase the minimum payments on credit cards.[69] These two policies intended, in support of the policies of the Central Bank, to control the credit supply (Yorukoglu & Atasoy, 2010).

Loan-loss provisioning is another tool to ensure that banks build up buffers against losses (as was explained before). As a second measure, the BRSA allowed banks to restructure loans posing no problems, in order to ensure the smooth functioning of the loan relations between banks and non-financial institutions (Yorukoglu & Atasoy, 2010).[70]

Moreover, considering the fields in which there is growth and potential of important risk concentration, in order to take prudent measures and follow-up these risks, principles and procedures concerning the banks' TL[71] Bond issuances were permitted on 30 September 2010 by the BRSA.[72]

---

69 The Bank Cards and Credit Cards Law Regulation became effective on 1 March 2006. With this regulation, the total credit card limit determined for all customer cards should not be greater than two times his/her average net total monthly income for the first year and four times for the second year. The customer should supply the necessary documents, which are confirmed by related institutions, as evidence of his or her monthly income. Otherwise, the total limit for all the customer's cards is set at TRY 1,000. These controls on credit card limits are intended to restrict systemic risk by forestalling households' exposure to excessive risk.

70 Other measures applied by the BRSA: it allowed banks to reclassify the securities in their balance sheets from trading portfolio to investment portfolio once only. Furthermore, three liquidity ratios that are used to measure and assess the liquidity adequacy of banks were put into effect in 2007. Therefore, Turkish banks have already been operating within the framework of liquidity regulations, which the Basel Committee is currently trying to implement at an international level. These ratios had a strong positive effect on the resilience of Turkish banks when facing the global financial stress (Yorukoglu & Atasoy, 2010; BAT, 2009). The sound financial positions of Turkish banks put them under less pressure in their lending activities through the positive effect of capital buffer (Atıcı & Gursoy, 2011).

71 Turkish currency.

72 Pursuant to the Resolution No. 3875.

However, the BRSA manifested that the capital adequacy ratio of the issuer bank could not be below 12% as of the date of application compared to the legislative threshold of 8% (Paksoy & Tiftikci, 2012). Furthermore, a bank must present to the BRSA a detailed report including the benefit and cost analysis, the effect of the issuance on the bank's financial structure and detailed evaluations concerning risks which may originate from the issuance.[73] This report is to be used in measuring, monitoring and controlling these risks (BRSA, 2010).

Finally, regarding the liquidity ratio in Basel III,[74] the ratio reported by all banks in the Turkish banking sector is parallel (even more conservative in some items) to the Liquidity Coverage Ratio of the Basel III Framework (BRSA Vice Chairman Speech, 2011). Regulation on the "Measurement and Evaluation of Liquidity Adequacy of Banks" has been in place since November 2006.[75] Although an official timetable for the full adoption of Basel III in Turkey has not been announced by the BRSA, the regulations are expected to be implemented between 2013 and 2019 in accordance with the transition period provided for by the Basel Committee.

3.1.2. *Capital Adequacy Regulation in the Russian Banking Sector*

Russia experienced a financial meltdown in 1998. Three years after the crisis, at the end of 2001, the Government of the Russian Federation and the Central Bank of Russia issued a joint declaration called the "Strategy for the Development of the Banking Sector in the Russian Federation" (the Strategy) setting out the strategy for banking reform in Russia and calling for certain legislative steps and structural changes to be taken during the following five years. This was followed by the introduction of the "Federal Law on the Central Bank of the Russian Federation" in 2002 which was an important step in banking reform. Finally, four years after the 1998 crisis, this law introduced new provisions related to banking regulation and supervision (CBR, 2002).[76] Among the measures aimed at increasing the stability of the Russian banking sector was an increase in the capital adequacy requirements to encourage the establishment of a better-capitalised banking sector.[77]

---

73 Considering the possible stress conditions as well as the application principles.

74 Basel III is the new version of the Basel Accords. It will be ultimately phased in by 2018. Basel III will increase the capital adequacy ratios and introduce new global regulatory requirements on bank liquidity and bank leverage.

75 Redrafted in June 2007 and January 2009.

76 For more on this, see CBR Annual Report 2002, section II.2.1.

77 The capital adequacy requirement for the Russian banks was 6% as of 1 February 1997 and 7% as of 1 February 1998 Bank of Russia Instruction No. 1 of 30 January 1996, "On the Procedure for Regulating the Activities of Credit Organisations", www.cbr.ru/eng/analytics/standart_acts/currency_regulations/print.asp?file=i1_e.htm.

3.1.2.1. Developments after the 1998 Crisis

In 2001, three years after the 1998 crisis, the Russian banking sector was still suffering from shortcomings that created obstacles to banking sector development, concealed banks' risk exposure and distorted the capital quality of the banking sector. These shortcomings were false reporting, non-compliance with mandatory standards, failure to observe the procedure and deadlines for submitting reports and publishing them in the general press, and failure to observe the procedure for creating loan loss reserves. The restructuring process did not eliminate most of the unsound banks from the sector, which further distorted the asset quality of the banking sector.[78] Serious defects in law enforcement, inadequate transparency in balance sheets, a low level of market discipline, and low level of corporate governance resulted in the distortion of accounting operations by some banks (CBR, 2000; 2001). Due to the violation of the reporting procedures in order to conceal the actual level of risk banks assume, their performance on the balance sheets was exaggerated. These situations, accompanied by the flaws in the internal control systems and incompetence and negligence of bank employees, led to violations committed by the banks. In fact, banks were still manipulating their end-of-period balance sheets to ensure their compliance (CBR, 2000).

After the introduction of the Basel Accord in 1999,[79] in April 2000, Russian banks started to include market risk[80] in the evaluation of capital adequacy.[81] Three years after the 1998 crisis, with the Development Strategy in 2001, the CBR started to work on bringing the banking regulation system into compliance with the Basel standards. A new version of the CBR's Regulation[82] on calculating capital was adapted in order to bring the calculation of the capital adequacy requirement in line with the Basel Core Principles.[83] In 2001, the Bank of Russia introduced a criterion that expanded the range of credit institutions required to calculate market risks to be included in the capital adequacy calculation. Between 2001 and 2003, the number of credit institutions that included market risk calculations increased from 703 to 848 (CBR, 2002).

---

78 See section 2.3.1. Besides, the 2004 IMF Report emphasised the need for amendments to the Bankruptcy Law in order to facilitate certain and speedy resolution processes.

79 See Balin (2008).

80 In 1993, the Basel Committee proposed a procedure to incorporate market risks on banks' capital requirements through a standard approach which was also used for credit risks under the 1988 Basel Accord (Basel I).

81 It was calculated in accordance with the procedure set by the Bank of Russia's Regulation No. 89-P, dated 24 September 1999 (On the Market Risk Calculation Procedure for Credit Institutions). The enforcement started in 1 April 2000 (CBR, 2003).

82 "On the Methodology of Calculating Credit Institutions' Own Funds (Capital)". The new version stipulated that the revaluation gains should not be included in the calculation of additional sources of credit institutions' capital more than once in three years (CBR, 2002).

83 Capital Adequacy Requirement refers to Core Principle 6 (CP 6) of the "Basel Core Principles for Effective Banking Supervision".

The new Banking Law (2002) stipulated that the CBR may set prudential requirements for banks.[84] Therefore, the CBR became authorised to establish ten compulsory standards for banking groups, including the capital adequacy ratios (CBR, 2002).[85] Accordingly, the CBR is authorised to introduce various capital adequacy requirements (CAR) applicable to banks.[86] The Banking Law also specified the procedure for fining banks by the CBR for non-compliance with the specified prudential requirements. The law empowered the CBR to recommend the founders of a credit institution to take actions to increase its equity capital to the required level (CBR, 2002). Another amendment to the law and the subsequent changes in CBR regulations was that the CBR became authorised to revoke the banking licence from a credit institution, but only if the credit institution's capital adequacy ratio fell below 2%.[87]

As was explained in Chapter 1,[88] the minimum capital adequacy requirements set by the regulators should reflect the risk that banks undertake and also must define the components of banks' capital. The quality of these components is important in the sense that it enables the bank to absorb losses. In 2003, the CBR issued a regulation[89] designed to improve the quality of credit institutions' capital and defined the "own funds" in line with the Basel standards.[90]

After 2001, although still above the required level the aggregate capital adequacy ratios of banks decreased steadily. The average capital adequacy registered in 2002 was 22.2 against 24.4 in 2001. This ratio continued to decline to 19.1% in 2003, due to the fact that the credit institutions' aggregate risk increased faster than their capital as was also evidenced in 2002. The capital

84 According to the articles 62, 64, 65, 67, 70, and 71 of the Banking Law.

85 In accord with the Article 62 of the Law.

86 Articles 62, 67 and 72 of the Banking Law.

87 Based on the amendments made to the Federal Law "On Banks and Banking Activities" and the subsequent changes in Bank of Russia regulations requirements. In accordance with Article 20, section 10 of the BL (395-I) the CBR is obliged to revoke a bank's licence if its bank's capital adequacy ratio falls below 2% (IMF, 2011a; b).

88 Chapter 1, section 6.1.1.

89 Bank of Russia Regulation No. 215P, dated 10 February 2003, "On the Methodology of Determining Own Funds (Capital) of Credit Institutions" and Bank of Russia Ordinance No. 1246U, dated 10 February 2003, "On Actions to be Taken upon the Discovery of the Evidence (Signs) of the Formation of Own Funds (Capital) or a Part Thereof, Using Inappropriate Assets".

90 This Regulation No. 215-p was replaced in 2006. The Federal Law No. 247FZ, dated 29 December 2006, Ordinance No. 1793U, dated 20 February 2007, On Amending Bank of Russia Regulation No. 215P, dated 10 February 2003, on the Methodology of Calculating the Capital of Credit Institutions, defined the term "subordinated loan".
It established the conditions to include subordinated loans in the sources of additional capital. The amendments made to this regulation in the following year extended the list of subordinated instruments included in capital calculation. These amendments correspond to international banking and supervisory practices. They aim to contribute to the growth in the capitalisation of the Russian banking sector (CBR, 2006; 2007).

adequacy ratio decreased from 19.1% to 17.0% in 2004 as again banks' risk-weighted assets grew faster than their equity capital (CBR, 2004) (see Table 19).

Moreover, the findings of the 2003 IMF Financial System Stability Assessment (FSSA) showed that although Russian banks were well capitalised in 2002 and in 2003, the quality of capital was questionable and loan loss provisioning was not reflecting actual credit risks.[91] The report emphasised the weakness of the banking sector in terms of the supervisory and regulatory framework and warned against a possible banking shock, which in fact happened in 2004. One of the recommendations of the 2003 IMF report referred to the tightening of the definition of capital and enforcement of capital requirements. Furthermore, the report mentioned that a CBR study of 30 banks at that time indicated that those banks had significantly overstated their capital level and actually had negative net worth. The same report also mentioned that the changes in the laws were not always accompanied by immediate reviews of regulations and that there was considerable overlap in the number of guidelines.[92]

The adoption of a new Regulation on Mandatory Ratios of Banks[93] by the CBR in 2004[94] was an important step because this regulation formed the foundation of the CBR's prudential supervision. Firstly, regarding capital adequacy requirements, the CAR ratio was increased to tighten the regulatory framework. Banks with capital of €5 million and more were required to hold a risk-weighted capital-asset ratio of 10%, and banks with capital less than €5 million were required to hold 11%.[95] Secondly, this regulation required credit

---

91 Loan-loss provisions in accounting have a central role in determining the asset quality (particularly loan quality) problems. However, banks may have the incentives to underreport their provisions. See, Chapter 1, section 6.1.1 and 6.1.4.

92 In 2002, the CBR drafted and received the approval for the Regulations "On the Procedure for Making Allowances for Estimated Losses" and "On the Procedure for Making and Use of Allowances for Estimated Loan Losses" (CBR, 2002). This regulation was changed in August 2004 with the introduction of a new loan classification and provisioning procedure called "Bank of Russia Regulation No. 254P, dated 26 March 2004, On the Procedure for Making by Credit Institutions Loan Loss Provisions and Provisions for Loan Debts and Similar Debts" (CBR, 2004).

93 Regulation No. 110-I.

94 Pursuant to the Federal Law No. 86-FZ, dated 10 July 2002, "On the Central Bank of the Russian Federation (Bank of Russia)" which superseded the CBR Instruction No. 1 "On the Procedure for Regulating the Activities of Credit Organisations", approved by the Order of the CBR No. 02–430 dated 1 October 1997, as amended (Instruction No. 1).

95 This new regulation of the Bank of Russia Instruction No. 110 I, dated 16 January 2004 "On Banks' Required Ratios", replaced Bank of Russia Instruction No. 1, dated 1 October 1997, "On the Regulation of Banking Activities," starting from 1 May 2004. Pursuant to this new regulation, changes were made to the calculation of market risk in calculating the amount of risk-weighted assets regarding certain off-balance sheet items. The CBR also extended the concept of risk-weights to all other ratios that include assets in the denominator (Tompson, 2004).

institutions to comply with the required ratios on a daily basis[96] in order to eliminate the motivation for the accounting manipulations mentioned above and contribute to asset quality (Tompson, 2004).[97]

In spite of these developments, financial intermediation in the Russian banking sector did not develop as intended between 2001 and 2005 (see Table 21). The Russian banking sector experienced instability and a liquidity deficit in 2004 called a *mini-crisis*.[98] This crisis resulted from the actions taken by the CBR and a crisis of confidence among Russian banking customers. During July 2004, the CBR revoked the banking licences of several Russian banks. The resulting uncertainty in the Russian banking system led to the collapse of the interbank lending system and to liquidity pressure for many Russian banks. The collapse of several Russian banks caused panic among depositors. Even reliable larger banks became subject to deposit withdrawals (Tompson, 2004).

Table 21. Russian banking sector 2001–2005

	Assets/GDP	Capital/GDP	Loans/GDP	Deposits/GDP
2001	35.3	5.1	14.8	7.6
2002	38.3	5.4	16.6	9.5
2003	42.3	6.2	20.3	11.5
2004	42.1	5.6	22.9	11.7
2005	45.1	5.7	25.3	12.8

Source: CBR (2001, 2002, 2003, 2004, 2005; Caner et al. (2007).

3.1.2.2. Developments after 2005

In 2005, the CBR started to prepare for the introduction of international capital adequacy standards established by the Basel New Capital Accord (Basel II) by studying the nature and scale of the changes that must be made to laws and regulations. The Government of Russia and the CBR published a new strategy for the development of the Russian banking sector regarding the period from 2005 to 2008, which replaced the 2001 joint declaration of "the Strategy". Several

In December 2011, a new law was introduced that incrementally increases the minimum capital requirements to RUB 300 million (around €7.4 million) by 2015. At the time of writing this book, minimum capital requirements are RUB 90 million (around €2.3 million).

96 These ratios were calculated on the reporting date (the first day of each month) and in case of non-compliance the bank could be fined.

97 Tompson (2004) adds that the mandatory ratios under the new instruction were not covering key issues such as the quality of capital and liability concentration which, according to him, would have a distorting effect on the disclosure by disabling market observers to detect risks in banks.

98 See footnote 3.

regulations were issued in 2005[99] by the Bank of Russia to make changes for the specification of methods in calculating the assets included in the capital adequacy ratio and in calculating the prudential ratios limiting a bank's credit risks (CBR, 2005).

However, the average capital adequacy ratio of Russian banks continued to decline after 2004. Although this decrease was in part the result of rapid credit growth, some banks were not able to raise enough capital as their businesses were expanding. Not all banks were meeting the 10% capital adequacy requirement. Several banks were still not meeting the minimum requirement on the basis of international financial reporting standards (IFRS) (IMF, 2006). The trend towards a gradual decline in the average capital adequacy ratio continued as the growth in banking sector assets exceeded the growth in banking sector capital, leading to an increase in banks' balance sheets. In 2005, the average capital adequacy ratio decreased from 17.0% to 16.0%. In 2006, it decreased from 16.0% to 14.9%. Only in 2007, unlike the situation in previous years, did the average capital adequacy ratio increase from 14.9% to 15.5% as the banking sector total capital grew faster than the assets (see Table 19).

3.1.2.3. Impact of the Global Crisis

In 2008, the global financial crisis adversely affected the dynamics of the banking sector average capital adequacy ratio. It contracted from 15.5% as of 1 January 2008 to 14.5% as of 1 October 2008 (see Table 19). However, due to measures taken by the government at the end of the year, specifically the extension of subordinated loans (i.e. quasi capital)[100] to several large banks reversed this trend and the banking sector capital adequacy ratio increased to 16.8% in 2008 (CBR, 2008). In 2009, due to the growth in the banking sector's capital, the CAR increased from 16.8% to 20.9%. It decreased to 18.1% in 2010. This was caused by the slowdown of the capital growth rate compared to the considerable growth of risk-weighted assets (CBR, 2010).

In order to improve the incorporation of Pillar 1 of Basel II to its regulatory framework, the Bank of Russia issued two regulations in 2009. The regulation[101] in November 2009 was introduced in order to improve the regulation on "Banks Required Ratios" (dated 2004). This established a procedure for implementing Basel II simplified approach to credit risk assessment. Moreover, another

99 Ordinance of 18 February 2005 No. 1549-U, Ordinance of 6 July 2005, No. 1592-U and Ordinance of 29 July 2005, No. 1599-U "On Amending Bank of Russia Instruction of 16 January 2004, No. 110-I On Banks Prudential Ratios".

100 Subordinated loans are listed as one of the items that constitute supplementary capital. Ashcraft (2006) finds that that an increase in the amount of subordinated debt in regulatory capital has an important positive effect in helping a bank recover from financial distress.

101 Ordinance No 2324-U "On Amending Bank of Russia Instruction No. 110-I", dated January 2004, on Banks' Required Ratios.

regulation in 2009[102] on the Procedure for Calculating Operational Risk established a procedure for the inclusion of *operational risk* in the calculation of capital adequacy ratio.[103]

In 2010, CBR continued to take steps to apply Basel II in the Russian banking sector. Amendments to the Bank of Russia regulations regarding the procedure for the calculation of required ratios and operational risk (introduced in November 2009) became effective in July 2010. These regulations implemented a simplified standardised approach to the assessment of credit risk and a basic indicator approach to the calculation of operational risk under Basel II. As of 1 January 2010, the minimum equity capital of an operating bank cannot be less than 90 million roubles (€2,234,570) and as of 1 January 2012, not less than 180 million roubles (€4,469,148). From June 2010, the Bank of Russia is to phase in operational risk coverage (at first 40%, then 70% and finally 100%) which banks should ensure when calculating the capital adequacy ratio (CBR, 2010).[104]

3.1.3. Discussion

The qualitative analysis regarding the post-crisis periods in Turkish and Russian banking sectors suggests that the restructuring process implemented following the crisis period was more comprehensive and more disciplined in Turkey compared to Russia. This had a significant positive impact on the Turkish banks' asset quality compared to the Russian banks where the existence of problematic banks in the sector still has a distorting effect on the asset quality. Hence, the analysis suggests that the asset quality remained a problem in the Russian banking sector partly due to the existence of the problematic banks (such as the so-called *pocket banks*), even in the aftermath of the 1998 crisis.[105] Whereas in Turkey many problematic banks' licences were cancelled or transferred to the SDIF immediately after the 2001 crisis, the restructuring process in Russia was not achieved successfully. Many of these Russian weak banks continued to operate

---

102 Regulation No. 346-P as of November 2009.

103 In November 2009 the CBR issued three regulations: (1) Ordinance No. 2321-U "On Amending Bank of Russia Regulation No. 313-P, dated November 2007, on the Procedure for Calculating Market Risk by Credit Institutions", (2) Ordinance No. 2322-U of November 2009, "On Amending Bank of Russia Regulation No. 283-P, dated March 2006, on the Loss Provision Procedure for Credit Institutions", and (3) Ordinance No. 2323-U of 3 November 2009, "On Amending Bank of Russia Regulation No. 254-P, dated 26 March 2004, on the Procedure for Making by Credit Institution Provisions for Possible Losses on Loans, Loan and Similar Debts". This provided the necessary changes regarding the transition within the framework of the capital adequacy calculation system.

104 Operational risk is connected with the conclusion and execution of deals, organisational issues and the implementation of business processes in a bank.

105 This situation was aggravated by the weak accounting and enforcement standards in Russia compared to the strict enforcement of the accounting standards by the BRSA in Turkey. These issues will be explained in detail in the following sections regarding disciplinary power of the regulatory authority and private monitoring practices in both countries.

distorting the overall asset quality of the banking sector. In fact, the total funding of restructuring measures amounted to $0.52 billion (16 billion roubles) in Russia (a very modest amount compared to the usual banking sector restructuring costs which arise following deep banking crises) (Steinherr et al., 2004). The total cost of the restructuring of the Turkish banking sector was $53.6 billion which was almost equivalent to one third of the national income (BRSA, 2010).

Table 22 shows some of the developments in the balance sheet activities of both countries' banking sectors during 2001 and 2005. The table shows that the Turkish banks recovered more quickly than the Russian banks in terms of the achievement of financial intermediation in their respective post-crisis periods. In fact, Russia experienced further crises in 2004 and in 2008. Looking at the non-performing loan (NPL) ratios in both countries, we see that in Turkey this ratio was very low during the global crisis compared to Russia (see Table 23).[106]

The 2010 IMF Report emphasises that generous accounting and provisioning rules continue to mask the extent of systemic risks, the severity of the deterioration of the loan portfolio, and the adequacy of capital in the Russian banking sector. The report insists on strengthening the loan classification and provisioning system, which are important for the health of a loan portfolio and for understanding a bank's capital adequacy (IMF, 2010).

Table 22. Banking sector indicators in Turkey and Russia 2001–2005

	Russian Banking Sector				Turkish Banking Sector			
	Assets/ GDP	Capital/ GDP	Loans/ GDP	Deposits/ GDP	Assets/ GDP	Capital/ GDP	Loans/ GDP	Deposits/ GDP
2001	35.3	5.1	14.8	7.6	95.9	8.6	21	66.1
2002	38.3	5.4	16.6	9.5	77.3	9.3	17.8	50.2
2003	42.3	6.2	20.3	11.5	70	10	18.6	43.5
2004	42.1	5.6	22.9	11.7	71.4	10.7	23.2	44.6
2005	45.1	5.7	25.3	12.8	81.6	11	30.8	50

Source: CBR Banking Supervision Reports (2001–2006), Caner et al. (2007).

Table 23. Non-performing loans to total gross loans 2003–2011

	2003	2004	2005	2006	2007	2008	2009	2010	2011
Turkey	11.5	6	5	3.9	3.6	3.8	5.6	3.8	3.1
Russia	5	3.8	2.6	2.4	2.5	3.8	9.5	8.2	8

Source: The World Bank (2003–2011), http://data.worldbank.org/indicator/FB.AST.NPER.ZS/countries?page=2.

106 In fact, the NPL to total gross loans decreased from 29.3% in 2001 to 3.1% in 2011 (World Bank).

Although above the minimum required level, the average capital adequacy ratios of Russian banks had a declining trend between 2000 and 2006, compared to the increasing trend of CAR in the Turkish banking sector during the same period (see Table 19). More importantly, some banks were not able to meet the minimum requirement ratio. The annual CBR banking supervision reports repeatedly refer to violations of capital adequacy requirements by several banks. Conversely, despite close scrutiny by Turkish authorities, there has been no publicly reported breach by a Turkish bank of the BRSA imposed capital adequacy requirements.

3.2. OFFICIAL DISCIPLINARY POWER

As explained in Chapter 1,[107] the public interest view argues that bank supervisors can overcome market imperfections. Strong official supervision in the public interest view contributes to preventing banks from engaging in overly risky behaviour and hence improves banks performance and stability. An independent supervisory agency would be able to insulate regulators from political pressures and from bankers (Barth et al, 2006: 55). This argument is also supported by my results of the empirical analysis, which showed that higher official disciplinary power is positively and significantly associated with higher efficiency results.

Following Pasiouras (2008),[108] the *official disciplinary power* variable used in the empirical analysis of this research measures the extent to which official supervisory authorities have the authority to take specific actions to prevent and correct problems in the banking sector. It is analysed in three sections: *Prompt corrective power* measures the extent to which the law establishes predetermined levels of bank solvency deterioration that force automatic enforcement actions, such as intervention, and the extent to which supervisors have the requisite, and suitable powers to do so. *Restructuring power* measures the extent to which supervisory authorities have the power to restructure and reorganise troubled banks. *Declaring insolvency power* measures the extent to which supervisory authorities have the power to declare a deeply troubled bank insolvent (see Table 24).[109]

107 See section 5.1.

108 See Appendix A.

109 Barth et al. (2001a; 2006: 121–132) decompose *official supervisory action variable* into five parts. However, since the empirical analysis in this research is based on the questions selected by Pasiouras (2008), I only include one part of the questions which is *the official supervisory power.* Other parts are titled as Supervisory Forbearance Discretion, Loan Classification Stringency Provisioning Stringency Diversification Index. *Supervisory forbearance discretion* measures the degree to which supervisory authorities may engage in forbearance when confronted with violations of laws or regulations or with other imprudent behaviour on the part of banks. Since forbearance is a long-standing problem in Russia, I will touch upon this part in brief.

Table 24. Components of official disciplinary power

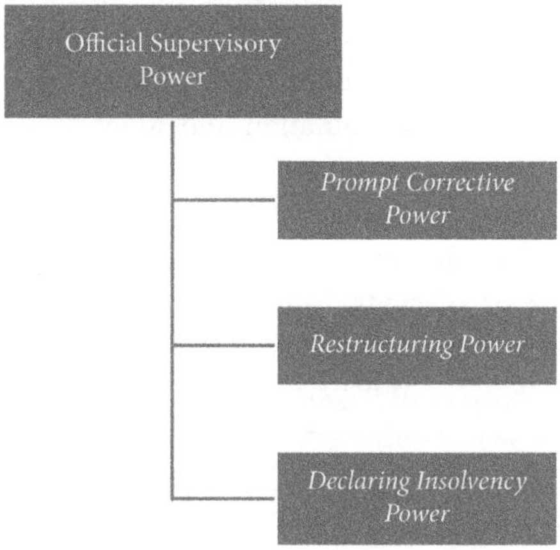

On top of the prudential regulations and banking laws, establishing a sound supervisory regime is very important in ensuring their implementation and compliance by the banks (Cetin, 2009; Hüpkes, 2000). Hüpkes states (2000: 31–32): "If it is determined by the supervisory authority that a bank does not comply with prudential requirements, this contravention must be addressed immediately and sufficiently before it leads to more serious problems". Lastra (2006) adds that supervision is a process that starts from the beginning of the business life of a supervised entity and continues until its end and it consists of four stages: *licensing, supervision, sanctioning* and *crisis management*. Based on this fact, the sanctioning process is crucial regarding the enforcement of prudential regulations because the success of banking regulations depends on their effective efficient enforcement (Lastra, 2006;[110] Hüpkes, 2000: 31). According to Hüpkes (2000), enforcement of prudential regulations might comprise remedial measures against a bank or its directors, managers and shareholders. Following these arguments, penalties and sanctions for failures to comply with the regulations should be clearly specified in a banking law (Cetin, 2011).

Examining the role of the regulatory/supervisory agency becomes especially important when it comes to analysing two emerging markets such as Russia and Turkey where the way of doing business and banking in the form of corruption and connected lending used to be considered normal practices of doing

[110] The categorisation of sanctions by Lastra (2006) is very similar to the classification of Barth, et al. (2001b) I used in my empirical analysis in terms of their content. The first category refers to "*institutional sanctions*" such as financial penalties, cease and desist orders, prompt corrective actions, and revocation of licences. The second category refers to "*personal sanctions*" such as temporary or permanent inability to be a banker, fines, loss of job, call of attention, management overhaul, and imprisonment that directly penalises the management (Lastra, 2006: 89).

business.[111] However, whereas this continues to be a major problem in Russia, doing banking in Turkey has transformed itself with the establishment of the BRSA. Kaymak (2009) argues that the BRSA case shows its originality as an emerging country banking regulatory and supervisory authority. The BRSA experience shows that banking regulation and supervision requires more than enacting laws to founding supervisory and regulatory authorities, making it very important for an emerging market economy to comply with the proposed standards and regulations (Kaymak, 2009).

Following the crisis periods, although both countries needed much improvement in their regulatory frameworks, (especially with regard to connected-lending practices, transparency and consolidated accounts), the key problem had been the lack of enforcement rather than the regulatory framework (Steinherr et al., 2004; Steinherr, 2006). One difference between the two countries is that the 2001 crisis in Turkey shifted the focus of the newly born BRSA from supervision to restructuring and rehabilitation in the first place whereas in Russia, there was no official program for more than four years with any serious restructuring plan. The requirements for a successful banking restructuring were not met (Steinherr et al., 2004; Thiessen, 2004). Thiessen (2004) argues that following the 1998 crisis, the banking system was rather stabilised through central bank credit and forbearance in rule enforcement of the CBR.[112] After the 1998 crisis, the CBR provided liquidity to banks that faced liquidity problems. However, these measures were flawed because the process was not transparent and the criteria in selecting the banks that received support from the government was not defined. Besides, there was no control regarding the use of provided funds (Thiessen, 2004). In fact, Thiessen (2004) argues that the CBR and the government were not successful in promptly implementing a transparent bank restructuring program (even over several years after the 1998 crisis) and enforcing prudential regulations for banks such as the enforcement of liability for any overdue debt. In spite of the Bankruptcy Law that came into effect in March 1998, many large enterprises or large debtors to producers continued to enjoy leniency. As a result, the leniency of the CBR in terms of the violation of prudential rules, and its provision of uncollateralised "stabilisation credits" to banks in very generous amounts, (mostly uncollateralised) created incentives for bank managers to lobby for further leniency and government support, to continue to take high risks and to distribute profits in spite of the solvency problems (Thiessen, 2004).

In the end, most of the bankrupt banks were not liquidated after the 1998 crisis. In fact, compared to other countries that wound down 20–40% of their

111 See section 2.1.1 and 2.3.1.

112 Based on Beck's (2004) empirical analysis' findings, Steinherr (2006) argues that the limited effect of the 1998 crisis on the growth rates is due to good luck provided by the real devaluation of the rouble and the increase in the world market price of oil. Therefore the failures became less visible. This argument is also supported by Thiessen (2004).

banks following a crisis, the Russian banking system experienced only a 12% decline in the number of its banks over the year following the 1998 crisis. Moreover, the number of licences withdrawn between the start of the crisis until the end of March 1999 is fewer than the number withdrawn in the same period of the previous year[113] (Ippolito, 2002) (see Table 17).[114] The number of institutions liquidated due to violation of legislation increased after the crisis. However, in spite of having lost their licences, many banks were not liquidated (Thiessen, 2004).[115]

Looking at the indexes concerning the disciplinary power, there is a considerable difference between Russia and Turkey, where the Turkish regulatory agency has a higher disciplinary power (see Table 25). BRSA has a rule-based approach (IFC, 2009). In contrast, Claeys et al. (2005) results indicate regulatory forbearance by the CBR. His argument is strengthened by Malyutina and Parilova (2001) who argue that although the CBR stated the prudential requirements, it did not apply them by tolerating their violations.

Table 25. Index on official disciplinary power in Turkey and Russia*

	1999	2000	2001	2002	2003	2004	2005	2006	2007	2008	2009	2010
Turkey	4	6	9	9	9	9	9	9	9	9	9	9
Russia	5	5	8	8	8	8	6	6	6	6	6	6

* This variable takes values between 0 and 10, with higher values indicating higher power of the supervisory authority.

3.2.1. *Official Disciplinary Power of the Banking Regulatory Authority in Turkey*

The Turkish Banking Law gives statutory recognition to two institutions in the banking sector: the Banking Regulations and Supervision Agency (BRSA) and the Savings Deposit Insurance Fund (SDIF) (Cetin, 2011). The Banking

113 The total number of revoked bank licences in 1998 was 152 compared to 282 in 1997 (CBR Report, December 1998 & December 1997). In 1999, licences of only 24 banks were revoked (CBR Report, January 2000).

114 Thiessen (2004) argues that the issue of forbearance might have its pros and cons relative to restructuring of a banking system. There can be an optimal degree of forbearance in a crisis situation depending on factors such as the nature of the shock and its degree of permanence and on the authorities' ability to carry out an effective restructuring program. But based on many country cases of banking crises used by the cited empirical literature on banking crises, which were examined individually, the literature finds that forbearance and delaying implementation of a comprehensive restructuring program tends to raise the real economic costs of such crises and only make things worse (Thiessen, 2004).

115 Thiessen (2004) adds that in the view of many observers the lack of government action with regard to implementing serious banking restructuring measures continued through several years after the crisis.

Regulation and Supervision Agency (BRSA) was established by the former Banks Act No. 4389 effective as of June 1999. Following the foundation of the BRSA, several regulations were introduced to improve its autonomy and accountability and to empower its administrative capacity.[116] Pursuant to the Banks Act (1999), the BRSA embodied all public institutions which were responsible for the banking sector's supervision.[117]

After the BRSA became fully operational in August 2000, all banking evaluation and supervision departments at the Treasury and the monitoring department at the Central Bank were closed, so that the overlaps between the Turkish Treasury and Central Bank in regulating the financial markets were brought to an end (Aysan & Al, 2007). Their personnel were transferred to the new agency. The Banks Act (1999) delegated to the BRSA the primary authority to regulate and supervise the Turkish banking sector (Cetin, 2011). This new structure gave the BRSA a wide range of authority in monitoring the conditions of all banks in Turkey through off-site analysis of bank balance sheets and income reports and through on-site examinations. In other words, its supervisory process was made stronger with the unification of on-site audit and off-site audit (Aysan & Al 2007; Altunbas et al., 2009: 55). Following the 2001 crisis, in addition to the banking restructuring program, the supervisory field of BRSA was expanded in order to increase the institutional capacity. All resolutions related to banks were given to the authority of BRSA. These included: (i) the principles and procedures related to the redefinition of loans, (ii) application of rules related to banks' consolidated audit in line with the international standards, and (iii) regular monitoring of banks' compliance with the requirements (Paksoy & Tiftikci, 2010).

Regarding on-site and off-site supervision of banks, the BRSA is authorised with extensive powers over the banks regarding (i) their compliance with the laws such as lending limits, capital and liquidity requirements and shareholding limits, (ii) the relation and balance between the consolidated and non-consolidated risk structures and internal control systems of the financial institutions and (iii) compliance with the corporate governance principles. In order to facilitate its supervision over the financial institutions, the BRSA may send (1) an observer to the general assembly meetings of the banks; (2) evaluate the structure, conformity and reliability of the annual financial reports prepared by the independent audit firms; and (3) request any consolidated and non-consolidated information (or financial statements) from banks and their subsidiaries, (including those classified as confidential) (Paksoy & Tiftikçi, 2010).

116 Following the establishment of BRSA, its autonomy and accountability was strengthened and the scope of its surveillance and supervision was expanded first by the Law No. 4491 in 19 December 1999 and then secondly by the Law No. 4743 dated 31 January 2002 (BRSA, 2010).

117 Pursuant to the Banks Act (1999), the SDIF was also administered and represented by the BRSA.

Although in its first years, the BRSA had to deal with the most urgent problem of the restructuring process, following the resolution process of troubled banks,[118] the BRSA continued to issue several prudential regulations to establish a sound regulatory framework (Kaymak, 2009).[119]

With the enactment of Act No. 5020 in December 2003, the management of the SDIF was separated from the management of the BRSA. Pursuant to this law,[120] the SDIF became a separate entity. More importantly, this Act provided a powerful framework for effectively penalising persons who are responsible for putting at risk and damaging the stability of the financial system by misbehaviour in management as well as persons causing loss to depositors. Bakır and Önis (2010) argue that the former legal environment was conducive to the establishment of a rent-seeking coalition through statutory decrees in banking. The authors indicate that the Statutory Decree No. 512 enacted in 1993 legally protected corrupt bank managers by: (1) removing their individual liability in unlawful acts, which would lead to loss and bankruptcy of a bank, and (2) removing the clause stipulating the exclusion of such bankers from any bank management activities. Hence, in order to create deterrence, Act No. 5020 brought heavy imprisonment and penalty relating to banking crimes (BRSA, 2010).

In 2003, the BRSA tightened branch supervision. It issued a regulation on support services. It increased the scope of audits by increasing the number of auditors conducting on-site supervision, made amendments in legislation to implement information systems audit in banks, issued regulations concerning internal systems and corporate management to establish transparency and accountability in internal audit, internal control and brought more severe rules in granting licences with amendments in legislation and brought tighter applications to off-shore banking (BRSA, 2010). In fact, every move and transaction of a bank became regulated.

The Banks Act (1999) was amended nine times following its introduction. Its systematic became deteriorated, and hence it was unable to support the sub-regulations. It became insufficient for a broad supervision and maintaining good governance. Therefore it was replaced by the Banking Law No. 5411 in 2005. This

118 According to the BRSA 2006 report, 20 banks were taken over by the SDIF and resolved from 1997 until 2003. 12 of these banks were found to be misusing their financial positions for the benefit of majority shareholders causing major significant losses. Besides, these bankers had taken loans from state banks and other SDIF banks as well. Hence, the total share of non-performing loans in the banking sector's gross loans was 29.3% as a result of these connected-lending practices (BRSA, 2006).

119 A number of regulations were issued and put into force on the following areas: capital adequacy, risk management, lending limits and loan loss provisioning, accounting standards, independent auditing, bank capital strengthening program, special finance institutions, and supervision and cooperation agreements with foreign supervisory authorities (BRSA, 2010).

120 The "Law on Making Amendments to Some Laws". The Law No. 5020 came into force in 26 December 2003. It was related to amendments in Certain Laws and Banks Act (1999).

law increased the scope of duties, authority and responsibilities of the BRSA because the regulation and supervision of non-bank financial institutions were transferred from the Treasury to the BRSA in January 2006. The aim was to improve consolidated supervision and facilitate integration in markets (BRSA, 2006; Steinherr et al., 2004).

The success of banking regulations depends on their effective enforcement (Lastra, 2006). Sanctions for failures to comply with prudential regulatory requirements must be clearly specified in the law as the efficiency of banking regulations depends on their effective enforcement (Lastra, 2006; Cetin, 2011). The current Banking Law (2005) consists of many prudential standards for banks. More importantly, the Banking Law (2005) established an effective sanctioning regime to ensure the implementation of these standards. Since one of the reasons of the crisis experienced in Turkey in 2001 was illegal practices conducted by managers and controlling shareholders, the Banking Law draws a comprehensive framework for the liability of these persons (Cetin, 2011). This law introduced personal liability and breach of the certain provisions of the law can constitute criminal liability.[121]

The implementation of prudential standards is monitored by the BRSA since the institutions under the scope of this Law and their activities are subject to supervision of the BRSA, and as such this supervisory power allows the BRSA to apply the sanctions specified in the Banking Law when a bank violates the regulatory requirements.[122]

The sanctioning regime in the Turkish Banking Law consists of *institutional sanctions* and *personal sanctions*. The institutional sanctions in the Banking Law consist of three categories; *prompt corrective actions*, *revocation of licence and closure*, and finally *financial penalties*. Personal sanctions consist of management overhaul and loss of job, temporary prohibition from employment in the banking sector, financial penalties, criminal liability, and civil liability of managers and controlling shareholders (Cetin, 2011) (Table 26).

Prompt corrective actions aim at dealing with banks in financial distress or banks that have breached regulatory requirements. This system allows the BRSA to take early action. It is worth noting that the codification of these measures is crucial to eliminate regulatory forbearance and the abuse of

---

121 The academic literature uses *deterrence-based enforcement theory* in explaining the social goal of enforcement policies. The foundations of this theory first appeared by Becker in 1968 and since then, Becker's theory has been accepted as a general law and economics framework for the analysis of law enforcement. The idea is that if market players act rationally in deciding whether to obey the law, enforcement policies must deter these players from law-breaking by creating an incentive scheme that makes them better-off obeying the law, rather than violating it. If people know that law-breaking triggers sanctions, they may be deterred from breaking the law (Ogus, 2004 in Oded (2012: 29–33).
For more on the deterrence-based enforcement theory, see Becker, (1968); Cooter & Ulen, (2007); Oded, (2012).

122 Article 65 of the Banking Law.

supervisors' discretion (Hüpkes, 2000: 36–37). The regulation of prompt corrective action specifies the pre-conditions to take *corrective, rehabilitating* and *restrictive* measures[123] under the Articles 68–70 of the Banking Law.[124] The evaluation takes place based on the financial situation of the bank (such as asset quality, profitability etc.) and based on the contravention of the prudential regulatory requirements such as the capital adequacy requirement, liquidity requirement etc.[125] If the pre-conditions have already occurred as ascertained by the BRSA, then the agency shall require the bank to take the necessary measures immediately. The aim of this design is to create an early-warning system.

Table 26. Sanctioning regime in Turkey

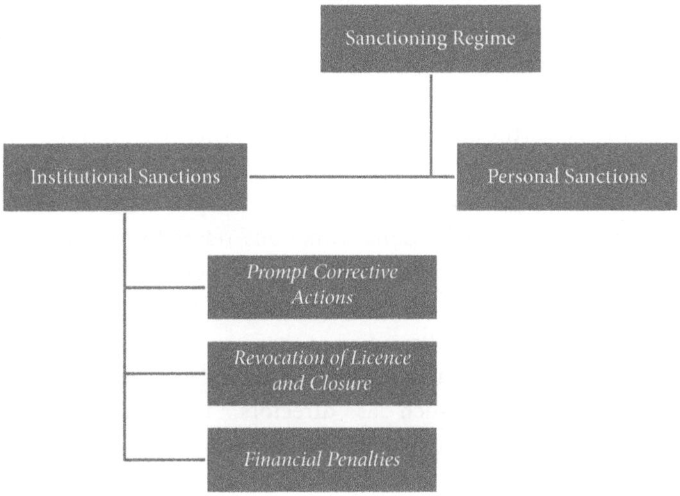

However, if the bank under supervision has not taken those measures, or has been unsuccessful even with the measures, then the BRSA starts the licence revocation process. Article 68 gives the BRSA the power to call on the board of directors of the relevant bank to take and implement corrective measures specified in the Law as deemed appropriate by the BRSA, within the time period

123 The regulation of prompt corrective action is codified in detail in the Banking Law under "Supervision and Measures to be Taken"; Articles 68–70 of the Banking Law.

124 In cases where: (i) the assets of a bank are unlikely to meet its obligations in terms of maturity or the bank doesn't comply with the capital adequacy or liquidity requirements; (ii) the profitability of a bank is not sufficient to reliably perform its activities due to the distorted balance between revenues and expenses; (iii) the quality of a banks' assets has deteriorated and its financial structure is likely to weaken; (iv) the decision and practices of the bank breach the legislation; and (v) the bank fails to establish its internal control system or fails to operate the system efficiently (Paksoy & Tiftikci, 2012).

125 Article 67 of the Banking Law (2005) specifies these conditions in detail under "Cases where measures are required to be taken".

approved by the BRSA. If the bank fails to implement the measures laid down in Article 68, and the bank has more serious financial problems than the ones subject to corrective measures, then the BRSA has the authority to force the bank to take more radical and stronger measures under Article 69 called "rehabilitating measures".

"Restrictive measures"[126] is the last component of the prompt corrective actions to be taken. They directly affect the activities of the bank and are designed to prevent the financial failure of a bank that may spread within the whole banking system. These measures are interpreted as a last resort for banks before closure since they intend to keep the bank in the system by imposing several restrictions (Cetin, 2011). These measures include restricting or to temporarily suspending the bank's activities, dismissing some or all of the general managers, relevant unit or branch directors, sometimes even the board of directors. The prompt corrective action system aims at enabling a bank in financial distress to continue its activities in a sound manner and bring it back to viability. However, if these measures are not sufficient to prevent the failure of the bank, the BRSA has the power[127] of *revocation of licence and closure*[128] in order to protect financial stability and depositors' rights (Cetin, 2011; Banking Law, 2005).

The third part of the institutional sanctions refers to *financial penalties*[129] which specify the reasons and the amount of the penalties. The BRSA has the right to impose financial penalties on banks when they breach regulatory requirements (Banking Law, 2005).

Other than the institutional sanctions, banking laws may also impose some sanctions against persons such as directors, managers and controlling shareholders who fail to comply with the regulatory requirements (Hüpkes, 2000:41). These sanctions are called *personal sanctions*. Their purpose is to directly penalise the management or the controlling shareholders. In the Turkish Banking Law (2005), personal sanctions are specified under five titles: management overhaul and loss of job;[130] temporary prohibition from employment in the banking sector;[131] financial penalties;[132] criminal liability; and civil liability of managers and controlling shareholders.[133]

126 Article 70 of the Banking Law (2005).

127 Pursuant to the Article 71 of the Banking Law (2005).

128 "Revocation of license and closure" refers to the second part of institutional sanctions (See Table 25).

129 Financial penalties are laid down in Articles 146 and 148 of the Banking Law (2005).

130 Banking Act Article 68/1-a and 69/1-and Banking Act Article 70/1-c.

131 Banking Act Article 26/2.

132 Banking Act Article 18/1, 2 and 4, Banking Act art. 36, Banking Act art. 38.

133 These sanctions are laid down in Articles 106–110, 132–143 and 146–161 in the Banking Law (2005).

3.2.2. *Official Disciplinary Power of the Banking Regulatory Authority in Russia*

The Central Bank of Russia (CBR) is the primary authority responsible for the regulation of the banking sector in Russia and also acts as Russia's central bank. Until 2002, the CBR had been operating under the general terms of the Federal Law on the Central Bank of the Russian Federation (the Bank of Russia)[134] of 2 December 1990. This law was superseded by the Central Bank Law in 2002. The legal framework for banking supervision consists of the Federal Law on the Central Bank of the Russian Federation of 2002 (later it came to be called the Central Bank Law) and the Federal Law on Banks and Banking Activity promulgated in 1990 (later on it was referred to as the Banking Law).[135]

Banks are regulated under Chapter 10 of the Banking Law. According to the CBR Law and the Banking Law (BL), responsibility for the licensing and supervision of banks belong to the CBR. The CBR is also authorised to approve permissible activities, issue regulations, and enforce compliance with laws and regulations (IMF, 2011c).

As explained above, the first component of the official disciplinary power refers to the *prompt corrective actions* which aim at dealing with banks in financial distress or banks that breached regulatory requirements. Corrective actions enable supervisors to act at an early stage to address unsafe and unsound activities that could create risks to banks. Hence, the codification of these measures is crucial to eliminate the regulatory forbearance and abuse of discretion. The supervisors should also be possessed with an adequate range of supervisory tools to bring about timely actions (Hüpkes, 2006: 36–37; BIS, 2011). The powers of the CBR regarding *supervisory corrective actions* against credit institutions are established in the Federal Law (ECB, 2005).[136]

Regarding *restructuring power* in Russia, following the 1998 crisis, the Russian government and the CBR adopted a key policy document "On Measures to Restructure the Russian Banking System" which established the guidelines for the legislature and the extent of power of the CBR to restructure the banking sector. The amendments made to banking legislation in 2001 broadened the powers of the CBR to withdraw financially unsound banks from the market, before their financial problems would make them unable to serve their obligations to creditors (CBR, 2002). According to the Article 74 of the Banking

134 As amended on 26 April 1995.

135 Russian Federation Federal Law On the Central Bank of the Russian Federation (Bank of Russia).

136 "On the Central Bank of the Russian Federation" (in Articles 73 and 75), the Federal Law "On Banks and Banking" (in Articles 19, 20, 23.1), and the Federal Law "On Insolvency (bankruptcy) of credit institutions (in Articles 4, 7–17, 32,33 and 35 and the regulations of the Bank of Russia implementing them; the latter include, the Instruction No. 59 of the Bank of Russia "On corrective actions against credit institutions" (ECB, 2005).

Law, the CBR has the power to prohibit the reorganisation of a credit institution if its reorganisation may create grounds for the implementation of bankruptcy-prevention measures under the Federal Law on Insolvency (Bankruptcy) of Credit Institutions.[137]

The corrective actions set in the CBR Law[138] and the Banking Law[139] have several limitations. Firstly, the CBR lacks the authority to enforce cease-desist type orders whose infraction leads to automatic imposition of civil and penal sanctions on banks' directors and managers (Melecky et al. (2010).[140] The CBR lacks the authority to penalise or sanction individual bank directors (compared to Turkey where the bank directors have personal liability for misleading information). Secondly, Melecky et al. (2010) argue that the Russian banking supervisors are not required to make timely disclosure of enforcement actions. The enforcement tools given by the CBR Law do not allow for sufficient options to report imprudent practices at an early stage (IMF, 2011c). The 2008 IMF report also emphasises that the CBR lacks the authority to intervene at an early stage so as to minimise the cost of resolution and the disruption to creditors, including depositors.[141] Although the current legislative framework provides the CBR with the authority to intervene in commercial banks, including removing bank management, CBR still has limited ability to impose bankruptcy on commercial banks (IMF 2006). Hence, the CBR should be given more authority (IMF 2010). Thirdly, the CBR doesn't have the power to reduce or suspend the distribution of bonuses and other remuneration such as management fees to bank directors and managers (Melecky et al., 2010). It also lacks the power to establish limits on salaries paid out to directors and key bank personnel (IMF, 2011a) (compared to Turkey where the BRSA has the power to establish limits on dividends, bonuses and management fees).

The problem of regulatory forbearance has been emphasised in most of the IMF Reports for Russia. In fact, Malyutina & Parilova (2001) argue that the

---

137 Law No. 144-FZ "On the Restructuring of Credit Institutions" dated 8 July 1999 establishes the procedure for restructuring of credit institutions by implementing measures to overcome their financial instability and restore solvency or liquidate them in compliance with the Russian legislation.

138 Article 74 of the CBR Law.

139 Article 20 of the Banking Law.

140 They argue that Russia is the only BRIC country unequipped with legally enforced cease and desist orders.

141 In Russia, the following actions can be taken against banks: preventive actions through letters, meetings or consultations, penalties; actions restricting the activities of the banks; replacement of managers and revocation of banking licences. However, this range of power given to the CBR is less than recommended by the Basel Committee of Banking Supervision (BCBS). According to the Supervisory Guidelines for Dealing with Weak Banks (prepared by the Basel Committee of Banking Supervision in 2002), banking supervisors are empowered with 16 supervisory corrective actions. However, the CBR uses only nine of them. Not all the criteria for selecting corrective actions are applied in Russia. Besides, the actions taken are usually inadequate (ECB, 2005).

Russian banks enjoyed regulatory forbearance because the violation of prudential requirements has not been followed by timely licence withdrawal after the 1998 crisis. The CBR withdrew a licence only after a bank had been violating prudential ratios for a long time. This fact continued to be a problem since the 1998 crisis. According to the 2002 IMF Report, although there was a system of business laws including corporate, bankruptcy, contract, consumer protection and private property laws, and although the objectives and the institutional framework for regulation and supervision are broadly defined in the Banking Law, this system was neither consistently enforced nor provided a mechanism for fair resolutions in a timely manner. The changes in laws were not always accompanied by immediate reviews of regulations and guidelines.[142] The report recommended that the banking legislation should include provisions so that the banking supervision authority would gain sufficient power for prompt action.

Regarding the last component of disciplinary power, the CBR lacks the authority to declare bank insolvency. The power of declaring a bank insolvent in Russia is legally in the hands of courts where court approval is required for declaring insolvency (compared to Turkey where the BRSA has the power to declare bank insolvency) (Barth et al., 2012). Hence, the CBR is limited in superseding shareholders' rights (IMF 2006; Melecky et al., 2010). Finally, CBR lacks the power to require a bank to meet supervisory requirements (e.g. capital, liquidity etc.) that are stricter than the legal or regulatory minimum (compared to Turkey where the BRSA possess this power) (Barth et al., 2013). These limitations on the extent of power of CBR have a negative impact on discipline in dealing with problem banks (Melecky et al., 2010).[143]

The authority of CBR is deficient in preventing transactions between the bank and its affiliates as well. It lacks the regulatory power to require that lending to related parties should be done at market terms and sanction banks that do not comply. The regulatory framework for related party transactions has some shortcomings in the sense that it does not require that lending to related parties

[142] One of the amendments made to the Law was the development of an early warning system by the CBR. However, the analytical work done by the supervisors did not concentrate on the credit institutions that needed special attention. They ignored the risks reflected in the reviews (IMF FSSA, 2002).

[143] CBR lacks authority also in these areas: (i) suspending shareholders from participation in the management of the credit organisation, including their right to vote or accept dividends; (ii) requiring additional capital levels to be maintained against the risks specific to the bank, except to impose higher CAR as a sanction for violations of federal law; and (iii) requiring prior consent of the supervisory authority to incur a major expenditure or take on a new liability. Although Article 75 of the Federal Law on the Central Bank of Russian Federation stipulates that the Bank of Russia may take corrective actions under Article 74 of the said Law in case the assessment of a bank reveals any situation which would threaten the interests of depositors and creditors or the stability of the banking system, the Law does not explicitly recognise the right of the Bank of Russia to take supervisory corrective actions against credit institutions based on professional supervisory judgement (IMF, 2011a).

should be on the same terms and conditions as those offered to the public. Although the CBR has issued recommendations to banks on related party lending, they lack enforcement capacity (IMF, 2011a, 2011c). The narrow definition of related parties and connected relationships prevents the CBR from applying limits or imposing supervisory restrictions. Hence, appropriate powers should be given to the CBR to sanction and remove the persons affiliated with banks. This would have a strong signalling effect to deter other banks (IMF, 2011a).

Despite the fact that banking reforms were progressing, the actual implementation was slow and the problems of regulatory forbearance, enforcement of prudential standards and weaknesses in the resolution and crisis management framework, continued to be a problem in Russia (IMF, 2005, 2006, 2010). The weakness of the CBR in enforcement became evident in the 2004 mini-crisis, which revealed the need for the CBR to have more effective instruments to strengthen banking supervision and deal with problem banks. It was understood that there had only been very limited progress in implementing banking reforms since the 1998 crisis, notwithstanding the recent steps to strengthen the enforcement of prudential norms.[144] In fact, the 2003 IMF Report insisted on the need of the CBR to move to forcefully close those banks which were non-viable and overburdened with connected lending.

Taking into account the lessons of the 2008–2009 crisis, the CBR started to prepare proposals to receive sufficient power to require credit institutions to maintain their capital at a specified level, to make the management and directors of banks accountable for their performance and to sanction them. Russian lawmakers continue to legislate additional powers to the Bank of Russia with regards to the use of sanctions against credit institution chief executives and owners (CBR, 2009). In fact, long-standing weaknesses in banking supervision and regulation allowed rapid credit expansion and accumulation of large unhedged foreign exchange exposures in the run-up to the crisis. Prudential regulations to limit credit booms and greater powers for the CBR to supervise banks are needed (IMF, 2010). The 2011 IMF Report emphasises that the CBR lacks the legal authority to implement the supervisory process (Pillar 2 component) of Basel II (IMF, 2011a).

3.2.3. *Discussion*

The efficiency of a regulation determines the possibility of banks' exposure to excessive risk-taking behaviour (Malyutina & Parilova, 2001). Followed by that, the stance of a regulator significantly affects the behaviour of a bank (Mailath & Mester, 1994). However, the CBR's policy has been criticised for being passive

144 In fact, the IMF officials warned the CBR staff about the possibility of a major crisis in the future.

before and after the 1998 crisis compared to the BRSA's policy in the post-crisis period. As argued in Perotti (2000), Malyutina and Parilova (2001), Steinherr (2006), and Steinherr and Klär (2005), the main reason of the Russian crisis in 1998 was the imprudent behaviour of banks, encouraged by poor law enforcement and the absence of prudential regulation, which continued to be the case even after the crisis. Many banks violated the prudential ratios specified in the CBR's regulations; however they did not lose their licences. The qualitative analysis shows that the Turkish banking regulatory authority had implemented its restructuring power tools in a more disciplined way than the Russian regulatory authority in their respective post-crisis period.

More importantly, the qualitative analysis shows that the Turkish banking regulatory authority is empowered with a wider range of authorities than the Russian regulatory authority. The bank standards established by a regulatory authority would create the desired effect on preventing banks' risk-taking, if banks anticipate that these standards will be enforced. This proper enforcement involves licence withdrawal as the ultimate penalty for banks which repeatedly violate the rules (Schoors et al., 2005). However, the analysis regarding the power of the Russian banking regulatory authority (the CBR) shows that the enforcement authority of the CBR is deficient in several areas compared to the Turkish regulatory authority.

One major difference is that the CBR is unequipped with legally enforced cease and desist orders and that it lacks the power to sanction directors personally for non-compliance (even with regulations). In fact, the 2011 IMF report argues that because of this lack of power, the CBR is unable to enforce related party regulations. Additionally, the CBR lacks the authority to penalise a bank for non-compliance. The CBR's existing powers towards related borrowers are not in the form of supporting laws or regulations. Its ability to identify connected borrowers[145] on the basis of a "legal" relationship prevents the consideration of other, potentially binding "economic" relationships between connected parties (IMF 2011).

However, in Turkey bank directors are legally liable for misleading information. The enactment of Law No. 5020 in Turkey provided a powerful basis for penalising the persons who are responsible for risking the stability of financial system by misbehaviour in management. In addition to expanding the scope of regulation, this Act brought heavy imprisonment and penalty relating to banking crimes. Regarding connected-lending practices, new regulations implemented after the 200/2001 crisis introduced the concept of a "risk group" and replaced the narrow definition of the previous period which led to abuse of connected lending practices. The amount of exposure a bank can take with each

145 Connected-lending or lending to related parties occurs when a bank lends to its own shareholders or managers, including also the entities controlled by them or their family members (Bredenkamp et al.).

risk group has been determined very specifically. These limits are being monitored by the BRSA and the relevant information is also included in the publicly-disclosed audit financial statements (Steinherr et al., 2004).[146] Compared to Turkey, connected lending practice is regarded as a serious problem in Russia according to the 2011 IMF Report. Narrow definition of related parties and connected relationships prevents the CBR from applying limits or imposing supervisory restrictions.

Other differences in the power of Turkish and Russian banking regulatory authorities concern the power to suspend directors' decisions to distribute bonuses and management fees, declaring bank insolvency, requiring banks to meet supervisory requirements (e.g. capital, liquidity etc.) that are stricter than the legal or regulatory minimum. These limitations on the extent of power of the CBR have a negative impact on discipline in dealing with problem banks (Melecky et al, 2010).

These results suggest that the Turkish supervisory authority has more power than the Russian supervisory authority. Whereas enforcement in Russia seems to be a long-standing problem accompanied by the limitations granted to the CBR supervisory power, stricter disciplining power of the BRSA in Turkey contributed to the proper enforcement of banking law and regulations. This finding supports my empirical result on the positive impact of supervisory power on banks' efficiency.

3.3. PRIVATE MONITORING

Private monitoring is the third pillar of Basel II and aims at creating a market disciplining mechanism.[147] However, there is limited research in the literature about the costs and benefits of financial reporting and disclosure requirements. In addition, there is little guidance on the economic consequences of reporting and corporate disclosure (Leuz & Wysocki, 2008). In general, there are disagreements about the role of the private sector in monitoring banks. Barth et al. (2002) argue that the complexity and opacity of banks may make private sector monitoring difficult even in the most developed economies. Having this in mind, less-developed countries with poorly developed capital markets, weak accounting standards and legal environment may not be able to rely effectively on private monitoring since it may lead to exploitation of depositors and poor bank performance (Barth et al., 2002). This is in line with the findings in the empirical chapter that a higher degree of private oversight is negatively associated with banks' efficiency.[148] Barth et al. (2001b) find that the degree of

[146] The 2007 IMF report on Turkey's financial assessment recommends the BRSA to continue with the current limits.

[147] See Chapter 1, section 6.1.1.

[148] See Chapter 2, section 7.2.

private monitoring decreases as one moves from high income countries to lower income countries.[149]

Following Pasiouras (2008),[150] I measured private monitoring variables based on three indicators: (i) whether an outside licensed audit is required of the financial statements issued by the banks; (this would indicate the presence or absence of an independent assessment of the accuracy of financial statements released to the public); (ii) whether regulations require credit ratings for commercial banks (this would make the public aware of the overall condition of the banking industry as viewed by an independent third party); (iii) whether the income statements of banks include accrued[151] interest and principal on non-performing loans and whether banks are required to produce consolidated financial statements; (iv) whether banks must disclose their risk management policies and off-balance sheet items to the public;[152] and (v) whether directors are legally liable for erroneous information (Barth et al., 2001b). Looking at Turkey's and Russia's overall indexes in private sector monitoring, we see that until 2001 they both had the same degree. From 2001 until 2005, Russia's degree of private sector monitoring was higher than in Turkey's. However, from 2005 until 2010, Turkey had a higher degree of private oversight (see Table 27).

Table 27. Indexes on private monitoring in Turkey and Russia*

	1999	2000	2001	2002	2003	2004	2005	2006	2007	2008	2009	2010
Turkey	5	5	6	6	6	6	7	7	7	7	7	7
Russia	5	5	7	7	7	7	6	6	6	6	6	6

* This variable takes values between 0 and 10, higher values indicating policies that promote private monitoring.

There are in fact some differences in the measures. Starting in 2005, Turkish banks became obligated to disclose their risk management procedures to the public. This is not a requirement in Russia. Secondly, compared to Russia, directors of Turkish banks have been held legally liable for misleading information since 2005.

3.3.1. Private Monitoring in the Turkish Banking Sector

Turkey had a weak risk-management culture towards the end of the 1990s. This became evident in the 2000/2001 crisis when significant internal audit and risk

149 The UK is an exception. In fact, Barth et al. (2008) found that the UK authorities weakened private monitoring slightly.

150 See Appendix A.

151 Or unpaid.

152 Pasiouras (2008) also includes whether banks are required to disclose their off-balance sheet items to supervisors. See Appendix A.

management weaknesses emerged. The risks realised increased the losses in the balance sheets and hence caused the own funds of banks to deteriorate quickly.[153] The loss in the banking sector was around 10.5 billion TL,[154] corresponding to approximately 6% of the total assets of the banking sector. 19 banks were transferred to the SDIF due to the erosion of their equity (BRSA, 2010).

Private monitoring practices include internal control and audit practices, establishing a solid accounting system to provide for transparency of the banks' financial statements, information disclosure and consolidated supervision. The objective of these tools is to enable market participants such as creditors and investors to have a sufficient understanding of banks' operations.[155]

3.3.1.1. Internal Control and Audit Practices in Turkey

The objective of an internal audit is to analyse whether banks' assets are protected and whether the operations are carried out in compliance with policies in place. In this context, an internal audit is necessary to improve the risk management and control and governance processes. Banks use internal audit to evaluate their overall financial and non-financial operations. Internal audit of banks in Turkey is carried out by *the internal control unit, the audit unit* and *the risk management group* of the banks (Gencoglu et al., 2011).

One of the problems that led banks to financial losses during the 2001 crisis was the deficiency in internal audit systems, because error and fraud in banks' operations were not detected. The first steps regarding risk management practices in the Turkish banking sector were taken with the Restructuring Process after the 2001 crisis under the "Operational Restructuring of Public Banks". In February 2001 the Regulation on Internal Audit and Risk Management Systems of Banks was published. Pursuant to this regulation,[156] banks became required to establish internal audit and risk management systems and became obligated to report their activities quarterly. As a result, the reports started being analysed regularly and developments were monitored closely (BRSA, 2010). Pursuant to this regulation, banks are required to determine

---

153 The level of own funds which was already low had further decreased. Inflation accounting was not applied and the high inflation environment encouraged activity with foreign resources instead of own funds, which had affected the level and the quality of the own funds negatively. Furthermore, due to the unstable structure of the Turkish economy during the 2000–2001 period, the fund supply of the banking sector from international markets remained limited (BRSA, 2010).

154 10.5 billion YTL corresponds to approximately €4.5 billion.

155 See Chapter 1, section 6.1.3.

156 This regulation exists in the Banking Law (2005) under Article 29. Additionally, according to the Article 30 of the Banking Law (2005) internal control activities shall be carried out by the internal control department and the internal control personnel under the board of directors.

limits to risk that might emerge from their operations. These limits need to be approved by the Board of Directors (Gencoglu et al., 2011).[157]

With the Regulation on Internal Systems of Banks which became effective in 2006, banks were obliged to implement an internal auditing system, and conduct continuous audits together with periodic inspection (BRSA, 2010).[158] The audit unit periodically audits all domestic and foreign units, branches and affiliates. It controls whether these activities are conducted in accordance with the law and regulations. The risk management unit is responsible for the identification, measurement, monitoring and control of risk through policies.[159]

Regarding the external auditing of banks, a regulation on external audit was issued in January 2002 to determine the procedures and principles of external audit in compliance with the international standards (BRSA, 2010).[160] The BRSA, the Saving Deposit Insurance Fund (SDIF), the Banks Association of Turkey (BAT), the Central Bank in Turkey (CBRT) and independent external audit firms are the institutions that perform external audits of banks. The working principles of the independent audit firms are established by the BRSA (Gencoglu et al., 2011). If an audit firm detects any violation of law or any matter that might endanger the bank's existence, it shall notify the BRSA.[161] The aim of having an independent audit firm is to determine whether the banks' financial reports are prepared in line with the generally accepted accounting rules.[162] Henceforth, these reports have different qualifications from the reports prepared by the internal bank auditors (Delikanlı, 1998). The BRSA, as the principal regulatory authority, has the right to review these independent audit reports (Paksoy & Tiftikci, 2010).[163]

Following the 2001 crisis, Turkish authorities realised the importance of building a risk management approach in accordance with the international banking regulations. The effectiveness of internal audit, internal control and risk

157 For more on risks banks are subject to, see Chapter 1, section 2.4.

158 Accordingly, internal control systems and operations shall be presented by the internal control unit and top managements of related units.

159 Regulation on Banks' Internal Systems, 2006; Article 35.

160 This regulation was accompanied by a second regulation on external audit to increase the transparency of external audit application (BRSA, 2010). Regulation on External Audit Procedures, Regulation on External Audit Principles and Regulation on Authorization of Institutions to Perform External Audit and Termination of Authorities Temporarily or Permanently Thereof were issued on 31 January 2002.

161 Article 33 of the Banking Law (2005).

162 Generally Accepted Accounting Rules are the set of systematic guidelines used by auditors when conducting audits on banks' financial statements. These standards ensure the accuracy, and verifiability of the audit reports.

163 Banks are also required to submit these independent audit reports to the Central Bank. Prior to the Banks Act of 1999, the supervision was conducted by the Treasury and the Central Bank. In accordance with the Regulation on Authorization and Activities of Institutions to Perform External Audit in Banks published in 2006, banks are required to select an audit firm.

management systems have gained considerable importance so that the Turkish authorities introduced several regulations to improve the risk management of banks. However, Gencoglu et al. (2011) argue that the audit procedures are not very effective in the Turkish banking sector regarding the number of auditors, their technical knowledge and also political barriers. This argument can be related to the results of my empirical analysis suggesting a negative impact of private monitoring on banks' efficiency. The ineffective implementation of audit procedures might have an increasing impact on operational costs of a bank and hence negatively affect its efficiency.

3.3.1.2. Disclosure Requirements

As explained in the first chapter of this book,[164] the objective of disclosure requirements is to mitigate the asymmetric information problem in the banking industry. To ensure that depositors and other market participants have access to information about a bank's portfolio and degree of risk exposure, regulators can require banks to adhere to certain accounting principles and disclose a wide range of information about their financials. More public information about the risk profile and the quality of a bank's portfolio is likely to have a deterrent effect on banks' risk taking behaviour through increased market discipline since depositors and other creditors will be able to monitor and evaluate banks activities at a lower cost (Tchana, 2008; Frankel & Li, 2004; Mishkin, 2000).

Disclosure requirements in the forms of financial reporting are important in evaluating a bank's financial status because they reduce asymmetric information problems by disclosing timely and accurate information (Frankel & Li, 2004). In that context, accounting quality contributes to the quality of financial reporting (Sonderstrom & Sun, 2007). In 2002, the European Union (EU) issued a regulation requiring consolidated accounts for all companies listed in the EU to use International Financial Reporting Standards (IFRS) beginning 1 January 2005.[165] Barth et al. (2006b) show that IFRS increases accounting quality of financial reports.[166]

The first step to improve accounting standards in Turkey was the introduction of a regulation stating that the financial statements should be prepared with *inflation accounting principles* so that banks' performances became assessable in a healthier way (BRSA, 2010).[167] In order to bring the

164 Chapter 1, section 4.1.1.

165 Before 2005, companies followed a variety of country-specific Generally Accepted Accounting Principles (GAAP) (Soderstrom & Sun, 2007).

166 Barth et al. (2006b) findings show that firms that implement IFRS have more timely loss recognition, and more value relevance of earnings which provide evidence for higher accounting quality.

167 The Regulation on Procedures and Principles for the Special External Audit to be Performed published in February 2002 (in line with the Provisional Article 4 of the Banks Act (1999).

Turkish accounting standards in line with international regulations,[168] additions and amendments were made to *"Accounting Standards to be Applied by Banks, Uniform Accounting Plan and Prospectus"*[169] in 2002 (BRSA, 2010).[170] In November 2006, the BRSA issued a final regulation on the new accounting standards to ensure that the year-end balance sheets of all banks comply with the International Accounting Standards (IAS). According to the Banking Law (2005), Turkish banks became required to follow the BRSA's principles and procedures[171] in preparing annual reports.[172] Each bank must submit a copy of its annual report to the BRSA and publish it on its website. In 2005, the Turkish Accounting Standards Board[173] implemented harmonisation with IFRS (Yalkin & Demir, 2007).

Abad et al. (2000) and Niskanen et al. (1998) find that consolidated financial statements are more value relevant and reliable than non-consolidated[174] financial statements because they increase the quality of the information content. In Turkey, banks became required to consolidate their financial statements on a quarterly basis in line with certain consolidation principles established by the BRSA (BRSA, 2010). With the amendment to the Declaration of Consolidated Financial Statements, the preparation of consolidated financial statements was amended and made stricter in the sense that banks became obligated to prepare their consolidated financial statements quarterly instead of semi-annually and the four-month reporting period was decreased to two months (BRSA, 2010).[175]

3.3.2. Private Monitoring in the Russian Banking Sector

As was explained above, private monitoring practices include internal control and audit practices, establishing a solid accounting system to provide the transparency of the banks' financial statements, information disclosure and consolidated supervision.

---

168 Including the repo transactions.

169 Amendments were made twice: 13 December 2001 and 31 January 2002.

170 The Article 13 of the Banks' Act specified the principles on conducting external audit, providing transparency and uniformity in the accounting systems of banks, preventing unrecorded transactions, and preparing financial statements on time which would reflect the true condition of banks (BRSA, 2010).

171 These standards are determined in consultation with the Turkish Accounting Standards Board and international standards.

172 The Regulation on the Preparation and Publication of Annual Reports.

173 The Turkish Accounting Standards Board has the authority and power for the determination and application of Turkish Accounting Standards (Yalkın et al., 2007).

174 Non-consolidated financial statements report only the parent company's financial information, excluding the subsidiaries.

175 The Communiqué amending the Communiqué on Principles and Procedures relating to Declaration of Consolidated Financial Statements became effective, published in Official Gazette dated 5 July 2000; No. 24100.

3.3.2.1. Internal Control and Audit Practices

Internal controls and audit are important to evaluate the overall financial status of a bank. Having in mind the banking history of Russia, transparency becomes an important issue regarding the Russian banks. Alexander et al. (2000) argue that during the 1990s, the Russian banking sector was suffering from a lack of transparent and reliable financial statements. Off-site analysis was based on unreliable data. On-site examinations were infrequent. Moreover, supervisors didn't use their authority to require changes in unsafe practices and they lacked insight into how to make real improvements in bank safety and soundness. Although the figures published at the end of 1997 implied that the banks were highly capitalised and sound, these figures were actually overstated. They were hiding the true condition of banks due to non-transparent accounting standards (Alexander et al., 2000).

Following the 1998 crisis, some institutional modifications were commenced by the CBR. In 1998, the departments responsible for on-site and off-site supervision, for licensing of banks, bank auditors and bank rehabilitation were consolidated under a single Deputy Chairman. Furthermore, a high-level committee was established to ensure that the CBR's supervisory efforts were fully coordinated (Alexander et al., 2000).

Before the implementation of the banking reform in 2002, Russian banks were guided by two regulations on internal control[176] in 2002. These regulations failed to comply with the requirements of the Basel Committee's Core Principles[177] in organising and implementing internal controls. Besides, some of the credit institutions were regarding internal control as a mere formality or they were not obeying at all (CBR; 2002, 2003).[178] Following the introduction of the Federal Law on the Central Bank of the Russian Federation in 2002, the CBR decided to present the elements of an internal control service and some other non-binding standards in the form of regulatory requirements (CBR, 2002; 2003).

176 Regulation No. 509, dated August 1997 "On Organising Internal Controls in Banks" and Bank of Russia Ordinance No. 603-U, dated July 1999 "On the Procedure for Implementing Internal Control over Compliance by Credit Institutions with the Financial Market Legislation". In March 2009, Ordinance No. 2194-U "On the Organisation of Internal Controls in Credit Institutions and Banking Groups" amended the regulation of December 2003. It recommended measures that need to be taken to ensure continuity in the activities of credit institutions (CBR, 2009).

177 Principle 17: "*Supervisors must be satisfied that banks have in place internal controls that are adequate for the size and complexity of their business. These should include clear arrangements for delegating authority and responsibility; separation of the functions that involve committing the bank, paying away its funds, and accounting for its assets and liabilities; reconciliation of these processes; safeguarding the bank's assets; and appropriate independent internal audit and compliance functions to test adherence to these controls as well as applicable laws and regulations*".

178 The need to create effective internal control arose also from the legislation against money laundering.

The Banking Law provided the CBR with the authority to establish rules on internal control in a bank.[179] Hence, a new regulation enforced by the CBR in 2004[180] put emphasis on the Basel Committee's recommendations on internal controls aiming at improving the legal basis of internal controls in credit institutions. It provided the definition of internal control, the mechanism of internal control and the responsible bodies[181] involved in internal control (IMF, 2011a). This regulation attached special importance to the participation of boards of directors and executive bodies in this process. It also facilitated the conversion of Russian internal control practices to internationally accepted standards (CBR, 2004).

This regulation was followed by another regulation[182] in 2004 to improve the content of prudential reports in order to facilitate the early detection of problems. Pursuant to this regulation, banks' financial statements must be disclosed to public by the bank on a quarterly and yearly basis (CBR, 2004).

Regarding audit practices, the CBR is responsible to introduce international audit, accounting and reporting standards. According to the same regulation on internal control,[183] banks are subject to an independent review by an audit firm. External audit is important in assessing a bank's financial condition. Pursuant to the Banking Law, banks' consolidated financial statements must be audited by a licensed external auditor once a year.[184] The accounting rules are determined by the CBR but the auditing standards are not (IMF, 2011a). The CBR also has the right to conduct full or selective audits of any bank at any time and inspect all books and records of the bank.[185] Regarding external audit, the Banking Law requires that an independent auditor certifies banks' annual financial statements.

In spite of these developments, according to the 2005 CBR Annual Report, not much progress had been made in the internal control area. Specifically, the relations between banks and affiliated parties remained imperfectly transparent because the law did not require affiliated parties to disclose information to credit institutions about themselves and their activities. Furthermore, most banks were not really trying to identify such parties or disclose information about them. In 2006, the CBR tried to improve the regulation of banks by encouraging risk-based supervision. Risk-based supervision included the evaluation of banks'

179 Article 57 Central Bank Law (CBL).

180 Regulation No. 242-P, On Organising Internal Controls in Credit Institutions and Banking Groups.

181 Pursuant to Article 2.2 of Regulation 242-P internal controls shall be exercised by the management bodies, the auditor and chief accountant and other staff (IMF, 2011a).

182 List and Forms of Credit Institutions' Reports and the Procedure for Compiling and Submitting Them to the Bank of Russia.

183 Regulation No. 242-P.

184 Pursuant to the Article 42 Banking Law (BL) (IMF, 2011a).

185 Under CBR Regulation No. 2332-U dated November 2009, routine reporting is performed by banks on a daily, five day, ten day, monthly, quarterly, half yearly and yearly basis; and certain reporting is effected on an ad hoc basis.

performance based on the assessment of banking risks and their possible impact on the stability of credit institutions. In 2006, still no substantial progress was made in the disclosure of information by banks about their related parties. Only half of the credit institutions were disclosing information about their activities on the Bank of Russia internet site. As a result of ineffective internal controls, the number of banking licence revocations increased in 2006 (CBR, 2005, 2006).

3.3.2.2. Disclosure Requirements

As explained above, the objective of disclosure requirements is to mitigate the asymmetric information problem in the banking industry. To ensure that depositors and other market participants have access to information about a bank's portfolio and degree of risk exposure, regulators can require banks to adhere to certain accounting principles and disclose a wide range of information about their financials (Tchana, 2008; Frankel & Li, 2004; Mishkin, 2000). In that context, accounting quality contributes to the quality of financial reporting (Sonderstrom & Sun, 2007).

In Russia, the Central Bank of Russia has the authority to establish *accounting rules and procedures* for banks. The Bank of Russia's accounting and financial reporting is determined by the Federal Law on Accounting and Bank of Russia Regulation[186] on Accounting Rules in the Central Bank of the Russian Federation[187] and other Bank of Russia regulations issued in pursuance of these federal laws. It establishes a standard format for the presentation of a bank's accounts and instructions on how transactions are recorded within the accounts.[188] It requires that banks should prepare their financial statements according to the Directive of the CBR[189] on the Rules for the Preparation and Submission of Reports to the CBR by Credit Organisations dated 16 January 2004.[190]

As with Turkey, Russian banks were also suffering from weak risk management practices before the 1998 crisis. Accounting norms differed from international accounting standards. In fact, Russian accounting practices were not aiming to provide information about the true financial conditions of banks. Most of the financial data were based on the Russian Accounting Standards

186 Regulation No. 66-P, (dated 1 January 2006).

187 Bank of Russia Accounting Rules No. 66, dated 18 September 1997. In March 2007 this regulation was amended and since then accounting practices are regulated by CBR Regulation No. 302-P (CBR, 2007).

188 In accordance with the Directive of the CBR No. 7-U "On Preparation and Submitting of Accountancy by Lending Organisations to the CBR", dated 24 October 1997.

189 Regulation No. 1375-U.

190 In March 2007, a new accounting procedure was introduced "On Accounting Rules in Credit Institutions Domiciled in the Russian Federation Regulation No. 302-P". This directive was amended in 2009 under the Directive of the CBR No. 2332-U dated 12 November 2009 (CBR, 2004, 2005, 2010).

(RAS).[191] These standards were putting more emphasis on formal reporting requirements rather than on material elements and their economic meaning. Their focus was on verifying the banks' statistical reports. However, no qualitative analysis was made about the true value or risk of a particular asset or about the quality of management (Barisitz, 2009).

In order to bring accounting standards in line with international standards, the International Financial Reporting Standards (IFRS) and the international accounting standards (IAS) were introduced in 2004 (Barisitz, 2009; CBR, 2004; 2005).[192] The IFRS implementation in Russia introduced *consolidated reporting* which did not exist under the Russian Accounting Standards. It was determined that the new Russian accounting standards would be developed in line with the IFRS principles (Bagaeva, 2008). Implementation of "consolidated reporting"[193] is important because it enables a comprehensive evaluation of a bank's financial condition to market participants by increasing the quality of the information content as explained above.[194] However, the implementation has been slow due to lack of availability of comprehensive education on IFRS, inadequate

---

[191] When banks were using Russian Accounting Standards (RAS), losses in balance sheets were concealed so that the banks that failed after the 1998 crisis continued to show a profit on their RAS accounts, despite the fact that they could no longer service their obligations (Tompson, 2004). Only 24% of Russian banks officially recorded losses in 1998, despite the fact that the CBR recognised the sector as a whole to be bankrupt after the crisis (Interfaks AiF, 25 March 1999, in Tompson, 2004).

[192] In November 2005, "On the Analysis of IFRS Statements for 2004" was published which specified the methods for examining consolidated and unconsolidated statements compiled by credit institutions in line with the IFRS, for the purpose of providing methodological support to Bank of Russia regional branches in analysing the activities of credit institutions. For the preparation to reach international accounting standards (IAS), the Bank of Russia drew up the plan for the Conversion of the Russian Banking Sector to IAS from 1 January 2004.

[193] On April 2003, the regulation on consolidated reporting was published to specify the requirements for the publication of consolidated reports. "On the Statements Published by Credit Institutions and Banking/Consolidated Groups". This was accompanied by "On Auditing Credit Institutions and Banking/Consolidated Groups dated July 2003. In April 2003, Bank of Russia Ordinance No. 55, "On Disclosure of Information by Credit Institutions" was issued. Regarding consolidated supervision "Regulation No. 246-P on the Procedure for Compiling Consolidated Statements by the Parent Bank of a Banking/ Consolidated Group" on January 2004 and "On Methodological Recommendations for Compiling consolidated Statements" were issued (both dated January 2004).

[194] Regarding the implementation of consolidated reporting in Russia, one of the main changes made to the Banking Law in 2002 was the introduction of consolidated accounting for a bank group. In conformity with the Banking Sector Development Strategy introduced in 2002, CBR formulated the principles for evaluating the level of consolidated risk assumed by credit institutions. It specified the procedure for compiling consolidated reports based on "Regulation No. 191-P dated July 2002" (CBR, 2002). The draft Federal Law "On Amending the Federal Laws on Banks and Banking Activities and on the Central Bank of the Russian Federation (Bank of Russia)" specifying the core provisions of consolidated supervision regarding credit institutions, banking groups and bank holding companies to disclose their operations was submitted to the Russian Government for approval in the first quarter of 2011 (CBR, 2010).

translations of standards from English into Russian, and lack of professionals with IFRS knowledge who could oversee the implementation and adherence to IFRS standards (Preobragenskaya & McGee, 2003). As of 2010, the CBR requires all banks to prepare supplementary IFRS financial statements, but there is no requirement to publish (IMF, 2011a).[195]

Another development in 2004 was that the CBR replaced the long-standing Instruction No. 1 on Banks' Mandatory Norms with the Instruction No. 110 (Tompson, 2004). Tompson (2004) argues that one of the most important innovations brought within this regulation was the requirement for prudential ratios to be available for inspection for every day of a bank's operation. Hence, all mandatory ratios must be in compliance at all times. On the other hand, this regulation reduced the number of mandatory prudential ratios from 18 to 10 which decreased the transparency of banks' financial status for the sake of depositors and investor understanding (Tompson, 2004).

As of January 2008, banks became more transparent. Over 84% of credit institutions disclosed information about their activities on the CBR website. As of the beginning of 2008, more than 61% of all operating credit institutions agreed to disclose information.[196] However, in 2008, there were still problems in establishing the risk management systems. Integrated risk management systems were developed mainly in large credit institutions. Risk management units in many other credit institutions were fragmented (CBR, 2007).

According to the 2008 CBR report, the most severe problems faced by the Russian banks during the 2008 crisis were caused by the *lack of coordination of bank risk management* and *strategy development*. According to the 2008 IMF Report's evaluation, although the banking law[197] clarifies the key provisions of consolidated supervision and disclosure, the CBR is unable to capture all related parties and affiliates due to the narrow definition of *consolidated supervision* in Russian legislation.[198] In fact, the 2009 CBR report also underlines that the 2008

Bank of Russia Ordinance No. 1114-U, dated 21 February 2002, "On Amending Bank of Russia Regulation No. 85-P, dated 5 August 1999, On the Procedure for Using Reported Data of Non-Credit Institutions Members of a Group in Compiling Consolidated Reports by Credit Institutions", regulated the procedure for using data of non-credit institutions members of a banking/consolidated group in calculating required ratios for the banking/ consolidated group and specified the procedure for including data of non-credit institutions members of banking/consolidated groups in consolidated statements (CBR, 2002).

195 On 27 July 2010 the Federal Law No. 208-FZ "On Consolidated Financial Statements" was adopted (Law No. 208-FZ). With this regulation, Russia introduced a legislative requirement on mandatory application of International Financial Reporting Standards (IFRS) by all public interest entities including credit institutions for the preparation of consolidated financial statements (CBR, 2010; Ernst & Young (2012): Implementation of IFRS in Russia in accordance with the Law "On Consolidated Financial Statements").

196 Pursuant to Bank of Russia Letter No. 165-T, dated 21 December 2006, "On Disclosure of Information by Credit Institutions."

197 The Federal Law "On Amending the Federal Law on Banks and Banking Activities."

198 At the beginning of 2008, the CBR enacted changes in Russian Accounting Standards. These changes eliminated some discrepancies between domestic and international accounting

crisis revealed serious internal problems in most of the banks. These included a lack of efficient risk management, high risk concentrations, poor transparency, and the use of manipulative schemes which allowed banks to avoid compliance with the regulatory requirements, including credit and liquidity risk mitigation requirements (CBR, 2009).

One major problem was that the heads of risk management departments lacked the necessary powers and status. Another major drawback in risk management was the lack of efficient control by their boards of directors (supervisory boards) over the decisions taken by senior management regarding the level of risk assumed by banks. Specifically, some credit institutions became financially unstable because their owners and management failed to formulate sensible credit, investment and liquidity management policies. This is attributed to the owners' and executives' excessive appetite for risk as well as the lack of an efficient mechanism to identify and assess the actual risks taken by credit institutions and inform their management about them (CBR, 2009). It should be noted that some credit institutions had problems that resulted from low risk diversification (high risk concentration). This risk concentration was caused by the risks associated with investment projects, securities issuances, and related parties (CBR, 2009).

After the 2008–2009 crises, in 2009, the CBR decided to improve the quality of banking regulation and promote a risk-based approach. It started to prepare the groundwork for the introduction of Basel II recommendations. Firstly, it plans to introduce new approaches to risk assessment, based on advanced financial practice and mathematical methods. Secondly, it will complement bank capital quantification with quality assessment, by formulating the general principles of risk-based supervision and setting market discipline requirements (CBR, 2009).[199]

3.3.3. *Discussion*

Although several important steps have been taken in Russia, risk management is still limited. One difference from Turkey is that public disclosure of risk management procedures is not mandatory in Russia. The lack of quality data and

principles but material differences remained (including consolidation and problem loan reporting and provisioning) (Trofimova et al. (2007), pp. 29–30 in Barisitz, 2009).

199 In 2009, the CBR prepared proposals that legislation should be amended in order to give it sufficient power in the following areas: (1) to require credit institutions to maintain their capital at a specified level; (2) to require credit institutions and banking groups to disclose information about their risk exposure and risk management procedures to a wide range of users; (3) to set banking risk management rules for credit institutions and banking groups, in order enable them to meet the requirements of Basel II Pillar 2; and (4) to make the management and boards of directors (supervisory boards) of credit institutions accountable for their institutions' performance, including risk management, and to sanction the chief executives and owners of credit institutions.

consolidated reporting in the Russian reporting standards is continuously emphasised in the annual IMF and CBR reports. On the other hand, the 2007 IMF report on Turkey underlines: "the Turkish banks' improved financial situation and risk management techniques, supported by a better framework of regulation, supervision, and intervention, have made the system more resilient". The 2010 IMF reports mentions again that the sub-regulations pursuant to the Banking Law in Turkey are in effect and implemented on a continuous basis.

In the 2009 IMF Report on Russia, the continuing deficiencies were stressed, with specific emphasis on generous accounting and provisioning rules and more importantly, regarding related party transaction disclosure requirements. These shortcomings continue to distort the CBR's ability to assess the quality of assets and adequacy of loan loss reserves. Hence, they increase uncertainty about the creditworthiness of Russian banks (IMF, 2009, 2011).[200]

According to the 2009 CBR Report, Russian lawmakers will continue to legislate additional powers to the Bank of Russia regarding the use of sanctions against banks' chief executives and owners. The aim is to make the owners and management of credit institutions accountable for the quality and results of their risk assessment and management policy, and to empower the Bank of Russia to use sanctions in case this policy proves ineffective (CBR, 2011a). The broadening of the CBR's powers in dealing with credit institutions in the event of mismanagement or dishonest practices aims at making bank managers more responsible when taking decisions that affect the interests of creditors and depositors (CBR, 2009). It also aims to define the requirements for risk management systems in banks.

These developments regarding information disclosure are important for the transparency of the banks' activities. However, the reporting requirements increase the regulatory burden and they are costly (Tompson, 2004). This argument is in line with my empirical findings on the negative effect of private monitoring on banks' performance. It suggests that these costs might negatively affect the banks' performances in Turkey and Russia. In fact, based on Gencoglu et al. (2011), I argue above that the audit procedures are not very effective in the Turkish banking sector regarding the number of auditors, and their technical knowledge. Hence, the negative impact might be caused by the costs and burden created by the ineffective implementation of audit components of the disclosure practices.

Regarding Russia, Tompson (2004) argues that the regulatory arrangements in Russia have been extremely burdensome in terms of the paperwork and

200 The 2009 IMF report also mentions that there are still important differences on the revenue recognition, consolidation, pension accounting, and application of fair value accounting. Shortcomings in reporting requirements for consolidated financial statements create significant uncertainty regarding the activities of banks' off-balance sheet activities. This weakness is compounded by the lack of adequate powers given to the CBR to monitor and supervise bank holding companies and sanction bank officers and directors (IMF, 2009, 2011a).

complicated instructions. Hence, the negative impact of private monitoring practices on Russian banks' efficiency can be explained with this ineffective regulatory burden. However, the ratio of increased non-performing loans in Russian banks' balance sheets and the number of failed banks compared to Turkey point to the fact that the negative impact of private monitoring practices have been less severe in the Turkish banking sector (see Table 23).

3.4. DEPOSIT INSURANCE SCHEME

As explained in the first chapter of this book, deposit insurance aims to protect banking systems and small, uninformed depositors from bank runs.[201] However, my empirical findings in the second chapter showed that deposit insurance had a negative effect on banks' efficiency.[202] This finding is in line with Detragiache and Demirgüç-Kunt (2002), and Laeven (2002) who emphasise that deposit insurance induces the moral hazard of banks. In the existence of such an insurance mechanism, banks would have the incentive to engage in riskier activities for higher returns since they know that any possible failure will be bailed out by the deposit insurance fund, which is ultimately backed by the government.

3.4.1. Deposit Insurance Scheme in the Turkish Banking Sector

The Savings Deposit Insurance Fund (SDIF) in Turkey was established under the auspices of the Central Bank[203] in 1983 as a public entity. Initially, it was administered by the Central Bank of Turkey. After the introduction of the Banks Act No. 4389 in 1999, the administration and representation of the SDIF was transferred to the BRSA in 2000. It was initially responsible only for insuring savings deposits. However, in the presence of financial crises, its duties have been enlarged. In 1994,[204] the Fund was allowed to intervene in order to strengthen the financial health of banks in trouble and to restructure them whenever that was necessary, not just to protect deposits. In December 2003, the SDIF gained its administrative and financial autonomy according to Act No. 5020 (Ayzit, 2004).

The SDIF is responsible and authorised for insuring savings deposits. The amount of deposits subject to insurance, the tariff of the insurance premium and other relevant matters are determined by the SDIF upon consultation with the Treasury, the BRSA, and the Central Bank. If a bank becomes insolvent or

201 Chapter 1, section 3.1.
202 Chapter 2, section 7.2.
203 According to the Decree Law No. 70 about banks.
204 With the Decree Law No. 538 dated 16 June 1994.

unable to operate, the SDIF takes over the bank, and restructures it financially. If however there is no recovery to save the financial strength of the bank despite the measures, the BRSA can either cancel the bank's operation licence or transfer the bank to the SDIF. When the bank is taken over by the SDIF, its debt is paid and its liquidation is completed. Bankruptcy proceedings are strictly regulated since the 2001 crisis and the SDIF has a wide range of authority in exercising the rules over the bankrupt banks (Paksoy & Tiftikci, 2010).[205]

The SDIF has significant legal powers for resolving failed banks. Under the Banking Law, the SDIF has the right firstly to transfer the assets, as well as the deposits and participation funds subject to insurance to another bank, and then ask the BRSA to revoke the operating licence of the failed bank; secondly, to provide financial support to the intervened bank by increasing its capital and/or liquidity; and finally, to sell the financially restructured bank or organise a merger with another bank (IMF, 2012). The deposit insurance framework broadly conforms to best international practice (IMF, 2012).

Since the establishment of the deposit insurance scheme in 1983, the coverage of deposit insurance has changed several times. The deposit insurance was made unlimited in the crisis of 1994[206] and remained so until 2000. Although this full coverage system was conceived as a temporary measure at that time to prevent a possible bank panic, it was not removed until 2000 due to a lack of political will. In 2000, it was changed to a new limited guarantee system. However, this didn't last long and with the emergence of the 2000/2001 crisis it was changed back to full guarantee ("blanket guarantee") (BRSA 2010).[207]

Following the 2001 crisis, the deposit guarantee system was effectively used in order to deal with the problem banks. The number of banks was reduced as a result of take-overs by the SDIF or mergers. In order to prevent the negative side effect of deposit insurance regarding moral hazard, the blanket guarantee provided by the deposit insurance scheme was cancelled when the 2001 crisis was over. Another resolution was issued on July 2003.[208] This resolution determined that the temporary full guarantee practice was to be abolished starting on July 2004. Blanket deposit insurance, which had caused a moral

---

205 Pursuant to Article 15 of the Banks Act (1999) and Article 111 of the Banking Law (2005). SDIF is authorised to insure savings deposit, restructuring and strengthening the financial soundness of the banks; transfer, merge, sell or liquidate such banks; execute and conclude the follow-up and collection of transactions of the Fund, manage the Fund's assets and resources and perform other duties assigned thereto by the Law.

206 Turkey experienced financial crises during the 1980s and in 1994. However, I will not discuss them as my empirical analysis covers only the period from 1999 onwards.

207 During the twin crisis of 2000–2001 it was changed back to full guarantee for a short time. Within this scope, the BRSA issued a resolution (BRSA Resolution No. 151) in January 2001 concerning the application of this guarantee. According to this resolution, deposit insurance guarantee would be applied by the SDIF by taking over the shares of banks which had violated the related articles of Banks Act (BRSA, 2010).

208 BRSA Resolution No. 1084.

hazard problem and unfair competition among banks, was ended in July 2004 and deposit insurance was aligned with the EU levels. The guarantee limited to YTL[209] 50,000 (around €21,000) was adopted (BRSA, 2010)[210] which was in line with the EU level.[211]

Önder and Özyıldırım (2008) found that the generous deposit insurance mechanism created moral hazard for banks during 1988 and 2000 in Turkey.[212] They argue that the perception of complete insurance encouraged bank managers to engage in risky activities, especially after 1994. Capital to assets ratio decreased by 1.63% and non-performing loans increased by 11.8%, the ratio of liquid assets to deposits decreased by 43.29% and many banks decreased their capital adequacy ratio. These results suggest that banks took risks during the generous deposit insurance period in Turkey (Önder & Özyıldırım, 2008). The first-stage analysis of the empirical work conducted in Chapter 2[213] of this book shows that the average efficiency scores of Turkish banks have a declining trend between 1999 and 2004. Taking also into account the negative impact of deposit insurance found in the second-stage regression analysis, the above-mentioned arguments provide support to my results suggesting that the moral hazard effect of deposit insurance might have negatively affected the performance of Turkish banks during the full coverage time period.

In May 2008, the risk-based premium practice[214] was adopted (BRSA, 2010).[215] With the introduction of this risk-based insurance premium tariff in 2008, banks paid insurance premiums according to the risk they create within the system so that they were encouraged to take fewer risks and comply with the

209 YTL is the Turkish currency.

210 With the BRSA Resolution No. 1083.

211 According to the Directive 94/19/EC of the European Parliament and of the Council of 30 May 1994 on deposit-guarantee schemes, the minimum guarantee level was established as €20,000. When the financial crisis hit in autumn of 2008, the EU Member States decided that the level of deposit protection should be increased in the EU. A Directive adopted in March 2009 required the coverage to be increased from a minimum of €20,000 to at least €50,000 by June 2010 and to a uniform level of €100,000 by the end of 2010. (European Commission Report on Deposit Guarantee Schemes, 2010: Review of Directive 94/19/EC on Deposit Guarantee Schemes).

212 This argument is also supported by Bakır and Öniş (2010).

213 See Chapter 2, Table 13.

214 The idea in risk-based deposit insurance premiums is that the risk-based premiums will discourage insured banks from taking excessive risks because if a bank is subject to higher premiums, it will think twice before undertaking a risky activity. Banks that have a higher risk exposure will pay higher insurance premiums (Prescott, 2002). However, Prescott (2002) argues that the risk-based deposit insurance premiums alone cannot control moral hazard in deposit insurance. He points out that this argument requires the deposit insurer to be able to observe the risk characteristics of a bank's investment portfolio. However, it is not easy for outsiders to evaluate a bank loan or a complicated portfolio of financial derivatives. Under these conditions, risk-based deposit insurance premiums are not enough to control moral hazard (Prescott, 2002).

215 The Regulation on Saving Deposit Subject to Insurance and Premiums to be collected by the Savings Deposit Insurance Fund.

prudential regulations (BRSA, 2010). According to the BRSA Report (2010), imposing a blanket guarantee at the proper time to prevent bank runs and revoking it when the crisis ended contributed to market discipline in the Turkish banking sector (BRSA, 2010). This argument provides support to the increasing trend in the efficiency scores of Turkish banks, found in Chapter 2, Table 13 after the introduction of the limited deposit insurance system in 2004.

According to the 2012 IMF Report, the SDIF is authorised with sufficient resolution tools provided by the Banking Law to use least cost resolution tools such as mergers, insured deposit transfers, and bank liquidation processes while the deposit insurance framework is in line with the EU and international practices. The same report evaluates the banking resolution and deposit insurance systems in Turkey as well designed.

3.4.2. Deposit Insurance Scheme in the Russian Banking System

Following the 1998 crisis, in order to restore competition in the deposit market, promote financial stability and increase trust in the banking system, the Federal Law on Insurance of the Deposits of Natural Persons was introduced as of 23 December 2003 as one of the reform initiatives following the 1998 crisis. The introduction of the deposit insurance system in Russia was one of the major reforms in the Russian banking regulation in the post-1998 crisis period (Tompson, 2004).

In January 2004, the Deposit Insurance Agency (DIA) was established as an independent entity and the first round of admissions into the deposit insurance scheme was completed at the end of March 2005 (IMF, 2005; ECB, 2005). The primary functions of the DIA are to determine the deposit insurance premium, receive payments from registered banks, make reimbursements to depositors in case of bank failures and manage the Deposit Insurance Fund. In late 2004, the government made an amendment to the Law on Insolvency (Bankruptcy) of Credit Institutions and the DIA also became responsible for managing the bankruptcy proceedings to liquidate insolvent banks (Camara & Negret, 2006).

When the system first started, in order to prevent moral hazard in the insurance scheme, all deposits up to 100,000 RUB (approximately €2,480) were insured. However, this ratio was increased gradually in the next years. In August 2006, the coverage was expanded up to a maximum of 190,000 RUB (approx. €4,700) and in March 2007, the upper limit for reimbursement was raised to 400,000 RUB (approx. €9,910). In October 2008 the CBR increased the coverage to 700,000 RUB (approx. €17,361) as an adjustment against the global crisis (Peresetsky, 2008; Barisitz, 2009).

During the 2004 crisis, the Russian government enacted a law providing temporary deposit insurance to all banks in order to mitigate depositors' panic. Hence, irrespective of their qualifications, all Russian banks were guaranteed blanket deposit insurance for deposits up to 100,000 RUB (€2,480) from July 2004 until the end of 2006 (IMF, 2004). On one hand, the introduction of the deposit insurance scheme (DIS) increased the banking sector's reliance on depository funding. Private deposits have grown with the introduction of DIS (Camara & Montes-Negret, 2006).

On the other hand, the absence of effective consolidated supervision hinders the monitoring of connected-lending practices. Hence, a true assessment of the banks' financial health is not possible. Although banks have to meet a number of prudential standards in order to be accepted into the deposit insurance system, institutions which account for nearly all deposits were eventually admitted into the system suggesting the weak enforcement of prudential standards (Barisitz, 2009).

There have been some changes in the resolution mechanism of failed banks and procedures for bank exits as of late 2008. The initiative to undertake resolution intervention still belongs to the Banking Supervision Committee of the CBR. As one of the legislative responses to the global crisis, major amendments to the powers and tools at the disposal of the Deposit Insurance Agency (DIA) for resolving failing banks were approved by the Russian Duma in October 2008. In practice, in cases of distress, both the CBR and the DIA are likely to evaluate the financial condition of particular banks that might be subject to resolution. The DIA has up to ten days to decide on its participation before engaging in a bank rescue operation. The CBR's Supervision Committee must approve the DIA's Action Plan within ten days of its submission (Melecky et al., 2010).

However, Vernikov (2007) argues that there are only minor additional benefits from introducing deposit insurance into a banking sector that is dominated by state-owned banks which enjoy de facto guarantees of performance from the state. He adds that when a comprehensive deposit insurance scheme was introduced in 2005, almost 70% of household deposits were held by major public sector banks.[216] It had practically no disciplining effect on the market participants since the introduction of deposit insurance meant simply the conversion of an implicit state guarantee into an explicit protection, removing some agents from the household deposit market. The only change has been an inflow of deposits into new private accounts at national private banks offering high interest rates, suggesting a building moral hazard problem (Vernikov, 2007). The introduction of the deposit insurance scheme (DIS) may aggravate moral hazard problems in an environment that lacks transparency and sound governance standards. The DIS should only be adopted after the foundations of the banking system become solid (Camara & Montes-Negret, 2006).

---

216 Such as Sberbank; Sberbank is government-owned and it is the largest bank in Russia. Central Bank of Russia is the majority shareholder of Sberbank.

3.4.3. *Discussion*

The above-mentioned argument of Camara and Montes-Negret (2006) is supported by my empirical findings that deposit insurance affects banks' efficiency negatively. Cross national research's findings show that the seriousness of moral hazard depends on the institutional environment (Tompson, 2004). Demirgüç-Kunt and Detragiache (1999) also found that deposit insurance increases banking system fragility in countries with weak institutions. Followed by that, where the rule of law and regulatory quality is weak, implementation of deposit insurance is likely to contribute to financial instability (Tompson, 2004). In fact, the World Bank governance indicators show a higher level in regulatory quality for Turkey compared to Russia (See Table 28). *Regulatory quality* is an index based on worldwide governance indicators prepared by the World Bank. It reflects the perceptions of the ability of the government to formulate and implement sound policies and regulations that permit and promote private sector development. The indexes show a lower level in Russia supporting the need for a sounder institutional environment compared to Turkey.[217]

Table 28. Regulatory quality in Turkey and Russia

	2000	2002	2003	2004	2005	2006	2007	2008	2009	2010
Turkey	0.301	0.075	0.048	0.102	0.278	0.293	0.323	0.282	0.304	0.382
Russia	−0.522	−0.293	−0.22	−0.114	−0.17	−0.447	−0.335	−0.453	−0.402	−0.395

Source: World Bank Governance Indicators.[218]

The qualitative analysis of this chapter's suggestions is in line with this description of a poor institutional and regulatory environment in Russia and hence with the above-mentioned argument. Based on my empirical findings on the negative effect of deposit insurance, the introduction of deposit insurance in Russia should be accompanied by the improvements in the enforcement of law.[219] Furthermore, following the introduction of the deposit insurance, the efficiency results of Russian banks show a declining trend after 2005 (see Chapter 2, Table 9).

217 Thiessen (2004) shows in his paper that the annual evaluation of financial sector reforms by the EBRD regarding the quality level of financial system supervision and regulation was relatively low even before the crisis and that it fell afterwards to very low standards until about 2002.

218 http://info.worldbank.org/governance/wgi/faq.htm. The estimate of governance ranges from approximately –2.5 (weak) to 2.5 (strong) governance performance.

219 This argument is also supported by Thompson (2004). As he mentions: "The introduction of deposit insurance therefore needs to be accompanied – preferably preceded – by major improvements in bank transparency, prudential regulation and the administration of law".

Although during the 2008–2009 crisis the DIA resolved a large number of banks, Melecky et al. (2010) argue that it is not clear whether the least cost measures were adopted. During the crisis, the Deposit Insurance Agency did not need to use the Deposit Insurance fund as a bank restructuring tool. The funds used during the crisis were either provided from investors, the CBR or the Federal Budget (IMF, 2011). Since the current system of deposit insurance is very new, it has been tested only in the latest crisis and hence it might be too early to decide on the performance of the DIA regarding the possible trade-offs between protection of depositors, protection of creditors and minimising of losses and disruptions to the overall financial system (Melecky et al., 2010).

The difference between the trend of efficiency scores in Turkish and Russian banks (taking also into account the negative impact of deposit insurance on banks' efficiency) suggests that a deposit insurance scheme should only be adopted after the foundations of a banking system become solid. In an environment with weak regulatory quality, connected lending practices, and a lack of reliable data such as there is in the Russian banking sector, a deposit insurance mechanism might aggravate the moral hazard problem. Besides, as argued above, the proper implementation of the deposit insurance mechanism in Turkey suggests that its negative impact on Turkish banks has been lower compared to Russian banks.

3.5. ENTRY REQUIREMENTS

Economic theory provides conflicting results about the impact of entry restrictions on banks' efficiency. Keeley (1990) argues that banks with monopolistic power have greater franchise value, which would give them an incentive for prudent behaviour. On the other hand, Shleifer and Vishny (1998) do not support entry restrictions by emphasising the positive effects of competition. Demirgüç-Kunt, Levine and Min (1998) and Wang and Bayraktar (2006) support the view that the regulatory restrictions do have negative effects on competition in banking. Barth et al. (2004) found that the percentage of entry applications denied is greater for low-income countries than for high-income countries, and that developing countries place more limitations on foreign bank ownership of domestic banks and foreign bank entry through branching than developed countries.

According to the results of my empirical analysis, regulations related to entry requirements have a negative effect on the efficiency of banks.[220] Barth et al. (2002) classify entry restrictions among the competition regulatory variables. Although they include limitations on foreign bank entry, following Pasiouras (2008), the index[221] I used measures only the specific legal requirements for

[220] Chapter 2, section 6.2.

[221] See Appendix A.

obtaining a licence to operate as a bank. The more information required by the regulatory authorities when deciding upon whether or not to issue a licence, the more restrictive will be entry into banking (Barth et al., 2006a). Looking at Turkey and Russia, until 2005, Russia had higher stringency in entry restrictions. Starting in 2005, they both receive the same degree of stringency in entry restrictions (see Table 29).

Table 29. Indexes on entry restrictions in Turkey and Russia*

	1999	2000	2001	2002	2003	2004	2005	2006	2007	2008	2009	2010
Turkey	3	6	6	6	6	6	8	8	8	8	8	8
Russia	8	8	7	7	7	7	8	8	8	8	8	8

* This variable takes values between 0 and 8.

3.5.1. *Entry Requirements in the Turkish Banking Sector*

In Turkey, the number of banks increased quickly after the financial liberalisation process started in the 1980s. Weaknesses in granting licences made entrance into the sector very easy. Firstly, bank licences were issued based on political criteria. Secondly, political authority was under pressure from bank lobbies so that it refrained from taking adequate regulatory action (Özkan, 2003). The qualifications required in persons who wanted to become a bank owner were low, making entrance into the sector easy. Besides, the decision of licence revocation was difficult, which made exit not easy. All these factors contributed to the increase in the number of banks (BRSA, 2010).

Following the 2001 crisis, the operating licences of many banks were annulled or transferred to the SDIF due to their illegal operations. Before 2000, commercial banking licences were given by the Ministry of Treasury. Starting in 2000, according to the Article 7 of the Banks Act (1999),[222] the establishment of a bank in Turkey or the opening up a branch in Turkey by a bank established abroad needs the permission of the BRSA, provided that the establishment conditions laid down in the Banking Law are fulfilled.

In order to obtain a licence to operate as a bank in Turkey, the submission of the following legal documents has been required since 1999: financial projections for the first three years, financial information on potential shareholders and sources of funds to be disbursed in the capitalisation of new banks, draft by law, and background experience of future managers and directors. After 2005, the BRSA has brought more severe rules in granting licences with amendments in legislation (BRSA, 2010). The amount of specific legal submissions required to obtain a banking licence increased with the 2005 Banking Law (Article 6 and

222 Article 6 of the Banking Law (2005).

Article 7). Intended organisation charts and market differentiation intended for a new bank were included in the entry requirements. Moreover, before 2000, there was not a specified amount for the minimum capital entry requirement. Starting in 2000, the minimum capital entry requirement was determined as twenty million YTL.[223] In 2005, this amount became thirty million YTL (approx. €12,650,000).[224]

The results of my empirical analysis suggest that entry regulations have a negative impact on efficiency. As argued above, entry restrictions have a negative effect on competition. During the 2001 crisis, it was observed that there were extensive dominant partner abuses in the SDIF banks. This led the BRSA to follow a stricter policy in the licensing process in terms of the qualifications and the intentions of entrepreneurs, the capacity of institutions in risk management, internal processes and corporate management principles (BRSA, 2010). The negative effect of this regulation can be explained by the BRSA's emphasis on financial stability at the expense of competition since as Kaymak (2009) argues; "competition brings risks" is still the underlying approach of the BRSA.[225] In fact, Abbasoglu et al. (2007) found that the degree of competition had decreased between 2001 and 2005. Looking at the period between 2005 and 2010, Macit (2012) found that the level of competition also decreased during this time period. Hence, the declining trend in competition in the Turkish banking sector can be explained as a negative effect of the entry restrictions.[226]

3.5.2. *Entry Requirement in the Russian Banking Sector*

According to the Banking Law in Russia, the Central Bank of Russia is the licensing authority. Under the Federal Law of the Central Bank of the Russian Federation, the Bank of Russia (The CBR) is authorised to take decisions regarding the authorisation of credit institutions, issuance of banking licences to credit institutions, and suspension and revocation of such licences in accordance with the procedures stipulated by the Federal Law on Banks and Banking (ECB, 2005). The registration of banks and the licensing of their activities is designated according to the Bank of Russia Instruction No. 75-I, dated 23 July 1998, on the Procedure for Applying Federal Laws Regulating the Procedure for Registering Credit Institutions and Licensing Banking Activities. Regarding the specific legal submissions, all of the requirements mentioned above are necessary to

223 YTL is the Turkish currency. 20 million YTL corresponds to approx. €8,500,000.

224 For more on the entry requirements, see Articles 6, 7, 8, 9, 10, 11, 12, 13, 14, 15 of the Banking Law (2005) under the section "Permissions for Establishment and Operation".

225 Kocaoglu (2010) also argues that banking issues have been more important for the BRSA rather than competition related matters. The competition-fragility view argues that competition encourages excessive risk-taking which would lead to less stability (Allen & Gale, 2004). For more on the "competition-fragility" strand of literature, see Weill and Fungacova, 2009; Allen & Gale, 2004.

226 The OECD Peer Review Report (2005).

obtain a licence to operate as a bank during the period of analysis.[227] The Federal Tax Authority has the responsibility to authorise credit institutions, following the decision of the CBR. It must be approved by the Federal Antimonopoly Authority regarding compliance with the anti-monopoly legislation requirements (ECB, 2005).

The Bank of Russia Regulation No. 218-P, dated March 2003, on the Procedure for and the Criteria of Evaluating the Financial Condition of Corporate Founders of Credit Institutions introduced a methodology for evaluating the financial condition of corporate founders of credit institutions through the use of a set of standard indicators. This regulation was amended in 2005 as on the Procedure and Criteria for Evaluating the Financial Position of Individual Founders of a Credit Institution.[228] It applies to individuals who intend to acquire shares in a bank confirming the sources of funds paid by the individuals as a contribution to the authorised capital of a bank (CBR, 2005).

Bank of Russia Ordinance No. 1624-U amended the 2004 Regulation on the Decision Making Procedure in Respect to the State Registration of Credit Institutions and the Issue of Banking Licenses in order to improve the registration process of banks and the licensing procedure of banking operations.[229] It contains a more detailed list of documents a credit institution is required to present to the Bank of Russia. In order to increase the transparency of the structure of founders when creating a new credit institution, the Law tightened the requirement by expanding the range of activities for which additional banking licences are required (CBR, 2004).

Bank entry in Russia has been easy during the 1990s when the CBR issued a very large number of banking licences. However, since the middle of the 1990s the number of banks started to decrease. The same argument discussed above for Turkish banks applies also to Russian banks where competition in the banking sector is also a problem.[230]

3.5.3. *Discussion*

According to the qualitative analysis of this chapter, the number of barriers required as part of the licensing process is similar for both Turkish banks and

227 According to Barth et al. (2003) and (2008) survey, only "market differentiation intended for a new bank" was not obligatory between 2001 and 2004. Hence, I measured the index based on this finding.

228 Regulation No. 268-P.

229 In 2006, the regulation "On the Procedure and Criteria for Evaluating the Financial Position of Individual Founders of a Credit Institution" was replaced by the Ordinance No. 1763-U "On Amending Bank of Russia Regulation No 268-P", dated April 2005. In 2007, the Bank of Russia amended its Instruction No. 109-I, dated January 2004, "On the Bank of Russia Decision-Making Procedure in Respect of the State Registration of Credit Institutions and Licensing Banking Operations".

230 See Meleckey et al. (2010) and Weill et al. (2010).

Russian banks. Imposing basic requirements before a banking licence is accepted or rejected would enhance the overall performance of the banking sector, because in that way only the banks with higher quality would be allowed to enter the banking sector (Barth et al., 2006a: 111). In fact, considering both countries' banking histories characterised by pervasive connected-lending and corruptive practices and abuses of banks' sources by their governments, imposing entry restrictions to better assure the quality of entrants gains a particular importance.

On the other hand, the negative impact of this regulation on efficiency found in Chapter 2 suggests its distorting effect on competition. My analysis on entry regulations regarding both Turkish and Russian banks suggests that following the financial crises in their history, both countries chose to tighten their licensing procedures. However, empirical results revealed that this regulation had a negative impact on banks' performance. Hence, it would be advisable for both countries to re-evaluate and improve their licensing policies in order to prevent the distortion of competition in the banking sector.

4. GOVERNMENT OWNERSHIP OF BANKS IN TURKEY AND RUSSIA

In many emerging markets, the key players in the banking industry are controlled by the state (Caner et al., 2007). This is also true for both Turkey and Russia where state banks' involvement in financial intermediation is significantly high. Barth et al. (2001b) describe the presence of government-owned banks as the fraction of the banking system's assets in banks that is 50% or more government-owned. According to the literature (such as La Porta et al., 2000; Schleifer & Vishny, 1998; Barth et al., 2010), state ownership of banks is associated with lower levels of efficiency, and government intervention over the banking sector is associated with slower financial development, as well as lower growth and productivity. My empirical findings also suggest a negative relationship between the share of government-owned banks and the banks' performance. In fact, many researchers encourage policy makers in developing countries to privatise their holdings in the banking sector to improve the efficiency (Mahlberg et al., 2011).

4.1. GOVERNMENT OWNERSHIP OF BANKS IN TURKEY

Before the 2000/2001 crisis, the Turkish banking sector was dominated by the state. In fact, according to Steinherr et al. (2004) state banks were the main contributor to the 2001 crisis. For years, these state banks had been misused by politicians, who allocated them to different political parties and to certain favoured groups to provide subsidised credits for their political constituencies. However, these banks were not compensated for the losses incurred by such lending activities. Instead, they were forced to book these losses as claims on the government, called "duty" losses (Özkan, 2003; Akyürek, 2006; Bredenkamp et al., 2009; Steinherr et al., 2004). These claims provided little income and no cash flow. Hence, banks had to fund themselves increasingly short-term in the interbank market, which subjected them to liquidity risk and interest rate risk as the liabilities grew. Moreover, state banks were not required to provide reserves for bad loans, to comply with prudential regulations applied to private banks, and they were also not subject to any serious supervision. This situation created the basis for regulatory forbearance and allowed massive distortion in the banking system (Özkan, 2003; Bredenkamp et al., 2009).

Following the second pillar of the restructuring process after the 2001 crisis,[231] state-owned banks were recapitalised and restructured financially and operationally within the Restructuring Program. Since 2003, the share of government-owned banks in the total banking sector shows a declining trend. In 2003, the share of government-owned banks was 39.27%. As of 2010, this ratio declined to 31.5% (BAT, 2010) (See also Table 30).

4.2. GOVERNMENT OWNERSHIP OF BANKS IN RUSSIA

The Russian banking sector is dominated by state-owned banks. The continuing dominant position of state banks was one of the main weak areas in the post-crisis period. Following the 1998 crisis, the banking sector has not undergone an ownership transformation process regarding the state's direct participation in the sector where these banks continued to dominate the market in terms of the volume of transactions and number of branches. In fact, the relative role of the biggest state banks[232] increased following the crisis.[233] The significant public share and the CBR's ambiguous role as the supervisor and also as the main shareholder of the largest bank in Russia[234] still continues (Mahlberg et al., 2011).

As shown in the second chapter[235] of this book and supported by Barth et al. (2010), Caprio and Martinez (2000) and de Nicolo (2000), state ownership and intervention have a negative impact on banks' efficiency and stability. The dominant position of the state has a distorting effect on credit allocation and competition. In Russia, state-owned banks benefited from privileged access to

231 See section 3.1.1.

232 Particularly Sberbank and Vneshtorgbank.

233 As of August 2011, the share of Sberbank's assets in the banking sector's total assets increased from to 24.35 in 2007 to 27% in 2010 (Fungacova & Jakubik, 2012; CBR, 2006–2010).

234 Sberbank.

235 Chapter 2, section 6.2.

state funds, and exemption from some regulatory norms.[236] These banks were continuously encouraged to fund personal projects and election campaigns for local authorities and to fund government deficit and finance unprofitable credits for state-owned enterprises (Tompson, 2004).

As of the end of 2001, the loan share of larger state banks was 35% compared to 20% at the end of 1998. Sberbank held of 70% of household deposits and overall 23% of the banking sector assets (IMF, 2003). The government had a stake of around 25% in 400 banks. In 2003, the government took over VTB, the second largest bank in Russia, from the CBR instead of privatising it. The 2003 IMF Report emphasised the need to level the playing field between state and private banks and prevent the dominant position of Sberbank in the market. In 2003, the share of government-owned banks was 36% in the banking sector (CBR, 2003). The state held majority stakes in 23 banks which accounted for 72% of retail deposits, 34% of capital, 38% of assets, and 39% of outstanding credit to the private sector. However, the CBR continued to hold the majority stake at Sberbank which created several conflicts of interest by acting as the banking sector regulator and simultaneously as the largest single creditor and the owner of its biggest bank.

In 2004, the government was still the owner of the largest banks through Sberbank;[237] and the system in 2004 was still heavily dependent on state banks (Steinherr, 2006). No major bank privatisation had occurred. The banking sector remains predominantly state-controlled as of the end of 2010[238] (Fungacova & Jakubik, 2012). In January 2010, the fifty largest banks were in control of 80% of the total assets in the banking sector. Among these fifty banks, the biggest five banks are government-owned and they control 48% of the total assets in the banking sector (IMF, 2011c).

The 2008–2009 crises in Russia revealed again the structural weaknesses of the Russian banking sector regarding the small and medium-sized banks, which were affected by the crisis due to their weak deposit base, given the dominance of state-owned banks (Fidrmuc & Süss, 2009). At the start of the crisis, state-controlled banks already accounted for over half of the banking sector and the country's five biggest banks were state-controlled. As one of the measures

236 For example, the government has established a number of corporations that have the special legal status of a non-commercial organisation and that are not subject to Bankruptcy Law nor controlled by the Audit Chamber (OECD, 2009).

237 CBR owns 57.6% of Sberbank (Fungacova & Jakobik, 2012).

238 In October 2010, the Russian government approved a programme to sell shares in various large state enterprises over the next five years, including banks. In February 2011, VTB conducted a second public offering resulting in the sale of a further 10% stake. However, even so, the Russian state still owns about 75% of VTB. Similarly, the Central Bank of Russia (CBR), which currently holds a 57.6% stake in Sberbank, plans to retain a 50%-plus-one-share majority in the giant bank even after selling 7.6% of its shares in the near future. Although referred to as a "privatisation programme", the state will maintain controlling voting shares in major banks and other "strategic" enterprises (Fungacova & Jakubik, 2012).

implemented to restore financial stability following the 2008–2009 crises, the government took over troubled banks via these state-controlled banks, boosting the state's presence in banking. These banks acquired other banks during the crisis and hence they increased their market share (Jakobik & Fungacova, 2012).[239] The increase of the share of government-owned banks in the total banking sector assets was around 16.8% between 2007 and 2010 (See Table 30).

Table 30. Percentage of government-owned banks in Turkey and Russia

	1999	2000	2001	2002	2003	2004	2005	2006	2007	2008	2009	2010
Turkey	34.60	34.20	32.70	39.36	39.27	38.35	33.27	31.00	30.25	30.38	32.20	31.56
Russia	41.90	68.00	35.50	37.50	36.00	38.10	40.70	37.80	39.20	40.50	43.90	45.80

Source: BRSA, BAT, CBR Annual Banking Supervision Reports (1999–2010).

5. CONCLUSION

This chapter has discussed the regulatory variables that cause the difference in the empirical analysis of Chapter 2 of this book, described across two geographical dimensions of variability, Russia and Turkey. The aim was to show that Turkey has implemented a stricter and more comprehensive banking reform than Russia in their respective post-crisis periods, that is, the post-2001 period for Turkey and the post-1998 period for Russia. Banking reforms implemented in Turkey involved stronger capital structures, stricter enforcement of the banking law through more disciplinary power granted to the regulatory authority and better risk management policy compared to the reforms implemented in Russia.

The analysis regarding the capital adequacy requirements suggests that asset quality remained a problem in the Russian banking sector due to weak accounting and enforcement standards compared to the strict enforcement of the accounting and supervision standards by the BRSA in Turkey. The average capital adequacy ratios have been higher in Turkey compared to Russia during the period of analysis. In fact, the capital adequacy ratios in Russia continuously declined between 2000 and 2006 (see Table 19). Some Russian banks were not even able to meet the minimum requirement ratio. On the other hand, in Turkey, there has been no news of banks breaching the capital adequacy requirements imposed by the BRSA.

Regarding the official disciplinary power of the regulatory authorities in both countries, the analysis of this chapter shows that the Turkish banking regulatory authority is empowered with a wider range of authority than the Russian regulatory authority. Emerging markets suffer from enforcement problems

[239] Sberbank, Bank VTB, Gazprombank, Rosselkhozbank, VTB-24.

(Vives, 2006). This argument suggests that the disciplinary power of supervisory and regulatory authorities and hence enforcement becomes an important issue in emerging markets. Aysan and Al (2006) argue that the BRSA experience proves that banking regulation and supervision requires more than enacting laws. For an emerging country where corruption and connected-lending practices have become a way of doing business for such a long time, complying with the standards proposed by the regulatory authorities is extremely important. This argument applies well to both Turkey and Russia.

The analysis regarding the power of the Russian banking regulatory authority (the CBR) shows that the enforcement authority of the CBR is deficient in several areas compared to the Turkish regulatory authority. One major difference is that the CBR lacks the power to sanction directors personally for non-compliance. On the contrary, the enactment of Law No. 5020 in Turkey provided a powerful basis for penalising the persons who are responsible for endangering the stability of the financial system by mismanagement. In fact, compared to the Russian regulatory authority in the post-crisis period, the Turkish BRSA had a very strict stance in the enforcement of banking regulations.[240]

Several important steps have been taken in the risk management practices, including information disclosure requirements in both countries. However, the analysis of this chapter shows that the lack of quality data in the Russian reporting standards is still a problem. There are continuing deficiencies related to generous accounting and provisioning rules and more importantly, in related party transaction disclosure requirements. These shortcomings continue to distort the CBR's ability to assess the quality of the assets and the adequacy of loan loss reserves. Hence, they increase uncertainty about the creditworthiness of Russian banks. Turkey has been more disciplined in implementing a comprehensive risk management system. However, the negative effect of this regulation might be due to its regulatory burden and costs caused by the amount of information disclosure requirements. In fact, Vives (2006) argues that reliance on transparency and disclosure requirements is limited in emerging markets. It may be problematic for them to move towards a disclosure approach in regulation since information problems are more acute and the production of information is more problematic in these countries. Hence, competitive pressures and market discipline should not be set at the same level as in developed countries (Vives, 2006).

The empirical findings of Chapter 2 show that deposit insurance affects banks' efficiency negatively due to moral hazard by banks. Tompson (2004) argues that the extent of moral hazard depends on the institutional environment. The qualitative analysis of this chapter is in line with the concept of a poor

240 According to the interview of Kaymak (2009) with the BRSA officials, one factor with the positive effect on BRSA's performance was the strong chair-man profile of the BRSA. The strong leadership made the BRSA the decisive authority of the banking sector.

institutional and regulatory environment in Russia and consequently, it supports the above-mentioned argument. Deposit insurance is a new system in Russia. However, in an environment with weak regulatory quality, and lack of reliable data such as in the Russian banking sector, a deposit insurance mechanism might aggravate the moral hazard problem. Compared to Russia, a deposit insurance system has existed in Turkey since 1983 and the qualitative analysis shows that it is better designed in Turkey. Since moral hazard depends on the institutional environment, the solid environment in Turkey reduces the negative effect (moral hazard) of deposit insurance on Turkish banks.

Finally, regarding entry restrictions, according to the qualitative analysis of this chapter, the number of barriers required as part of the licensing process is similar in both Turkish banks and Russian banks. My analysis on entry regulations regarding both Turkish and Russian banks suggests that following the financial crises in their history, both countries chose to tighten their licensing procedures. In fact, considering both countries' banking histories which are characterised by pervasive corruptive practices, the imposition of entry restrictions to ensure a higher quality of entrants, gains particular importance. However, the negative impact of these regulations on banks' efficiency suggests that its adverse effect on competition prevails.

CONCLUSION

This book has analysed the impact of regulatory variables on banking performance in two emerging countries, Turkey and Russia, with the aim of understanding which banking regulations might contribute to financial stability so that the policymakers in emerging countries can work on these regulatory policies.

The first chapter of this book analysed the function of banking regulation in supporting financial stability. For this purpose, it reviewed the basic concepts in banking, the economic rationale of banking regulation and their role for the financial stability. Due to the banks' role as financial intermediaries in the economy, bank failures are viewed as the most serious failures compared to other industries. Contagion of these failures occurs quickly, spreads more broadly within the industry and, results in large losses to depositors of these banks. More importantly, a bank failure contagion spreads beyond the banking industry and damages the whole financial system and economy. Therefore, the major goal of banking regulation and supervision is to prevent banks from engaging in overly risky activities so that the depositors, other savers and the economy at large are protected from systemic failures.

An efficient banking system is the key to financial stability. Regulation aims to improve the efficiency of a banking sector and hence support financial stability. However, the theoretical discussion in Chapter 1 indicated that the efficiency of certain solutions regarding banking regulation is open to debate. The literature finds conflicting results about the impact of regulations related to capital adequacy requirements, the power of regulatory bodies, information disclosure requirements, deposit insurance and entry regulations on banks' performance and hence, financial stability. Some of the regulations contribute to banks' performance by preventing the risk-taking incentive of banks and thereby supporting financial stability, whereas some of them might have a detrimental effect on financial stability. Besides, banks react differently to regulation under different institutional settings. This implies that conclusions that hold for two emerging countries, particularly Turkey and Russia in the present study, might not apply to advanced countries.

With this fact in mind, Chapter 2 of this book presented an empirical analysis to understand whether different regulatory practices implemented in Turkey and Russia had any impact on their banking sectors' performance during 1999 and 2010. I have employed a two-stage Data Envelopment Analysis (DEA).

The first stage DEA findings indicate that the performance of Turkish banks had an increasing trend from 2005 until 2010 whereas Russian banks' efficiency was declining gradually from 2005 to 2010. The second-stage regression analysis examined the differences in these efficiency scores between Turkish and the Russian banks. I investigated whether the regulations related to capital adequacy requirements, the power of regulatory bodies, the information disclosure requirements, deposit insurance and the entry regulations had any significant impact on banks' performance. The findings of the regression analysis suggest a strong link between these regulations and the differences in the trend of efficiency scores between Turkish and Russian banks.

The empirical analysis provides support for stricter capital adequacy standards and for the development of powerful regulatory/supervisory agencies, but not for a private monitoring approach based on information disclosure. There is also no empirical case for deposit insurance schemes and entry regulations, at least as far as the two countries of interest – Turkey and Russia – are concerned. This implies that the banking regulatory authorities in emerging markets should focus on maintaining high levels of capital adequacy requirements and on developing powerful supervisory agencies for the sake of the enforcement of regulations. These results are suggestive of more general policy implications on which regulations might be important for emerging countries and why. The policymakers in emerging countries could possibly concentrate on these items of banking regulation.

Emerging countries typically suffer larger exogenous shocks than developed countries. They have weaker institutional settings and weaker financial shock absorbers than advanced countries. The discussion in Chapter 3 suggests that the policy responses should be tailored according to the needs of emerging countries. Specifically, *regarding their lack of capacity for policy commitment*, having capital buffers in the banking system and a strong authority capable of enforcing regulations can contribute to financial stability in emerging markets. On the other hand, the results of Chapter 2 indicate that the entry restrictions implemented in these countries have a negative effect on efficiency. This can be attributed to the negative effect of entry restrictions on competition in the banking sector. Considering this negative effect, it would be advisable for both countries to re-evaluate their licensing policies in order to prevent the distortion of competition in the banking sector.

The negative effect of higher requirements for private monitoring can be associated with increasing costs to meet information disclosure requirements such as consolidated accounts, disclosure of off-balance sheet items to the public and to the supervisors, disclosure of risk management procedures to the public, audits by certified auditors and obtaining credit ratings from rating agencies. This increase in costs might undermine the performance of banks. In fact, these results regarding entry requirements and private monitoring suggest that – as argued by Vives (2006) – the level of competition and market discipline should not be set at the same level in emerging countries as in advanced countries.

Finally, the negative effect of deposit insurance supports the argument of Demirgüç-Kunt and Detragiache (1999), who argue that the deposit insurance mechanism is likely to increase banking system fragility in countries with weak institutions. At least, the blanket guarantees provided by the state should be temporary and should be cancelled when a crisis is over.

The contribution of this research is fourfold. Firstly, the literature incorporating the regulatory environment in the factors influencing a bank's efficiency is in its infancy. This work tries to fill a gap by providing evidence on the regulatory factors that have an impact on banks' performance. Secondly, international comparisons of banking performance have not been discussed extensively in the existing literature. This work contributes to the literature by providing international evidence on the impact of regulations. Thirdly, to the best of my knowledge, there is no work which compares Turkey and Russia's banking performance from a law and economics perspective. Most studies which concentrate on banking focus on sectorial differences rather than the regulatory differences. This research carries out an economic analysis of the differences in performance between two countries' banking sectors based on the differences in the legal environment where the banks operate. To the best of my knowledge, this is the first study that applies this methodology to Turkey and Russia.

Finally, this study mainly relies on the database of regulatory indicators of the World Bank survey "The Bank Regulation and Supervision Survey". This dataset allows the international comparison of various features of the bank regulatory environment. However, the regulatory data for the Turkish banking sector is integrated by unique interviews made with the officials of the banking regulatory authority. The data for the Russian banking sector is based on the World Bank survey as well. In order to provide an updated version of the latest survey of the World Bank regarding the years 2009 and 2010 in Russia, an interview was also carried out with the officials of the banking regulatory agency in Russia.

This study has a number of limitations, which could be fruitfully addressed by future research. To begin, this research has used a non-parametric method for the efficiency analysis of banks. Parametric and non-parametric techniques have advantages and disadvantages. Due to the limitations of Data Envelopment Analysis (DEA) – which is the core empirical methodology employed in this work – some researchers prefer to apply both parametric and non-parametric methods in their analyses. In the future, in order to establish the consistency or inconsistency among the parametric and nonparametric findings, an application of a parametric linear programming technique such as Stochastic Frontier Approach might provide another perspective and another set of results for discussion. A further study on the comparison of results would provide stronger support for the findings while suggesting some insights on the advantages and the drawbacks of the different models.

In contrast to parametric frontier models, the incorporation of environmental variables in DEA models is still being researched and it offers a wide variety of proposals to be considered, for instance, risk-adjusted efficiency measures. An analysis by Pastor (2002) applies a three-stage sequential technique, based on the DEA model and on the decomposition of risk into its internal and external components, for obtaining efficiency measures adjusted for risk and the environment. It seems that this technique allows the incorporation of environmental variables in DEA analysis. The implementation of this technique on the subject of this work might allow for more detailed empirical investigations in the future.

With this work, I tried to identify the characteristics of a regulatory framework that would support the efficient performance of banks. A major finding of this research is that banking regulation needs to be adapted to the needs of emerging countries, particularly in the case of Turkey and Russia. This might be instructive for the policymakers of these countries. My analysis is based on a specific list of questions following the literature regarding each regulatory variable of interest. However, the original World Bank survey contains a more detailed list of questions for a few more regulatory variables. By applying the survey for each of these questions, one could obtain more information about the regulatory policies in Turkey and Russia and hence provide a more comprehensive analysis. This too would be an interesting avenue for future research.

APPENDIX A

Variable	Category	Description
Regulatory Variables		
CAPTREQ	Capital Requirements	This variable takes values between 0 and 9, with higher values indicating grater stringency. It is determined by adding 1 if the answer is yes to questions 1–7 and 0 otherwise, while the opposite occurs in the case of questions 8 and 9 (i.e. yes = 0, no = 1). (1) Is the minimum required capital asset ratio risk-weighted in line with Basle guidelines? (2) Does the ratio vary with individual bank's credit risk? (3) Does the ratio vary with market risk? (4–6) Before minimum capital adequacy is determined, which of the following are deducted from the book value of capital: (a) market value of loan losses not realised in accounting books? (b) unrealised losses in securities portfolios? (c) unrealised foreign exchange losses? (7) Are the sources of funds to be used as capital verified by the regulatory/supervisory authorities? (8) Can the initial or subsequent injections of capital be done with assets other than cash or government securities? (9) Can initial disbursement of capital be done with borrowed funds?
OFFDISCPLINE	Official Disciplinary Power	This variable takes values between 0 and 10, with higher values indicating higher power of the supervisory authorities. It is determined by adding 1 if the answer is yes and 0 otherwise, for each one of the following ten questions: (1) Can the supervisory authorities force a bank to change its internal organisational structure? (2) Are there any mechanisms of cease-desist type orders whose infraction leads to automatic imposition of civil & penal sanctions on banks directors & managers? (3) Can the supervisory agency order directors/management to constitute provisions to cover actual/potential losses? (4) Can the supervisory agency suspend director's decision to distribute dividends? (5) Can the supervisory agency suspend director's decision to distribute bonuses? (6) Can the supervisory agency suspend director's decision to distribute management fees? (7) Can the supervisory agency supersede bank shareholder rights and declare bank insolvent? (8) Does banking law allow supervisory agency to suspend some or all ownership rights of a problem bank? (9) Regarding bank restructuring & reorganisation, can supervisory agency remove and replace management? (10) Regarding bank restructuring & reorganisation, can supervisory agency remove and replace directors?

PRVTMONITOR	Private Monitoring	This variable takes values between 0 and 10, with higher values indicating policies that promote private monitoring. It is determined by adding 1 if the answer is yes and 0 otherwise, for each one of the following ten questions: (1) Does accrued, though unpaid interest/principal enter the income statement while loan is non-performing? (2) Are financial institutions required to produce consolidated accounts covering all bank and any non-bank financial subsidiaries? (3) Are off-balance sheet items disclosed to supervisors? (4) Are off-balance sheet items disclosed to public? (5) Must banks disclose their risk management procedures to public? (6) Are directors legally liable for erroneous/misleading information? (7) Is an external audit compulsory? (8) Are there specific requirements for the extent of audit? (9) Are auditors licensed or certified? (10) Do regulations require credit ratings for commercial banks?	
DEPOSITINSUR	Deposit Insurance Scheme	Dummy variable that takes the value of one if there is an explicit deposit insurance scheme and zero otherwise.	
ENTRY	Entry Requirements	This variable examines whether there are specific legal submissions required to obtain a license to operate as a bank. It is determined by adding 1 if the answer is yes and 0 otherwise, for each one of the following eight questions: (1) Draft by law, (2) Intended organisation chart, (3) Financial projections for first three years, (4) Financial information on main potential shareholders, (5) Background experience of future directors, (6) Background experience of future managers, (7) Sources of funds to be disbursed in the capitalisation of new banks, (8) Market differentiation intended for new bank?	
Control Variables			
Bank-Specific Characteristics			**Source/ Database**
EQAS	Capital Strength	Equity/assets	Bankscope & BAT*
ROE	Profitability	Pre-tax profit/equity	Bankscope & BAT*
EXPTA	Expenses Management	Non-interest expenses/average assets	Bankscope & BAT*
LOANTA	Loan Activity	Loans/total assets	Bankscope & BAT*
Macroeconomic Conditions			
GDP	Overall economic conditions	Real GDP growth	GMID, OECD

Market Structure			
OFGOVBANKS	Presence of government-owned banks	Fraction of the banking system's assets in banks that are 50% or more government-owned	CBR & BRSA
Institutional Environment			
GOVNTINTERV	Government intervention in the economy	This is an index of government intervention in the economy. It measures government's direct use of scarce resources for its own purposes and government's control over resources through ownership. The index takes values between 1 and 5, with higher values indicating higher levels of government consumption in the economy and higher share of revenues received from state-owned enterprises and property.	Heritage Foundation
REGQUALITY	Regulatory quality	This is an index reflecting the perceptions of the ability of the government to formulate and implement sound policies and regulations that permit and promote private sector development. The index takes values between 1 and 10, with higher values indicating higher levels of regulatory quality.	WB Governance Indicators

Notes: WB: World Bank
CBR: Central Bank of Russia
BRSA: Banking Regulation and Supervision Agency
BAT: The Banks Association of Turkey
WB Governance Indicators: World Bank governance indicators prepared by D. Kaufmann, A. Kraay & P. Zoido-Lobaton

APPENDIX B

Robustness Test: Wilcoxon-Mann-Whitney Test

Each DEA sample for both countries consists of two groups of banks: domestic banks and foreign banks. Constructing frontiers specific to each of these groups provides more flexible, homogenous and thus more appropriate findings than estimating a single size frontier (see Bauer et al., 1993 and Isik and Hasan, 2002). Before calculating the efficiency scores for each country, it is necessary to test statistically the difference between the two groups of domestic and foreign banks in terms of efficiency. The aim is to test their comparability. The result will enable us to pool domestic bank and foreign banks together when calculating their efficiency scores. In order to fulfil this purpose, the rank-sum test developed by Wilcoxon-Mann-Whitney can be used to identify whether the differences between two groups of domestic banks and foreign banks are significant (Cooper et al., 2006: 221–224). If the test concludes that the two groups of domestic and foreign banks belong to the same population, both groups of banks' DEA scores will be estimated by pooling both groups for each country.

For each country, I represent the data in two groups by D= {d1,d2, ..., dm} which refers to domestic banks, and F = {f1,f2, ..., fn} which refers to foreign banks. By ranking the data, we arrive at a variable called *S* statistic which follows an approximately normal distribution with mean m(m+n+1)/2 and variance mn(m+n+1)/12. By normalising *S*, we have:

$$T = \frac{S - m(m + n + 1)/2}{\sqrt{mn(m + n + 1)/12}}$$

where *T* has an approximately standard normal distribution. *T* serves to test whether the hypothesis that the two groups belong to the same population or whether they differ significantly. The hypothesis will be rejected if $T \leq -T\alpha/2$ or $T \geq T\alpha/2$, where $T\alpha/2$ corresponds to the upper $\alpha/2$ percentile of the standard normal distribution.

The *T* statistic for the group of Turkish banks is –1.27. If we choose the significance level $\alpha = 0.05$ (5%), then it holds that $T0.025 = 1.96$. Since $T = -1.27 > -1.96$, we do not reject the null hypothesis at the significance level 5%. We arrive at the same conclusion for Russian banks where T is equal to 0.49. Since $0.49 < 1.96$, we do not reject the null hypothesis that the two groups of domestic and foreign banks belong to the same population. Hence, the common frontier approach will be used in the calculations of efficiency scores for both types of banks with the assumption that they use the same production technology.

APPENDIX C
List of Failed Banks

Bank Name	Acquired By	Involvement	Date
Svyat bank	VEB	Direct state bailout	23/09/2008
KIT Finance	Alrosa	State controlled	10/10/2008
Soyuz	Gazenergoprombank	State controlled	11/10/2008
Globex	VEB	Direct state bailout	17/10/2008
VEFK*	DIA	Direct state bailout	21/10/2008
Sobinbank*	Gazenergoprombank	State controlled	15/10/2008
Severnaya Kazna *	Alfa Bank	DIA	09/12/2008
Russky Bank Razvitiya	Otkritie	DIA	13/12/2008
Russian Capital Bank	Nat. Reserve Bank	CBR support	14/01/2009
Elektronika*	Nat. Reserve Bank	DIA	01/12/2008
Gubernsky Bank*	Sinara Group	DIA	11/11/2008
Nizhegorodpromstroybank*	Sarovbusinessbank	DIA	17/11/2008
Bank 24.ru*	Probusinessbank	DIA	07/12/2008
Yarsotbank*	Promsvyazbank	CBR support	21/10/2008
Potenzial*	Solidarnost Bank	DIA	10/11/2008
Gasenergobank*	Probusinessbank	DIA	14/11/2008
Bashinvest*	Binbank	DIA	24/11/2008
Moscow Zalogovy Bank	Bank of Moscow	DIA	29/12/2008
Moskovsky Kapital	Nomos Bank	DIA	19/12/2008
Nizhniy Novgorod*	Promsvyazbank	DIA	28/11/2008
Russian Develop. Bank	DIA	DIA	06/11/2008
Investment Bank Trust*	National Bank Trust	Merger	20/11/2008
APR Bank*	Onexim Group	Merger	24/11/2008
MDM Bank*	URSA Bank	Merger	03/12/2008
Tharkhany Bank	Morskoy	DIA	22/12/2008
Kauri Bank	Licence revoked	Licence revoked	10/02/2009
Econats Bank	Licence revoked	Licence revoked	22/12/2008
Peace Bank	Licence revoked	Licence revoked	22/12/2008
Bank Eurasia Center	Licence revoked	Licence revoked	22/12/2008

Bank Name	Acquired By	Involvement	Date
Sakhalin Vest*	Licence revoked	Licence revoked	22/12/2008
West Bank Premier	Licence revoked	Licence revoked	22/12/2008
Lefco Bank	Licence revoked	Licence revoked	12/11/2008
Sibcontact	Licence revoked	Licence revoked	06/02/2009
ZelAK Bank	Licence revoked	Licence revoked	18/01/2009
Bank Sochi	Licence revoked	Licence revoked	17/11/2008
Setevoi Neftyanoy Bank*	Licence revoked	Licence revoked	16/12/2008
Agrokhimbank*	Licence revoked	Licence revoked	30/12/2008
Baltcreditbank	Licence revoked	Licence revoked	19/12/2008
Net Oil Bank	Licence revoked	Licence revoked	19/12/2008
Inkasbank*	Licence revoked	Licence revoked	19/02/2009
Sudcombank*	Licence revoked	Licence revoked	19/02/2009
Prikamye Bank	Licence revoked	Licence revoked	19/01/2009
Uraykombank	Licence revoked	Licence revoked	10/02/2009
Integro*	Licence revoked	Licence revoked	27/11/2008
Kurganprombank*	Licence revoked	Licence revoked	27/11/2008
Gazinvestbank	Licence revoked	Licence revoked	17/12/2008

* Banks whose equity is below €5 million.
Source: Fidrmuc and Süss, 2009.

REFERENCES

Abad, C., J. Laffarga, A. García-Borboll, M. Larrán, J. Pinero and N. Garrod (2000): "An evaluation of the value-relevance of consolidated versus unconsolidated accounting information: Evidence from quoted Spanish firms" *Journal of International Financial Management and Accounting*, Vol. 11, Issue 3, pp. 156–177.

Abbasoglu O.F., A.F. Aysan, and A. Gunes (2007): "Concentration, Competition, Efficiency and Profitability of the Turkish Banking Sector in the Post-Crises Period" Munich Personal RePEc Archive (MPRA) Paper No. 5494.

Acharya, V.V., T. Cooley, M. Richardson and I. Walter (2011): "Market Failures and Regulatory Failures: Lessons from Past and Present Financial Crises" ADBI Working Paper No. 264.

Admati, A.R., P.M. DeMarzo, M.F. Hellwig and P. Pfleiderer (2011): "Fallacies, Irrelevant Facts, and Myths in the Discussion of Capital Regulation: Why Bank Equity is Not Expensive" The Rock Center for Corporate Governance at Stanford University Working Paper Series No. 86, Stanford GSB Research Paper No. 2063.

Admati, A.R., P.M. DeMarzo, M.F. Hellwig and P. Pfleiderer (2012): "Debt Overhang and Capital Regulation" The Rock Center for Corporate Governance at Stanford University Working Paper Series No. 114.

Adrian, T., and H.S. Shin (2008): "Liquidity, Monetary Policy and Financial Cycles" Current Issues in Economics and Finance, Federal Reserve Bank of New York, Vol. 14, No. 1.

Akyürek, C. (2006): "The Turkish Crisis of 2001: A Classic?" *Emerging Markets Finance and Trade,* Vol. 42, Issue 1, pp. 5–32.

Alexander, W.E., D.S. Hoelscher, and M. Fuchs (2000): "Banking System Restructuring in Russia" IMF Conference on Post-Election Strategy Moscow, April 5–7, 2000.

Alexandru, C.G., and R.M. Laurentiu (2008): "The Assessment of Banking Performances: Inidcators of Performance in Bank Area" MPRA Paper No. 11600.

Alhadeff, D.A. (1962): "A Reconsideration of Restrictions on Bank Entry" *The Quarterly Journal of Economics,* Vol. 76, No. 2, pp. 246–263.

Allen, F. and D. Gale (2004): "Competition and Financial Stability" *Journal of Money, Credit, and Banking*, Vol. 36, No. 3.

Allen, F. and R.J. Herring (2001): "Banking Regulation versus Securities Market Regulation" Wharton School, University of Pennsylvania WP 01–29.

Allen, L. and A. Rai (1996): "Operational Efficiency in Banking: An International Comparison" *Journal of Banking and Finance*, Vol. 20, pp. 655–672.

Allen, L., A. Saunders and G.F. Udell (1991): "The Pricing of Retail Deposits: Concentration and Information" *Journal of Financial Intermediation*, Vol. 1, No. 4, pp. 335–361.

Altunbas, Y., A. Kara, and Ö. Olgu (2009): *Turkish Banking: Banking under Political Instability and Chronic High Inflation,* Palgrave Macmillan Publishing.

Altunbas, Y., D. Maude and P. Molyneux (1995): "Efficiency and Mergers in the UK Retail Banking Market" Institute of European Finance Working Paper, pp. 1–40.

Aly, H.Y., R. Grabowski, C. Pasurka and N. Rangan (1990): "Technical, Scale, and Allocative Efficiencies in US banking: An empirical investigation" *Review of Economics and Statistics*, Vol. 72, pp. 211–218.

Anayiotos. G., H. Toroyan and A. Vamvakidis (2010): "The Efficiency of Emerging Europe's Banking Sector before and after the Recent Economic Crisis" *Financial Theory and Practice*, Vol. 34, No. 3, pp. 247–267.

Angrist, J.D. and J.-S. Pischke (2008): "Mostly Harmless Econometrics: An Empiricist's Companion" Princeton University Press.

Aras, O.N. (2010): "Effects of the Global Economic Crisis on Turkish Banking Sector" *International Journal of Economics and Finance Studies*, Vol. 2, No. 1, pp. 113–120.

Arner, D.W. (2009): "The Global Credit Crisis of 2008: Causes and Consequences" Asian Institute of International Financial Law (AIIFL), Working Paper No. 3.

Arrow K.J., H.B. Chenery, B. Minhas and R.M. Solow (1961): "Capital-Labour Substitution and Economic Efficiency" *The Review of Economics and Statistics*, Vol. 43, pp. 225–250.

Asarkaya, Y. and S. Ozcan (2007): "Determinants of Capital Structure in Financial Institutions: the Case of Turkey" *Journal of BRSA Banking and Financial Markets*, No. 1, pp. 91–109.

Ashcraft, A.B. (2006): "Does the Market Discipline Banks? New Evidence from the Regulatory Capital Mix" Federal Reserve Bank of New York (FRB) of New York Staff Report No. 244.

Atici, G. and G. Gursoy (2011): "Financial Crises and Capital Buffer: Evidence from the Turkish Banking Sector" *Banks and Bank Systems International Research Journal*, Vol. 6, Issue 1, pp. 72–86.

Aysan, A.F. and H. Al (2006): "Assessing the Preconditions in Establishing an Independent Regulatory and Supervisory Agency in Globalized Financial Markets: The Case of Turkey" *International Journal of Applied Business and Economic Research*, Vol. 4, Issue 2, pp. 125–146.

Aysan, A.F. and S.P. Ceyhan (2007): "Market Disciplining Role of Crisis on the Restructuring of the Turkish Banking Sector" Munich Personal RePEc Archive (MPRA) Paper No. 5492.

Aysan, A.F. and S.P. Ceyhan (2008): "What Determines the Banking Sector Performance in Globalized Financial Markets? The Case of Turkey" *Physica A*, 387, pp. 1593–1602.

Ayzıt, M. (2004): "Dünyada ve Türkiye'de Mevduat Sigorta Sistemi Uygulamaları" TCMB 2004.

Bagaeva A. (2008): "An examination of the effect of international investors on accounting information" *Advances in Accounting, incorporating Advances in International Accounting* Vol. 24, Issue 2, pp. 157–161.

Bakır, C. (2009): "Wobbling but Still on its Feet: The Turkish Economy in the Global Financial Crisis" *South European Society and Politics,* Vol. 1, Issue 1, pp. 71–85.

Bakir, C. and Z. Önis (2010): "The Regulatory State and Turkish Banking Reforms in the Age of Post-Washington Consensus" *Development and Change*, Vol. 41, No. 1, pp. 77–106.

Balin, B.J. (2008): "Basel I, Basel II, and Emerging Markets: A Nontechnical Analysis" The Johns Hopkins University School of Advanced International Studies (SAIS).

Baltagi, B.H. and J.M. Griffin (1988): "A General Index of Technical Change" *Journal of Political Economy*, Vol. 96, pp. 20–41.

Banker, R.D., A. Charnes and W.W. Cooper (1984): "Some Models for Estimating Technical and Scale Inefficiencies in Data Envelopment Analysis" *Management Science*, Vol. 30, pp. 1078–1092.

Baltensperger, E. (1988): "Die Regulierung des Bankensektors" *Wirtschafts-wissenschaftliches Studium*, 17–2, 53–57; in Dragomir 2010: 43.

Barisitz, S. (2009): "Russian Banking in Recent Years: Gaining Depth in a Fragile Environment" in: "Current Trends in the Russian Financial System", SUERF Studies, SUERF – The European Money and Finance Forum, number 2009/2 edited by Morten Balling, August.

Barr, R., L.M. Seiford and T.F. Siems (1994): "Forecasting Bank Failure: A Non-Parametric Frontier Estimation Approach" *Recherches Economiques de Louvain*, Vol. 60, pp. 417–429.

Barrell, R. and S. Gottschalk (2006): "The Impacts of Capital Adequacy Requirements on Emerging Markets" NIESR Discussion Papers No. 269.

Barth, J.R., G. Caprio, Jr., and R. Levine (2001a): "Bank Regulation and Supervision: What Works Best?" The World Bank Development Research Group – Finance and Financial Sector Strategy and Policy Department, WP No. 2725.

Barth, J.R., G. Caprio, Jr., and R. Levine (2001b): "The Regulation and Supervision of Banks around the World: A New Database" World Bank Policy Research Working Paper No. 2588.

Barth, J.R., G. Caprio, Jr., and R. Levine (2002): "Bank Regulation and Supervision: What Works Best?" NBER Working Paper No. 9323.

Barth, J.R., G. Caprio, Jr., and R. Levine (2003): "Bank Regulation and Supervision: Lessons from a New Database", in: J.A. Murillo Garza (ed.), *Macroeconomic Stability, Financial Markets, and Economic Development*, Banco de Mexico.

Barth, J.R., G. Caprio, Jr., and R. Levine (2004): "Bank regulation and Supervision: What works best?" *Journal of Financial Intermediation*, Vol. 13, pp. 205–248.

Barth, J.R., G. Caprio, Jr., and R. Levine (2006a): "Rethinking Bank Regulation: Till Angels Govern" Cambridge University Press.

Barth J.R, G. Caprio, Jr. and R. Levine (2007): Guide to the 2007 World Bank Survey, available at http://econ.worldbank.org/ 2003–2007 Database by section.

Barth, J.R., G. Caprio, Jr., and R. Levine (2008): "Bank regulations are changing: But for better or worse?" World Bank Policy Research Working Paper 4646.

Barth, J.R., G. Caprio, Jr., and R. Levine (2013): "Bank Regulation and Supervision in 180 Countries from 1999 to 2011" NBER Working Paper No. W18733.

Barth, J.R., L.G. Dopico, D.E. Nolle and J.A. Wilcox (2002): "Bank Safety and Soundness and the Structure of Bank Supervision: A cross-country analysis" *International Review of Finance*, Vol. 3, pp. 163–188.

Barth, M., W. Landsman and M. Lang (2006b): "International accounting standards and accounting quality" Working Paper, Stanford University and University of North Carolina at Chapel Hill.

Barth, J.R., C. Lin, Y. Mac, J. Seadec and F.M. Song (2010): "Do Bank Regulation, Supervision and Monitoring Enhance or Impede Bank Efficiency?" Available from: http://papers.ssrn.com/sol3/papers.cfm?abstract_id=1579352.

Bascı, E (2006): "Credit growth in Turkey: Drivers and Challenges" in: Bank for International Settlements (ed.), *The banking system in emerging economies: how much progress has been made?* BIS No. 28, pp. 363–375.

Bator, F.M. (1958): "The Anatomy of Market Failure" *The Quarterly Journal of Economics*, Vol. 72, No. 3, pp. 351–379.

Bauer, P.W., A.N. Berger and D.B. Humphrey (1993): "Efficiency and Productivity Growth in US Banking" in: H.O. Fried, C.A.K. Lovell and S.S. Schmidt (1993), *The Measurement of Productive Efficiency: Techniques and Applications*, Oxford University Press, pp. 386–414.

Bayraktar, N. and Y. Wang (2008): "Banking Sector Openness and Economic Growth" *The Journal of Applied Economic Research*, Vol. 2, No. 2, pp. 145–175.

Beatty, A.L. and A. Gron (2001): "Capital, Portfolio, and Growth: Bank Behavior Under Risk-Based Capital Guidelines" *Journal of Financial Services Research*, Vol. 20, pp. 5–31.

Beccalli, E., B. Casu and C. Girardone (2006): "Efficiency and Stock Performance in European Banking" *Journal of Business Finance and Accounting*, Vol. 33, pp. 245–262.

Beck, T., A. Demirgüç-Kunt and R. Levine (2006): "Bank concentration, competition and crises" *Journal of Banking and Finance*, Vol. 30, pp. 1581–1603.

Becker, G.S. (1968): "Crime and Punishment: An Economic Approach" *The Journal of Political Economy*, Vol. 76, No. 2, pp. 169–217.

Belianin, A.V. (2005): "Signaling Bank Quality: An Evolutionary Approach to Money Market in Transition" Moscow State University - Higher School of Economics, Working Paper No. 9.

Beltratti, A. and R.M. Stulz (2009): "Why Did Some Banks Perform Better during the Credit Crisis? A Cross-Country Study of the Impact of Governance and Regulation" Charles A. Dice Center for Research in Financial Economics - Working Paper No. 2009–12; NBER Working Paper No. 15180.

Beltratti, A. and R.M. Stulz (2010): "The Credit Crisis around the Globe? Why Did Some Banks Perform Better?" Charles A. Dice Center for Research in Financial Economics - Working Paper No. 2010–05.

Benston, G.J. (2007): "Basel II and Bankers' Propensity to Take or Avoid Excessive Risk" *Atlantic Economic Journal*, Vol. 35, No. 4, pp. 373–382.

Benston, G.J. and C.W. Smith, Jr. (1975): "A Transactions Cost Approach to the Theory of Financial Intermediation" *The Journal of Finance*, Vol. 31, No. 2, pp. 215–231.

Berg, S.A., E.S. Jansen and F.R. Forsund (1992): "Malmquist Indices of Productivity Growth during the Deregulation of Norwegian Banking, 1980–89" *The Scandinavian Journal of Economics*, Vol. 94, pp. 211–228.

Berg, S.A., P.N.D. Bukh and F.R. Forsund (1995): "Banking Efficiency in the Nordic Countries: A Four Country Malmquist Index Analysis" Working Paper, University of Aarhus, Dinamarca.

Bergendahl, G. (1998): "DEA and Benchmarks – An Application to Nordic Banks" *Annals of Operations Research*, Vol. 82, pp. 233–249.

Berger, A. and D. Humprey (1997): "Efficiency of Financial Institutions: International Survey and Directions for Future Research" *European Journal of Operational Research*, pp. 175–212.

Berger, A.N. and C.H.S. Bouwman (2009): "Bank Liquidity Creation" *The Review of Financial Studies*, Vol. 22, Issue 9, pp. 3779–3837.

Berger, A., and S.M. Davies (1998): "The Information Content of Bank Examinations" *Journal of Financial Services Research*, Vol. 14, No. 2, pp. 117–144.

Berger, A.N. and D.B. Humphrey (1992): "Measurement and Efficiency Issues in Commercial Banking" in: Griliches Z. (ed.), *Output Measurement in the Service Sectors*, National Bureau of Economic Research, University of Chicago Press, pp. 245–279.

Berger, A.N. and L.J. Mester (1997): "Inside the Black Box: What Explains Differences in the Efficiencies of Financial Institutions?" *Journal of Banking and Finance*, Vol. 21, pp. 895–947.

Berger, A.N. and R. DeYoung (1997): "Problem Loans and Cost Efficiency in Commercial Banks" *Journal of Banking and Finance*, Vol. 21, pp. 849–870.

Berger, A.N. and T.H. Hannan (1998): "The Efficiency Cost of Market Power in the Banking Industry: a Test of the Quiet Life and Related Hypotheses" *Review of Economics and Statistics*, Vol. 80, No. 3, pp. 454–465.

Berger, A.N., R.J. Herring and G.P. Szego (1995): "The Role of Capital in Financial Institutions" *Journal of Banking and Finance*, Vol. 19, No. 3–4, pp. 393–430.

Bernanke, B.S. and M. Gertler (1987): "Financial Fragility and Economic Performance" NBER Working Paper No. 2318.

Besanko D. and A. Thakor (1992): "Banking Deregulation: Allocational Consequence of Relaxing Entry Barriers" *Journal of Banking and Finance*, Vol. 16, pp. 909–932.

Besanko, D. and G. Kanatas (1993), "Credit Market Equilibrium with Bank Monitoring and Moral Hazard" *Review of Financial Studies*, Vol. 6, No. 1, pp. 213–32.

Bhattacharya, A.W., A. Boot and A.V. Thakor (1998): "The Economics of Bank Regulation" *Journal of Money, Credit and Banking*, Vol. 30, No. 4, pp. 745–770.

Bhattacharya, S. and A. Thakor (1993): "Contemporary Banking Theory" *Journal of Financial Intermediation*, Vol. 3, pp. 2–50.

Bjurek, H. (1996): "The Malmquist Total Factor Productivity Index" *Scandinavian Journal of Economics*, Vol. 98, No. 2, pp. 303–313.

Black, F. (1975): "Bank funds management in an efficient market" *Journal of Financial Economics*, Vol. 2, Issue 4, pp. 323–339.

Blanchard, O., J. Caruana and R. Moghadam (2009): "Initial Lessons of the Crisis" IMF Working Paper.

Blum, J. (1999): "Do Capital Adequacy Requirements Reduce Risks in Banking?" *Journal of Banking and Finance*, Vol. 23, pp. 755–771.

Blum, J. and M. Hellwig (1995): "The macroeconomic implications of capital adequacy requirements for banks" *European Economic Review*, Vol. 39, pp. 739–749.

Blundell-Wignall, A., P. Atkinson and S.H. Lee (2008): "The Current Financial Crisis: Causes and Policy Issues" *OECD Journal: Financial Market Trends*, Vol. 2008, Issue 2.

Blundell-Wignall, A. and P. Atkinson (2008): "The Sub-prime Crisis: Causal Distortions and Regulatory Reform" in: P. Bloxham and C. Kent (ed.), *Lessons from the Financial Turmoil of 2007 and 2008*, Reserve Bank of Australia, 2008.

Bogetic, Z. (2008): "Russia's Financial Crisis: Causes, Consequences and Prospects" in: M. Balling (ed.), *Current Trends in the Russian Financial System*, SUERF – The European Money and Finance Forum Vienna 2009.

Bolt, W. and A.F. Tieman (2004): "Banking competition, risk and regulation" *Scandinavian Journal of Economics,* Vol. 106, No. 4, pp. 783–804.

Boorman, J. (2009): "The Impact of the Financial Crisis on Emerging Market Economies: The Transmission Mechanism, Policy Response and Lessons" Emerging Markets Forum 2009.

Boot, A.W.A. and A. Thakor (1993): "Self-interested bank regulator" *American Economic Review,* Vol. 83, Issue 2, pp. 206–212.

Borio, C. (2009): "Ten propositions about liquidity crises" BIS Working Papers No. 293, November 2009.

Boyd, J.H., R. Jagannathan and S. Kwak (2009): "What Caused the Current Financial Mess and What Can We Do about It?" CFA Institute, CFA Digest, Vol. 40, No. 2.

Brana, S., M. Maurel and J. Sgard (1999): "Enterprise Adjustment and the Role of Bank Credit in Russia: Evidence from a 420 Firm's Qualitative Survey" *Comparative Economic Studies*, Vol. 41, No. 4, pp. 47–69.

Bredenkamp, H., M. Josefsson and C.J. Lindgren (2009): "Turkey's Renaissance: From Banking Crisis to Economic Revival" in E. Brau and I. McDonald, *Successes of the International Monetary Fund: Untold Stories of Cooperation at Work*, Palgrave Macmillan.

Brunnermeier, M., A. Crockett, C. Goodhart, A. Persaud and H.S. Shin (2009): "The fundamental principles of financial regulation – Geneva reports on the world economy" Vol. 11, Centre for Economic Policy Research (CEPR).

Brunnermeier, M., and L.H. Pederson (2005): "Market Liquidity and Funding Liquidity" NYU Working Paper No. SC-AM-05-06.

Buch, C., and G. DeLong (2004): "Cross-Border Bank Mergers: What lures the rare animal?" *Journal of Banking and Finance*, Vol. 28, No. 9, pp. 2077–2102.

Buchs, T.D. (1999): "Financial crisis in the Russian Federation: Are the Russians learning to Tango", *Economics of Transition*, Vol. 7, Issue 3, pp. 687–715.

Buiter, W.H. (2007): "Lessons from the 2007 Financial Crisis" CEPR Policy Insight No.18.

Caballero, R.J. and P. Kurlat (2008): "Flight to Quality and Bailouts: Policy Remarks and a Literature Review" MIT Department of Economics Working Paper No. 08–21.

Calem, P. and R. Rob (1999): "The Impact of Capital-Based Regulation on Bank Risk-Taking" *Journal of Financial Intermediation*, Vol. 8, pp. 317–352.

Calomiris, C.W. (2008): "The Subprime Turmoil: What's Old, What's New, and what's Next" Columbia University, National Bureau of Economic Research (NBER).

Calomiris, C.W. (2009): "Financial Innovation, Regulation, and Reform" *Cato Journal*, Vol. 29, pp. 65–92.

Calomiris, C.W. and C.M. Kahn (1991): "The Role of Demandable Debt in Structuring Optimal Banking Arrangements" *The American Economic Review*, Vol. 81, No. 3, pp. 497–513.

Canakcı, İ.H. (2009): "Global Financial Crisis: Impact on the Prospects for the World Economy and Turkey" *International Economic Issues, Crisis Special*, pp. 7–14.

Caner, S., E. Ungan and S. Ozyıldırım (2007): "Transition to Market-Based Discipline of Banks: A Comparative Analysis of Russian Federation and Turkey" Bilkent University.

Caner, S., E. Ungan and S. Ozyıldırım (2008): "Depositors' Assessment of Bank Riskiness in the Russian Federation" *Journal of Financial Services Research*, Vol. 33, pp. 77–100.

Caner, S. and V.K. Kontorovich (2004): "Efficiency of the banking sector in the Russian Federation with international comparison" *Economics Journal of HSE* (Ekonomicheskii gurnal vysshei shkoly ekonomiki), Vol. 8, No. 3, pp. 357–375.

Cannata, F. and M. Quagliariello (2009): "The Role of Basel II in the Subprime Financial Crisis: guilty or not guilty?" CAREFIN Working Paper No. 3/09.

Caprio, Jr., G. and L.H. Summers (1993): "Finance and Its Reform: Beyond Laissez Faire" World Bank Policy Research Working Paper No. 1171.

Carey, M. (2000): "Dimensions of Credit Risk and Their Relationship to Economic Capital Requirements" NBER Working Paper No. 7629.

Carvallo O. and A. Kasman (2005): "Cost efficiency in the Latin American and Caribbean banking systems" *Journal of International Financial Markets, Institutions and Money*, Vol. 15, Issue 1, pp. 55–72.

Casu B. and C. Girardone (2006): "Bank Competition, Concentration and Efficiency in the Single European Market" The Manchester School, Vol. 74, No. 4, pp. 441–468.

Casu, B. and C. Girardone and P. Molyneux (2004): "Productivity Change in European Banking: A Comparison of Parametric and Non-Parametric Approaches" *Journal of Banking and Finance*, Vol. 28, No. 10, pp. 2521–2540.

Casu, B. and P. Molyneux (2003): "A Comparative Study of Efficiency in European Banks" *Applied Economics*, Vol. 35, No. 17, pp. 1865–1876.

Chapman, S.A. and M. Mulino (2001): "Explaining Russia's Currency and Financial Crisis" *Economic Policy in Transitional Economies*, Vol. 11, Issue 1, pp. 1–26.

Charnes, A., W.W. Cooper and E. Rhodes (1978): "Measuring the Efficiency of Decision Making Units" *European Journal of Operational Research*, Vol. 2, pp. 429–444.

Chernykh, L. and R.O. Edmister (2010): "Do Foreign Correspondent Relationships Indicate Bank Quality?" *International Scientific Journal*, Vol. 8., 2010/11, No. 2, pp. 63–76.

Chowdhury, A. (2003): "Banking reform in Russia: Winds of change?" Bank of Finland Institute for Economies in Transition, No. 5.

Čihák, M. and A. Tieman (2008): "Quality of Financial Sector Regulation and Supervision around the World" IMF Working Paper No. 08/190.

Čihák, M., A. Demirgüç-Kunt, M.S.M. Peria and A. Mohseni-Cheraghlou (2012): "Bank Regulation and Supervision around the World: A Crisis Update" The World Bank Policy Research Working Paper No. 6286.

Claeys, S. and K. Schoors (2007): "Bank supervision Russian style: Evidence of conflicts between micro- and macro-prudential concerns" *Journal of Comparative Economics*, Vol. 35, Issue 3, pp. 630–657.

Claeys, S., G. Lanine and K. Schoors (2005): "Bank Supervision Russian Style: Rules versus Enforcement and Tacit Objectives" William Davidson Institute Working Paper No. 778.

Cockerill, T., A. Ataullah, and H. Le (2004): "Financial Liberalization and Bank Efficiency: A Comparative Analysis of India and Pakistan" *Applied Economics*, Vol. 36, pp. 1915–1924.

Coelli, T. (1996): "A Guide to DEAP version 2.1: A Data Envelopment Analysis (Computer Programme. CEPA Working Paper 96/08, Department of Econometrics, University of New England, Armidale, Australia.

Coelli, T., D.S.P. Rao, and G.E. Battese (1998): "An Introduction to Efficiency and Productivity Analysis" Kluwer Academic Publishers.

Cooper, W.W., L.M. Seiford and K. Tone (2006): "Introduction to Data Envelopment Analysis and its Uses with DEA-Solver Software and References" Springer Science & Business Media, Inc.

Cooter, R. and T. Ulen (2007): *Law and Economics*, 5th edition, Addison-Wesley Series in Economics.

Cordella T. and E.L. Yeyati (2002): "Financial opening, deposit insurance, and risk in a model of banking competition" *European Economic Review*, Vol. 46, pp. 471–485

Cornwell, C., P. Schmidt and R.C. Sickles (1990): "Production Frontiers with Cross-sectional and Time-series Variation in Efficiency Levels" *Journal of Econometrics*, Vol. 46, pp. 185–200.

Curry, T., J.P. O'Keefe, J. Coburn and L. Montgomery (1999): "Financially Distressed Banks: How Effective Are Enforcement Actions in the Supervisory Process?" *FDIC Banking Review*, Vol. 12, No. 2, pp. 1–18.

Davies, H. (1998): "Averaging in a Framework of Zero Reserve Requirements: Implications for the Operation of Monetary Policy" Bank of England Working Paper No. 84.

De Grauwe, P. (2009): "Lessons from the Banking Crisis: A Return to Narrow Banking" CESifo Dice Report, Vol. 7, Issue 2, pp. 19–23.

De Nicolo, G. (2000): "Size, charter value and risk in banking: an international perspective" International Finance Discussion Papers No. 689, Board of Governors of the Federal Reserve System.

Debreu, G. (1951): "The Coefficient of Resource Utilization" *Econometrica*, Vol. 19, No. 3, pp. 273–292.

Del Gatto, M., A. di Liberto and C. Petraglia (2009): "Measuring productivity" IAREG WP5/01.

Delikanlı, I.U. (1998): "Bankaların Denetimi ve Gözetimi: Türkiye ve Avrupa Birliği Uygulamaları", Active Bankacılık ve Finans Dergisi, 1998/v No. www.makalem.com/Search/ArticleDetails.asp?nARTICLE_id=196

Delimatsis, P. (2012): "Financial Innovation and Prudential Regulation – The New Basel III Rules" Tilburg Law and Economics Center (TILEC) Discussion Paper No. 2012-016.

Dell'Arciccia, G., D. Igan and L. Laeven (2008): "Credit Booms and Lending Standards: Evidence from the Subprime Mortgage Market" IMF Working Paper No. 08/106

Demirgüç-Kunt, A., E. Detragiache and T. Tressel (2008): "Banking on the Principles: Compliance with Basel Core Principles and Banks Soundness" *Journal of Financial Intermediation*, Vol. 17, pp. 511–542.

Demirgüç-Kunt, A. and E. Detragiache (2002): "Does deposit insurance increase banking system stability? An empirical investigation" *Journal of Monetary Economics*, Vol. 49, No. 7, pp. 1373–1406

Demirgüç-Kunt, A. and H. Huizinga (1999): "Market Discipline and Financial Safety Net Design" CEPR Discussion Papers No. 2311.

Demirgüç-Kunt, A. and V. Maksimovic (1998): "Law, Finance and Firm Growth" *Journal of Finance*, Vol. 53, No. 6, pp. 2107–2137.

Demirgüç-Kunt, A. and H. Huizinga (1999): "Determinants of Commercial Bank Interest Margins and Profitability: Some International Evidence" *The World Bank Economics Review.*

Demirgüç-Kunt, A., L. Laeven and R. Levine (2004): "Regulations, Market Structure, Institutions, and the Cost of Financial Intermediation" *Journal of Money, Credit and Banking*, Vol. 36, pp. 593–622.

Demirgüç-Kunt, A., R. Levine and H.G. Min (1998): "Opening to Foreign Banks: Issues of Stability, Efficiency, and Growth" World Bank mimeo, July 1998.

Demirgüç-Kunt, A., R. Levine and H.G. Min (1998): "Foreign banks: Efficiency, stability, and growth" in S. Lee (ed.), *The Implications of Globalization of World Financial Markets*, Bank of Korea.

Den Hertog, J. (1999): "General Theories of Regulation" Economic Institute/CLAV, Utrecht University.

Denizer, C.A., M. Dinc and M. Tarımcılar (2007): "Financial Liberalization and Banking Efficiency: Evidence from Turkey" *Journal of Productivity Analysis*, Vol. 27, Issue 3, pp. 177–195.

Detragiache, E. and A. Demirgüç-Kunt (1998): "The Determinants of Banking Crises in Developing and Developed Countries" IMF Staff Papers, Vol. 45, No. 1.

Detragiache, E., A. Demirgüç-Kunt and Q. Merrouche (2010): "Bank Capital: Lessons from the Financial Crisis" World Bank Policy Research Working Paper No. 5473.

DeYoung, R. and I. Hasan (1998): "The Performance of de novo Commercial Banks: A profit efficiency approach" *Journal of Banking and Finance*, Vol. 22, pp. 565–587.

Diamond, D.W. (1985): "Optimal Release of Information by Firms" *The Journal of Finance*, Vol. 40, No. 4, pp. 1071–1094.

Diamond, D.W. and P.H. Dybvig (2000): "Bank Runs, Deposit Insurance, and Liquidity" *Federal Reserve Bank of Minneapolis Quarterly Review*, Vol. 24, No. 1, pp. 14–23.

Diamond, D.W. (1984): "Financial Intermediation and Delegated Monitoring" *The Review of Economic Studies*, Vol. 51, No. 3, pp. 393–414.

Diamond, D.W. (2007): "Banks and Liquidity Creation: A Simple Exposition of the Diamond-Dybvig Model" *Economic Quarterly*, Vol. 93, No. 2, pp. 189–200.

Diamond, D.W. and P.H. Dybvig (1983): "Bank Runs, Deposit Insurance, and Liquidity" *Journal of Political Economy*, Vol. 91, No. 3, pp. 401–419. Reprinted in the issue of the *Federal Reserve Bank of Minneapolis Quarterly Review*, Vol. 24, No. 1, pp. 14–23

Diamond, D.W. and R.G. Rajan (2001): "Liquidity risk, liquidity creation and financial fragility: A theory of banking" *Journal of Political Economy*, Vol. 109, pp. 287–327.

Dietch, M. and A. Lozano-Vivas (2000): "How the Environment Determines Banking Efficiency: A Comparison between French and Spanish Industries" *Journal of Banking and Finance*, Vol. 24, pp. 985–1004.

Distinguin, I. (2008): "Market discipline and bank supervision: the role of subordinated debt" Working Paper, University of Limoges, France.

Dorbec, A. (2010): "Russia to build confidence" BNP Paribas, Economic Research Department, July 2010.

Dragomir, L. (2010): "European Prudential Banking Regulation and Supervision – The Legal Dimension" Routledge.

Dreger, C. and J. Fidrmuc (2009): "Drivers of Exchange Rate Dynamics in Selected CIS Countries: Evidence from a FAVAR Analysis" DIW Berlin Discussion Papers, March 2009.

Duarte, J., X. Han, J. Harford and L. Young (2008): "Information Asymmetry, Information Dissemination and the Effect of Regulation FD on the Cost of Capital" *Journal of Financial Economics*, Vol. 87, pp. 24–44.

Dziobek, C. and C. Pazarbasıoglu (1998): "Lessons from Systemic Bank Restructuring" IMF Economic Issues No. 14.

Edwards, F.R. and E.R. Morrison (2004): "Derivatives and the Bankruptcy Code: Why the Special Treatment?" Columbia Law and Economics Research Paper No. 258

Eichengreen, B. and C. Arteta (2000): "Banking Crises in Emerging Markets: Presumptions and Evidence" Center for International and Development Economics Research (CIDER), Institute of Business and Economic Research, UC Berkeley.

Enria, A., L. Cappiello, F. Dierick, S. Grittini, A. Haralambous, A. Maddaloni, P.A.M. Molitor, F. Pires and P. Poloni (2004): "Fair Value Accounting and Financial Stability" European Central Bank Occasional Paper No. 13.

Etkin, L.P., M.M. Helms, U. Turkkan and D.J. Morris (2000): "The Economic Emergence of Turkey" *European Business Review*, Vol. 12, No. 2, pp. 64–75.

Fabozzi, F.J., H.A. Davis and M. Choudhry (2006): *Introduction to Structured Finance*, Wiley Finance.

Fabozzi, F.J., L.S. Goodman and D.J. Lucas (2007): "Collateralized Debt Obligations and Credit Risk Transfer" Yale ICF Working Paper No. 0706.

Fama, E.F. (1980): "Banking in the Theory of Finance" *Journal of Monetary Economics*, Vol. 6, Issue 1, pp. 39–57.

Fama, E.F. (1985): "What's Different about Banks?" *Journal of Monetary Economics*, Vol. 15, Issue 1, pp. 29–39.

Färe, R., S. Grosskopf and C.A.K. Lovell (1994): *Production Frontiers*, Cambridge University Press (10–13–25–51).

Färe, R. and D. Primont (1995): "Multi-Output Production and Duality: Theory and Applications" Kluwer Academic Publishers.

Farrel, M.J. (1957): "The Measurement of Productive Efficiency" *Journal of the Royal Statistical Society*, Vol. 120, pp. 253–281.

Favero, C.A. and L. Papi (1995): "Technical Efficiency and Scale Efficiency in the Italian Banking Sector: A Non-Parametric Approach" *Applied Economics*, Vol. 27, pp. 385–395.

Fernandez, A., and F. Gonzalez (2005): "How Accounting and Auditing Systems can counteract Risk-Shifting of Safety Nets in Banking: Some international evidence" *Journal of Financial Stability,* Vol. 1, pp. 466–500.
Fidrmuc, J. and P.J. Süß (2009): "The Outbreak of the Russian Banking Crisis" Volkswirtschaftliche Fakultät Ludwig-Maximilians-Universität München Discussion Paper No. 2009–16.
Flannery, M.J. and J.F. Houston (1999): "The Value of a Government Monitor for US Banking Firms" *Journal of Money, Credit, and Banking,* Vol. 31, No. 1, pp. 14–34
Focarelli, D. and A.F. Pozzolo (2001): "Where do Banks Expand Abroad? An Empirical Analysis" Banca d' Italia Research Department Working Paper.
Forsund, F.R. and L. Hjalmarsson (1974): "On the Measurement of Productive Efficiency" *Swedish Journal of Economics,* Vol. 76, pp. 141–154.
Forsund, F.R. and L. Hjalmarsson (1979): "Generalized Farrell Measures of Efficiency: An Application to Milk Processing in Swedish Dairy Plants" *Economic Journal,* Vol. 89, pp. 294–315.
Forsund, F.R., L. Hjalmarsson, S.A. Berg and M. Suominen (1993): "Banking Efficiency in the Nordic Countries" *Journal of Banking and Finance,* Vol. 17, pp. 371–388.
Frankel, R. and X. Li (2004): "Characteristics of a firm's information environment and the information asymmetry between insiders and outsiders" *Journal of Accounting and Economics,* Vol. 37, Issue 2, pp. 229–259.
Freeman, S. (1987): "Reserve Requirements and Optimal Seigniorage" *Journal of Monetary Economics,* Vol. 19, Issue 2, pp. 307–314.
Freixas, X. and J.-C. Rochet (1999): *Microeconomics of Banking,* MIT Press.
Freixas, X., B.M Parigi and J.-C. Rochet (2004): "The Lender of Last Resort: A Twenty-First Century Approach" MIT Press, European Economic Association.
Fried, H.O., C.A.K. Lovell and S.S. Schmidt (1993): *The Measurement of Productive Efficiency: Techniques and applications,* New York: Oxford University Press.
Fries, S. and A. Taci (2005): "Cost Efficiency of Banks in Transition: Evidence from 289 banks in 15-post communist countries" *Journal of Banking and Finance,* Vol. 29, pp. 55–81.
Fukuyama, H. (1993): "Technical and Scale Efficiency of Japanese Commercial Banks: A Non-Parametric Approach" *Applied Economics,* Vol. 25, No. 8, pp. 1101–1112.
Fungacova, Z. and L. Weill (2009): "How Market Power Influences Bank Failures: Evidence from Russia" Bank of Finland Institute for Economies in Transition Discussion Papers No. 12/2009.
Fungacova, Z. and P. Jakubik (2012): "Bank stress tests as an information device for emerging markets: The case of Russia" Bank of Finland Institute for Economies in Transition Discussion Papers No. 3/2012.
Gadanecz, B. and K. Jayaram (2008): "Measures of financial stability – a review" IFC Bulletin No. 31.
Gencoglu, Ü.G., G. İşseveroglu and Y. Ertan (2011): "Bank Audits and Risk Management in Turkey" *International Journal of Economics and Finance Studies,* Vol. 3, No. 1, pp. 239–250.
Gertler, M. (1988): "Financial Structure and Aggregate Economic Activity: An Overview" *Journal of Money, Credit and Banking,* Vol. 20, No. 3, Part 2: Recent Developments in Macroeconomics, pp. 559–588.

Gibson, M.S. (1995): "Can Bank Health Affect Investment? Evidence from Japan" *Journal of Business*, Vol. 68, No. 3, pp. 281–308.
Girardone, C., G.E. Chortareas and A. Ventouri (2012): "Bank Supervision, Regulation and Efficiency: Evidence from the European Union" *Journal of Financial Stability*, Vol. 8, pp. 292–302.
Goldstein, M. and P. Turner (1996): "Banking Crises in Emerging Economies: Origins and Policy Options" BIS Economic Papers No. 46.
Golovan, S.V. (2006): "Factors which influence the efficiency of Russian banks" *Applied econometrics (Prikladnaya ekonometrika)*, Vol. 2, pp. 3–17 (in Russian) in: A. Peresetsky, "Bank cost efficiency in Kazakhstan and Russia" Bank of Finland Discussion Papers, 1, 2010.
Gonzalez, F. (2005): "Bank regulation and risk-taking incentives: An international comparison of bank risk" *Journal of Banking and Finance*, Vol. 29, No. 5, pp. 1153–1184.
Goodhart, C.A.E. (2006): "A framework for assessing financial stability?" *Journal of Banking & Finance*, Vol. 30, pp. 3415–3422.
Gorton, G. (2008): "The Subprime Panic" Yale School of Management; National Bureau of Economic Research (NBER).
Gorton, G. (2009): "Slapped in the Face by the Invisible Hand: Banking and the Panic of 2007" Yale School of Management; National Bureau of Economic Research (NBER).
Gorton, G. (2010a): "Slapped by the Invisible Hand: The Panic of 2007" Oxford University Press.
Gorton, G. (2010b): "Questions and Answers about the Financial Crisis" NBER Working Paper.
Gorton, G. and G. Pennacchi (1990): "Financial Intermediaries and Liquidity Creation" *Journal of Finance*, Vol. 45, No. 1, pp. 49–72.
Gorton, G. and A. Metrick (2009): "Securitized Banking and the Run on Repo" NBER Working Paper No. 15223.
Gray, S. (2011): "Central Bank Balances and Reserve Requirements" IMF Working Paper No. 11/36.
Greenspan, A. (2005): "Bank Regulation" Bank for International Settlements, Central Bankers' Speeches, Speech given to the Independent Community Bankers of America National Convention, San Antonio, Texas, March 2005.
Grigorian, D.A. and V. Manole (2002): "Determinants of Commercial Bank Performance in Transition: An Application of Data Envelopment Analysis" IMF Working Paper No. 02/146.
Grosskopf, S. (1993): "Efficiency and Productivity" in: H.O. Fried, C.A.K. Lovell and S.S. Schmidt (eds.), *The Measurement of Productive Efficiency: Techniques and Applications*, Oxford University Press, pp. 160–194.
Gualandri, E., A. Landi, and V. Venturelli (2009): "Financial Crisis and New Dimensions of Liquidity Risk: Rethinking Prudential Regulation and Supervision" Center for Studies in Banking and Finance No. 09011.
Gunther, J.W. and R.R. Moore (2002): "Loss Underreporting and the Auditing Role of Bank Exams" prepared for a symposium on *The Impact of Economic Slowdowns on Financial Institutions and Their Regulators* sponsored jointly by the *Federal Reserve Bank of Boston* and the *Journal of Financial Intermediation*, 17–19 April 2002.

Gurley, J.G. and E.S. Shaw (1955): "Financial Aspects of Economic Development" *The American Economic Review*, Vol. 45, No. 4, pp. 515–538.

Hantke-Domas, M. (2003): "The Public Interest Theory of Regulation: Non-Existence or Misinterpretation" *European Journal of Law and Economics*, Vol. 15, pp. 165–194.

Hardy, D.C. (2006): "Regulatory Capture in Banking" IMF Working Paper No. 06/34.

Hauner, D. (2005): "Explaining Efficiency Differences among Large German and Austrian Banks" IMF Working Paper No. 04/140.

Hawkins, J. and D. Mihaljek (2001): "The banking industry in the emerging market economies: competition, consolidation and systemic stability – an overview" BIS Papers No. 4.

Hellmann, T., K. Murdock and J.E. Stiglitz (2000): "Liberalization, moral hazard in Banking and Prudential Regulation: Are capital controls enough?" *American Economic Review*, Vol. 90, pp. 147–165.

Hellmann, T.F., K.C. Murdock and J.E. Stiglitz (2000): "Liberalization, Moral Hazard in Banking, and Prudential Regulation: Are Capital Requirements Enough?" *The American Economic Review*, Vol. 90, No. 1, pp. 147–165.

Hellwig, M. (2008): "Systemic Risk in the Financial Sector: An Analysis of the Subprime-Mortgage Financial Crisis" Max Planck Institute for Research on Collective Goods, 2008/43.

Hellwig, M. (2010): "Capital Regulation after the Crisis: Business as Usual?" Max Planck Institute for Research on Collective Goods, Bonn 2010/31

Hendrickson, J.M. and M.W. Nichols (2001): "How does Regulation affect the Risk Taking of Banks? A US and Canadian perspective" *Journal of Comparative Policy Analysis: Research and Practice*, Vol. 3, pp. 59–83.

Heremans, D. and A.M. Pacces (2011): "Regulation of Banking and Financial Markets" Rotterdam Institute of Law and Economics, Working Paper Series No. 2011/04.

Heremans, D. and K. Bosquet (2011): "The Future of Law and Finance after the Financial Crisis. New Perspectives on Regulation and Corporate Governance for Banks" *University of Illinois Law Review*, Vol. 2011, Issue 5

Herring, R.J. and A.M. Santomero (2000): "What is Optimal Financial Regulation?" Wharton School, University of Pennsylvania WP 00–34

Herring, R.J. and R.E. Litan (1995): "Financial Regulation in the Global Economy" The Brookings Institution.

Hoenig, T.M. (1998): "Financial Modernization: Implications for the Safety Net" *Mercer Law Review*, Vol. 49, No. 3, pp. 787–792.

Hoggarth, G., R. Reis and V. Saporta (2001): "Costs of Banking System Instability: Some Empirical Evidence" *Journal of Banking and Finance*, Vol. 26, No. 5, pp. 825–855.

Horvitz, P.M. (1980). "A Reconsideration of the Role of Bank Examination" *Journal of Money, Credit and Banking*, Vol. 12, No. 4, pp. 654–659.

Hume, M. and A. Sentance (2009): "The Global Credit Boom: Challenges for Macroeconomics and Policy" *Journal of International Money and Finance*, Vol. 28, No. 8, pp. 1426–1461.

Hüpkes, E.H.G. (2000): "The Legal Aspect of Bank Insolvency: A Comparative Analysis of Western Europe, the United States and Canada" Kluwer Law International.

Ippolito, F. (2002): "The Banking Sector Rescue in Russia 2002" Bank of Finland Institute for Economies in Transition No. 12.

Isik, I. and M.K. Hassan (2002): "Technical, Scale and Allocative Efficiencies of Turkish Banking Industry" *Journal of Banking and Finance,* Vol. 26, No. 4, pp. 719–766.

Isik, I. and M.K. Hassan (2003): "Financial Disruption and Bank Productivity: The 1994 Experience of Turkish Banks" *The Quarterly Review of Economics and Finance,* Vol. 43, pp. 291–320.

Jackson, P. (1999): "Capital Requirements and Bank Behaviour: The Impact of the Basel Accord" BIS Working Paper No. 1.

Jackson, P.M. and M.D. Fethi (2000): "Evaluating the Technical Efficiency of Turkish Commercial Banks: An Application of DEA and Tobit Analysis" presented at the International DEA Symposium, University of Queensland, Brisbane, Australia, 2–4 July 2000.

Jemric, I. and B. Vujcic (2002): "Efficiency of Banks in Croatia, A DEA Approach" *Comparative Economic Studies,* Vol. 44, pp. 169–193.

Jones, D. (2000): "Emerging Problems with the Basel Capital Accord: Regulatory Capital Arbitrage and Related Issues" *Journal of Banking and Finance,* Vol. 24, Issues 1–2, pp. 35–58.

Jorda, O., M. Schularick and A.M. Taylor (2009): "Financial Crises, Credit Booms, and External Imbalances: 140 Years of Lessons" NBER Working Paper No. 16567.

Kane, E.J. (2009): "Incentive Roots of the Securitisation Crisis and Its Early Mismanagement" CEPR Policy Insight No. 32.

Kaparakis, E., S. Miller and A. Noulas (1994): "Short-Run Cost Inefficiency of Commercial Banks: A Flexible Stochastic Frontier Approach" *Journal of Money, Credit and Banking,* Vol. 26, No. 4, pp. 875–893.

Karas, A., K. Schoors and L. Weill (2008): "Are private banks more efficient than public banks? Evidence from Russia" Bank of Finland Institute for Economies in Transition Discussion Papers No. 3/2008.

Kashyap, A.K., R.G. Rajan and J.C. Stein (2008): "Rethinking Capital Regulation" presented in Federal Reserve Bank of Kansas City Economic Symposium on "Maintaining Stability in a Changing Financial System", 21–23 August 2008.

Kasman A. and C. Yildirim (2006): "Cost and profit efficiencies in transition banking: the case of new EU members" *Applied Economics,* Vol. 38, pp. 1079–1090.

Kaufman, G. (1994): "Bank Contagion: A Review of the Theory and Evidence" *Journal of Financial Services Research,* pp. 123–150.

Keeley, M. (1990): "Deposit Insurance, Risk, and Market Power in Banking" *American Economic Review,* Vol. 80, pp. 1183–1200.

Keister, T. and J. McAndrews (2009): "Why Are Banks Holding So Many Excess Reserves?" Federal Reserve Bank of New York Staff Reports No. 380, July 2009.

Kendall, S.B. (1992): "Bank Regulation under Nonbinding Capital Guidelines" *Journal of Financial Services Research,* Vol. 5, pp. 275–286.

Kim, D. and A.M. Santomero (1988): "Risk in Banking and Capital Regulation" *The Journal of Finance,* Vol. 43, No. 5, pp. 1219–1233.

Kocaoglu, N.K. (2010): "Development of Competition Policy in the Turkish Banking Sector: 1994–2005" Ankara Barosu Dergisi 2010/3.

Koehn, M. and A. Santomero (1980): "Regulation of Bank Capital and Portfolio Risk" *Journal of Finance,* Vol. 35, pp. 1235–1244.

Komulainen, T., I. Korhonen, V. Korhonen, J. Rautava and P. Sutela (2003): "Russia: Growth Prospects and Policy Debates" Bank of Finland Institute for Economies in Transition No. 3.

Koopmans, T.C. (1951): "An Analysis of Production as Efficient Combination of Activities" in T.C. Koopmans (ed.), *Activity Analysis of Production and Allocation*, Cowles Commission for Research in Economics, Monograph No. 13, New York.

Kumbakhar, S., A. Lozano-Vivas, C.A.K Lovell and I. Hasan (2001): "The Effects of Deregulation on the Performance of Financial Institutions: The Case of Spanish Savings Banks" *Journal of Money, Credit, and Banking*, Vol. 33, No. 1, pp. 101–120.

Kumbhakar, S., S. Ghosh and J. McGuckin (1991): "A Generalized Production Frontier Approach for Estimating Determinants of Inefficiency in United States Dairy Farms" *Journal of Business Economics and Statistics*, Vol. 9, pp. 279–286.

Kumbhakar, S.C. (1993): "Production Risk, Technical Efficiency and Panel Data" *Economics Letters*, Vol. 41, pp. 11–26.

La Porta, R., F. Lope-de-Silanes, A. Shleifer and R.W. Vishny (1998): "Law and finance" *Journal of Political Economy*, Vol. 106, No. 6, pp. 1113–1155.

La Porta, R., F. Lopez-de-Silanes and A. Schleifer (2002): "Government Ownership of Banks" *The Journal of Finance*, Vol. 57, No. 1, pp. 265–301.

La Porta, R., F. Lopez-de-Silanes, S. Djankov and A. Schleifer (2000): "The Regulation of Entry" Harvard Institute of Economic Research Discussion Paper No. 1904.

Laeven, L. (2002): "Bank Risk and Deposit Insurance" *The World Bank Economic Review*, Vol. 16, No. 1, pp. 109–137.

Laeven, L., A. Demirgüç-Kunt, and B. Karacaovalı (2005): "Deposit Insurance around the World: A Comprehensive Database" World Bank Policy Research Working Paper No. 3628.

Lambert-Mogiliansky, A., K. Sonin and E. Zhuravskaya (2003): "Capture of Bankruptcy: Theory and Russian Evidence" CEFIR Working Paper No. 3.

Leuz, C. and P. Wysocki (2008): "Economic Consequences of Financial Reporting and Disclosure Regulation: A Review and Suggestions for Future Research" Available from: http://papers.ssrn.com/sol3/papers.cfm?abstract_id=1105398.

Levine, R. (1998): "The legal environment, banks and long-term economic growth" *Journal of Money, Credit and Banking*, Vol. 30, No. 3, pp. 596–613.

Levine, R. (1997): "Financial Development and Economic Growth: Views and Agenda" *Journal of Economic Literature*, Vol. 35, No. 2, pp. 688–726.

Levine, R. (2003): "More on finance and growth: more finance, more growth?" The Federal Reserve Bank of St. Louis, 31–46, July.

Levine, R. (2004): "The Microeconomic Effects of Different Approaches to Bank Supervision" The Stanford Center for International Development (SCID) Working Paper No. 237.

Levine, R., A. Demirgüç-Kunt and T. Beck (2005): "Bank Supervision and Corruption in Lending" NBER Working Paper No. 11498.

Levine, R., and S. Zervos (1998): "Stock Markets, Banks and Economic Growth" *The American Economic Review*, Vol. 88, No. 3, pp. 537–558.

Levine, R., N. Loayza and T. Beck (2000): "Financial Intermediation and Growth: Causality and Causes" *Journal of Monetary Economics*, Vol. 46, pp. 31–77.

Levonian, M. (2001): "Subordinated Debt and the Quality of Market Discipline in Banking" Workshop on Applied Banking Research Oslo, Norway, 12–13 June 2001 at the Norges Bank.

Lindquist, K. (2003): "Banks' buffer capital: How important is risk" presented at BIS, March 2003.

Lovell, C.A.K. (1994): "Linear Programming Approaches to the Measurement and Analysis of Productive Efficiency" *Top*, Vol. 2, No. 2, pp. 175–248.

Lozano-Vivas, A., J.T. Pastor and I. Hasan (2000): "Cross-Border Performance in European Banking" Bank of Finland Discussion Papers No. 24/2000.

Macit, F. (2012): "Recent evidence on concentration and competition in Turkish banking sector" *Theoretical and Applied Economics*, Vol. 19, No. 8, pp. 19–28.

Mahlberg, B., U. Bernhard and P. Haiss (2011): "Russian Banking: The impact of ownership on efficiency and performance" Vienna University of Economics and Business, Institute for International Business, 2011.

Malmquist, S. (1953): "Index Numbers and Indifference Surfaces" *Trabajos de Estatistica*, Vol. 4, pp. 209–242.

Malyutina, M. and S. Parilova (2001): "The Determinants of Excessive Risk-Taking by Banks in Transition" Economics Education and Research Consortium - Russia and CIS.

Mason, J.R. (2009): "Regulating for Financial System Development, Financial Institutions Stability, and Financial Innovation" *Development, Stability, and Innovation.*

Matthews, K. and J. Thompson (2008): *The Economics of Banking*, 2nd edition, John Wiley & Sons.

Maudos, J, J.M. Pastor, F. Perez and J. Quesada (2002): "Cost and profit efficiency in European banks" *Journal of International Financial Markets, Institutions and Money*, Vol. 12, Issue: 1, pp. 33–58.

McDonald, H. (2009): "Using Least Squares and Tobit in Second Stage DEA Efficiency Analyses" *European Journal of Operational Research*, Vol. 197, Issue 2, pp. 792–798.

Melecky, M., D. Anzoategui and M.S.M. Peria (2010): "Banking Sector Competition in Russia" The World Bank Policy Research Working Paper No. 5449.

Merton, R.C. (1993): "Operation and Regulation in Financial Intermediation: A functional perspective", *Operation and Regulation of Financial Markets*, edited by P. England, Stockholm Economic Council in: X. Freixas and J.-C. Rochet (1999): *Microeconomics of Banking*, MIT Press.

Mishkin, F.S. (2004): *The Economics of Money, Banking and Financial Markets*, 7th edition, Addison-Wesley Series in Economics, Pearson Publications.

Mishkin, F.S. (2000): "Prudential Supervision: Why is it important and what are the issues?" NBER Working Paper No. 7926.

Mizobata, S. (2009) "The Economic Crisis in Russia: Fragility and Robustness of Globalisation" Kyoto Institute of Economic Research Discussion Paper No. 688.

Modibo, K.C. and F. Montes-Negret (2006): "Deposit Insurance and Banking Reform in Russia" World Bank Policy Research Working Paper No. 4056.

Mohammadi, A. and H. Ranaei (2011): "The Application of DEA based Malmquist Productivity Index in Organizational Performance Analysis" *International Research Journal of Finance and Economics*, Issue 62, pp. 68–76.

Montoro, C. and L. Rojas-Suarez (2012): "Credit at times of stress: Latin American lessons from the global financial crisis" BIS Working Papers No. 370.

Morroni, M. (1992): *Production Process and Technical Change*, Cambridge University Press.

Murillo-Zamorano, L.R. (2004): "Economic Efficiency and Frontier Techniques" *Journal of Economic Surveys*, Vol. 18, Issue 1, pp. 33–77.

Niskanen, J., J. Kinnunen and E. Kasanen (1998): "A note on the information content of parent company versus consolidated earnings in Finland" *European Accounting Review*, Vol. 7, Issue 1, pp. 31–40.

Norman, M. and B. Stoker (1991): *Data Envelopment Analysis: The Assessment of Performance*, Wiley.

Oded, S. (2012): "Inducing Corporate Proactive Compliance: Liability Controls & Corporate Monitors" Erasmus Universiteit.

Ogus, A. (1994): "Regulation, Legal Form and Economic Theory" in: L. Dragomir (2010): *European Prudential Banking Regulation and Supervision – The Legal Dimension*, Routledge.

Ogus, A. (2004): "Enforcing Regulation: Do We Need the Criminal Law?" in: H. Sjögren and G. Skogh (eds.), *New Perspectives on Economic Crime*, Edward Elgar Publishing, pp. 42–55.

Ono, S. (2004): "The Impact of the Russian Financial Crisis on the Efficiency of Russian Banks" *Economic Journal of Hokkaido University*, Vol. 33, pp. 151–176.

Oral, M., and R. Yolalan (1990): "An Empirical Study on Measuring Operating Efficiency and Profitability of Bank Branches" *European Journal of Operational Research*, Vol. 46, pp. 282–294.

Özatay, F. and G. Sak (2003): "Banking Sector Fragility and Turkey's 2000–01 Financial Crisis" The Central Bank of the Republic of Turkey (TCMB).

Özkan, F.G. (2003): "Currency and Financial Crises in Turkey 2000–2001: Bad Fundamentals or Bad Luck" University of York and CEPR, 12 March.

Pacces, A.M. (2010): "The Role and the Future of Regulation in the Financial Crisis: The Uncertainty Perspective" Erasmus School of Law, Erasmus University Rotterdam.

Pacces, A.M. and R.J. Van den Bergh (2011): "An Introduction to the Law and Economics of Regulation" in: A.M. Pacces and R.J. Van den Bergh, *Regulation and Economics*, Encyclopaedia of Law and Economics, 2nd edition, Edward Elgar Publishing; Rotterdam Institute of Law and Economics Working Paper No. 2011/03.

Paksoy, S. and S.N. Tiftikci (2010): "The Banking Regulation Review – Chapter III2: Turkey" in: J. Putnis (ed.), *Banking Regulation Review*, Law Business Research Ltd.

Pasiouras, F. (2006): "Estimating the technical and scale efficiency of Greek commercial banks: the impact of credit risk, off-balance sheet activities, and international operations" Working Paper No. 2006.17, School of Management, University of Bath, UK.

Pasiouras, F. (2008): "International Evidence on the Impact of Regulations and Supervision on Banks' Technical Efficiency: an Application of Two-Stage Data Envelopment Analysis" *Review of Quantitative Finance and Accounting*, Vol. 30, No. 2, pp. 187–223.

Pasiouras, F., M.-E.K. Agoraki and M.D. Delis (2011): "Regulations, competition and bank risk-taking in transition countries" *Journal of Financial Stability*, Vol. 7, pp. 38–48.

Pasiouras, F., S. Tanna and C. Zopounidis (2009): "The impact of banking regulations on banks' cost and profit efficiency: Cross-country evidence" *International Review of Financial Analysis* Vol. 18, pp. 294–302.

Pasiouras, F., S. Tanna and C. Zopounidis (2007): "Regulations, Supervision and Banks' Cost and Profit Efficiency around the World: a Stochastic Frontier Approach" University of Bath, School of Management Working Paper Series No. 2007.05.

Pastor, J.M. and L. Serrano (2005): "Efficiency, Endogenous and Exogenous Credit Risk in the Banking Systems of the Euro Area" *Applied Financial Economics*, Vol. 15, No. 9, pp. 631–649.

Pastor, J.M., F. Perez and J. Quesada (1997): "Efficiency Analysis in Banking Firms: An International Comparison" *European Journal of Operational Research*, Vol. 98, pp. 395–407.

Pastor, J.T., A. Lozano-Vivas and J.M. Pastor (2002): "An Efficiency Comparison of European Banking Systems Operating under Different Environmental Conditions" *Journal of Productivity Analysis*, Vol. 18, pp. 59–78.

Paul-Morrison, C.J. (1999): *Cost Structure and the Measurement of Economic Performance*, Kluwer Academic Publishers.

Peek, J., E.S. Rosengren and G.M.B. Tootell (1999): "Is Bank Supervision Central to Central Banking?" *The Quarterly Journal of Economics*, Vol. 114, No. 2, pp. 629–653

Penas, M.F. and G. Tümer-Alkan (2008): "Bank Disclosure and Market Assessment of Financial Fragility: Evidence from Banks' Equity Prices" TILEC Discussion Paper No. 2008–013.

Peresetsky, A. (2008): "Market discipline and deposit insurance in Russia" Bank of Finland Institute for Economies in Transition Discussion Papers No. 14.

Peresetsky, A. (2010): "Bank cost efficiency in Kazakhstan and Russia" Bank of Finland Institute for Economies in Transition Discussion Papers, 1, 2010.

Perotti, E. (2001): "Lesson from the Russian Meltdown: The Economics of Soft Legal Constraints" University of Amsterdam and CEPR Working Paper No. 379.

Platt, H.D (2010): "Where did all the liquidity go?" *Real Estate Finance Journal*, Summer 2010.

Posner, R.A. (1974): "Theories of Economic Regulation" NBER Working Paper No. 41.

Prescott, E.S. (2002): "Can Risk-Based Deposit Insurance Premiums Control Moral Hazard?" *FRB Richmond Economic Quarterly*, Vol. 88, No. 2, pp. 87–100.

Preobragenskaya, G. and R.W. McGee (2003): "Auditing in Russia" Conference of the International Academy of Business Disciplines, 2003.

Pyle, D.H. (1997): "Bank Risk Management: Theory" University of California, Berkeley, Working Paper No. RPF-272.

Qu, B., C. Jiang and J. Zhang (2012): "Risk-taking, concentration, and bank performance: Evidence from emerging economies" Middlesex University Business School Discussion Paper No. 151.

Rajan, R.G. and L. Zingales (1998): "Financial Dependence and Growth" *The American Economic Review*, Vol. 88, No. 3, pp. 559–586.

Rajan, R.G. (1996): "Is there a future in banking? Towards a new theory of the commercial bank" Northwestern University

Rajan, R.G. and D.W. Diamond: (1997): "Liquidity Risk, Liquidity Creation and Financial Fragility: A theory of banking" CRSP Working Paper No. 476.

Rajan, R.G. and D.W. Diamond: (2005): "Liquidity Shortages and Banking Crises" *The Journal of Finance*, Vol. 60, No. 2, pp. 615–647.

Ray, S. and E. Desli (1997): "Productivity Growth, Technical Progress, and Efficiency Change in Industrialized Countries: Comment" *American Economic Review*, Vol. 87, No. 5, pp. 1033–1039.

Resti, A. (1997): "Evaluating the cost-efficiency of the Italian banking system: What can be learnt from the joint application of parametric and non-parametric techniques" *Journal of Banking and Finance*, Vol. 21, pp. 221–250.

Rochet, J.-C. (2008): "Liquidity Regulation and the Lender of Last Resort" Banque de France, Financial Stability Review, Special Issue on Liquidity, No. 11.

Rogoff, K.S. and C.M. Reinhart (2009): "The Aftermath of Financial Crises" NBER Working Paper No. 14656.

Rosengren, E.S. and J. Peek (1995): "The capital crunch: Neither a borrower nor a lender be" *Journal of Money, Credit and Banking*, Vol. 27, pp. 625–638.

Samuelson, P.A. and S. Swamy (1974): "Invariant Economic Index Numbers and Canonic Duality: Survey and Synthesis" *American Economic Review*, Vol. 64, pp. 566–93.

Santomero, A.M. and R.D. Watson (1977): "Determining an Optimal Capital Standard for the Banking Industry" *The Journal of Finance*, Vol. 32, No. 4, pp. 1267–1282.

Santos, J.A.C. (2000): "Bank Capital Regulation in Contemporary Banking Theory: A Review of the Literature" BIS Working Paper No. 90.

Santos, J.A.C., V.V. Acharya and T. Yorulmazer (2010): "Systemic Risk and Deposit Insurance Premiums" Federal Reserve Bank of New York Economic Policy Review/ August 2010.

Sato, R. (1975): "The Most General Class of CES Functions" in: R. Sato (1999), *Production, Stability and Dynamic Symmetry: The Selected Essays of Ryuzo Sato*, Volume 2, Edward Elgar Publishing, pp. 3–13, pp. 14–19.

Sato, R. (1977): "Homothetic and non-homothetic CES Production Functions" in: R. Sato (1999), *Production, Stability and Dynamic Symmetry: The Selected Essays of Ryuzo Sato*, Volume 2, Edward Elgar Publishing, pp. 3–13.

Sato, R. (1999): *Production, Stability and Dynamic Symmetry: The Selected Essays of Ryuzo Sato*, Volume 2, Edward Elgar Publishing.

Scazzieri, R. and M. Landesmann (1993): *Production and Economic Dynamics*, Cambridge University Press.

Scharfstein, D. and V. Ivashina (2008): "Bank Lending During the Financial Crisis of 2008" EFA 2009 Bergen Meetings Paper.

Schmukler, S. (2008): "The Benefits and Risks of Globalization: Challenges for Developing Countries" in J. Stiglitz and J.A. Ocampo (eds.), *Capital Markets Liberalization and Development*, Oxford University Press, pp. 48–73.

Schooner, H.M. and M.W. Taylor (2010): *Global Bank Regulation*, Elsevier.

Schoors, K. (1999): "The Mired Restructuring of Russia's Banking System" *Russian Economic Trends*, Vol. 8, Issue 4, pp. 35–45.

Sealey, C. and J. Lindley (1977): "Inputs, Outputs, and a Theory of Production and Cost at Depository Financial Institutions" *Journal of Finance*, Vol. 32, pp. 1251–1266.

Seiford, L.M. (1996): "Data Envelopment Analysis: The evolution of the State of the Art (1978–1995)" *Journal of Productivity Analysis*, Vol. 7, pp. 99–138.

Seiford, L.M. and R.M. Thrall (1990): "Recent Developments in DEA: The Mathematical Programming Approach to Frontier Analysis" *Journal of Econometrics*, Vol. 46, pp. 7–38.

Seura, J. and C.R. Braun (2004): *An Eponymous Dictionary of Economics: A Guide to Laws and Theorems Named after Economists*, Edward Elgar Publishing.

Shleifer, A. and R. Vishny (1998): *The Grabbing Hand: Government Pathologies and their Cures*, Harvard University Press.

Sonderstrom, N. and K.J. Sun (2007): "IFRS Adoption and Accounting Quality: A Review" *European Accounting Review*, Vol. 16, Issue 4, pp. 675–702.

Stein, J.C. (2011): "Monetary Policy as Financial-Stability Regulation" NBER Working Paper No. 16883.

Steinherr, A., A. Tukel and M. Ucer (2004): "The Turkish Banking Sector: Challenges and Outlook in Transition to EU Membership" CEPS EU-Turkey Working Papers No. 4.

Steinherr, A. and E. Klär: (2005): "The Russian Banking Sector: Unsolved Problems Seven Years after the Crisis" German Institute for Economic Research - DIW Berlin Weekly Report No. 25/2005.

Steinherr, A. (2006): "Russian Banking since the Crisis of 1998" *Journal of Economic Change*, Vol. 39, pp. 235–259.

Stigler, G.J. (1971): "The Theory of Economic Regulation" *The Bell Journal of Economics and Management Science*, Vol. 2, No. 1, pp. 3–21.

Strahan, P.E. (2008): "Liquidity Production in 21st Century Banking" NBER Working Paper No. 13798.

Swank, J. (1996): "How Stable is the Multi-Product Translog Cost Function? Evidence from the Dutch Banking Industry" *Kredit und Kapital*, Vol. 29, pp. 153–172

Swindle, C.S. (1995): "Using CAMEL Ratings to Evaluate Regulator Effectiveness at Commercial Banks" *Journal of Financial Services Research*, Vol. 9, No. 2, pp. 123–141.

Tarr, D.G. (2010): "The Political, Regulatory and Market Failures that Caused the US Financial Crisis" World Bank Policy Research Working Paper No. 5324.

Tchana, F.T. (2008): "Regulation and Banking Stability: A Survey of Empirical Studies" MPRA Paper No. 9298.

Tektas, A. and E.N. Ozkan-Gunay (2006): "Efficiency Analysis of the Turkish Banking Sector in Pre-crisis and Crisis Period: A DEA Approach" *Contemporary Economic Policy*,Vol. 24, No. 3, pp. 418–431.

Thakor, A. (2013): "Bank Capital and Financial Stability: An Economic Tradeoff or a Faustian Bargain?" ECGI – Finance Working Paper No. 386.

Thießen, U. (2000): "Banking Crises in Transition Countries. Theory and Empirical Evidence: The Case of Russia" Deutsches Institut für Wirtschaftsforschung (DIW) Discussion Papers No. 193.

Thießen, U. (2004): "Financial System Development, Regulation and Economic Growth: Evidence from Russia" Deutsches Institut für Wirtschaftsforschung (DIW) Discussion Papers No. 400.

Thießen, U. (2005): "Banking Crises, Regulation, and Growth: The Case of Russia" *Applied Economics*, Vol. 37, Issue 19, pp. 2191–2203.

Thompson, E. (2002): "Turkish Bank Capital Adequacy - Too Little, Too Late" Fitch Ratings Special Report, 1 May 2002.
Tirole, J. (2010): "Illiquidity and all its friends" BIS Working Paper No. 303.
Tirole, J. and M. Dewatripont (1999): *The Prudential Regulation of Banks*, MIT Press.
Tirole, J., J.-C. Rochet and M. Dewatripont (2010): *Balancing the Banks: Global Lessons from the Financial Crisis*, Princeton University Press.
Tompson, W. (2004): "Banking Reform in Russia: Problems and Prospects" OECD Economics Working Paper No. 410.
Turner, P. (2006): "The banking system in emerging economies: how much progress has been made?" BIS Papers No. 28.
Uygur, E. (2010): "The Global Crisis and the Turkish Economy" Turkish Economic Association Working Papers No. 2010/3.
Van Hoose, D. (2006): "Bank Behaviour under Capital Regulation: What does the Academic Literature Tell Us?" Networks Financial Institute at Indiana State University Working Paper No. 04.
Vauhkonen, J. (2011): "The Impact of Pillar 3 Disclosure Requirements on Bank Safety" *Journal of Financial Services Research*, pp. 1–13.
Vernikov, A. (2007): "Russia's banking sector transition: Where to?" Bank of Finland Institute for Economies in Transition Discussion Papers No. 5.
Vives, X. (2006): "Banking and Regulation in Emerging Markets: The Role of External Discipline" *World Bank Research Observer*, Vol. 21, Issue 2, pp. 179–206.
Wang, Y., and N. Bayraktar (2006): "Banking Sector Openness and Economic Growth" World Bank Policy Research Working Paper No. 4019.
Walter, I. (1985): "Barriers to Trade in Banking and Financial Services, London" Trade Policy Research Centre, Thames Essay, no. 41.
Wheelock, D.C. and P.W. Wilson (2000): "Why do Banks Disappear? The Determinants of US Bank Failures and Acquisitions" *The Review of Economics and Statistics*, Vol. 82, Issue 1, pp. 127–138.
Wilmarth, Jr., A.E. (2011): "The Dodd-Frank Act: A Flawed and Inadequate Response to the Too-Big-to-Fail Problem" *Oregon Law Review*, Vol. 89, pp. 951–1057.
Wooldridge, J.M. (2003): *Introductory Econometrics – A Modern Approach*, Thomson.
Yalkın, Y.K., and V. Demir (2007): "International Financial Reporting Standards and Development of Financial Reporting Standards in Turkey" *Research in Accounting Regulations*, Vol. 20.
Yay, T., G.G. Yay and E. Yilmaz (2004): "Financial Crises, Financial Regulation and Turkey" University of Istanbul, Journal of Political Science Department, pp. 101–130.
Yeldan, E. (2002): "Behind the 2000/2001 Turkish Crisis: Stability, Credibility and Governance, for Whom?" Bilkent University.
Yıldırım, H.D. and G.C. Philippatos (2006): "Efficiency of banks: recent evidence from the transition economies of Europe, 1993–2000" *The European Journal of Finance*, Vol. 13, Issue 2, pp. 123–143.
Yıldırım, C. (2002): Evolution of Banking Efficiency within an Unstable Macroeconomic Environment: the Case of Turkish Commercial Banks" *Applied Economics*, Vol. 34, pp. 2289–2301.

Yolalan R., A. Reisman, M. Mercan and A.B. Emel (2003): "The Effect of Scale and Mode of Ownership on the Financial Performance of the Turkish Banking Sector: Results of a DEA-Based Analysis" *Socio-Economic Planning Sciences*, Vol. 37, pp. 185–202.

Yörükoğlu, M. and H. Atasoy (2010): "The effects of the global financial crisis on the Turkish financial sector" BIS Papers chapters, in: Bank for International Settlements (ed.), *The global crisis and financial intermediation in emerging market economies*, Vol. 54, pp. 387–405.

Zaim, O. (1995): "The Effect of Financial Liberalization on the Efficiency of Turkish Commercial Banks" *Applied Financial Economics*, Vol. 5, pp. 257–264.

About the author

Deniz (Akün) Ergun is currently working for the Garanti Bank in Istanbul, and has previously worked for HSBC Trinkaus INKA in Düsseldorf and KPMG Düsseldorf. She obtained her PhD in 2014 from the Erasmus University Rotterdam, Bologna University and Hamburg University as part of the European Doctorate in Law and Economics programme. She holds a Masters in Economics and Politics from the Albert Ludwigs University, Freiburg, and gained her Bachelors in Economics from the Koç University, Istanbul.

European Studies in Law and Economics

The European Studies in Law and Economics Series is an initiative of the board of the European Doctorate in Law and Economics programme. It is a peer-reviewed book series for a wide audience, including policy makers, legislators, economists, lawyers and judges. The volumes cover a broad range of topics. Each volume is devoted to promote the understanding of the effects of laws on human behaviour, thus providing the tools for a better assessment of the impact of laws on the economic system.

The European Doctorate in Law and Economics (www.edle-phd.eu) is the academic response to the increasing importance of the economic analysis of law in Europe. It is an excellence programme offered by the Universities of Bologna, Hamburg and Rotterdam and sponsored by the European Commission under the Erasmus Mundus scheme. It offers the unique opportunity to study Law and Economics on a PhD level in three different countries. The programme prepares economists and lawyers of high promise for an academic career in a research field of growing importance or for responsible positions in government, research organizations and international consulting groups.

The editors also invite authors from outside the European Doctorate in Law and Economics to submit publishing proposals. Please contact Kris Moeremans (k.moeremans@intersentia.be) for further information.

www.ingramcontent.com/pod-product-compliance
Ingram Content Group UK Ltd.
Pitfield, Milton Keynes, MK11 3LW, UK
UKHW051922100926
8556IPUK00021B/1322

9 781780 683003